ABODE
OF THE GODS

I felt I could go on like this for ever, that life had little better to offer than to march day after day in an unknown country to an unattainable goal.

HW Tilman, *Two Mountains and a River* (1949)

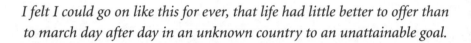

There are many ways to enjoy mountains: some persons engage their passion by cutting steps in impossible ice walls, others entrust their lives to one fragile piton in a rocky crevice, and still others, I among them, prefer simply to roam the high country.'

George B Schaller, *Stones of Silence* (1988)

ABODE OF THE GODS

TALES OF TREKKING IN NEPAL

Kev Reynolds

CICERONE

2 POLICE SQUARE, MILNTHORPE, CUMBRIA LA7 7PY

www.cicerone.co.uk

A catalogue record for this book is available from the British Library.
All photographs are by the author unless otherwise stated.

For Kirken Sherpa,
who makes the impossible possible,
and the porters of Nepal – unsung heroes of the Himalaya

Front cover Everest and Nuptse, the classic trekker's view from Kala Pattar

THE EARTH MOVED

At around midday on Saturday 25 April 2015 Nepal was shaken by an earthquake measuring 7.8 on the Richter scale. Just over two weeks later, a second major quake rocked the country, adding to the devastation wrought by the first.

In the Kathmandu Valley ancient buildings classified as Unesco World Heritage Sites – some that had fallen victim to an earlier earthquake in 1934 but had been painstakingly rebuilt – crumbled into heaps of rubble. Houses, hotels, restaurants and shops collapsed, trapping many people inside.

North and west of the capital the epicentre of the first quake sent out waves of destruction, releasing avalanches of snow, ice and rock onto unsuspecting villages. Communities that for decades had captivated newcomers to Nepal with their groups of thatched cottages strung along foothill ridges like those of Helambu, fell into ruin, while others were carried away by landslide.

The village of Langtang was overwhelmed by an avalanche released from Langtang Lirung, burying its houses, trekkers' lodges and their occupants – locals and visiting trekkers alike. A similar fate happened to Thame in the Bhote Kosi Valley, childhood home of Sherpa Norgay Tenzing, first man on Everest's summit in 1953 along with Ed Hillary. Everest Base Camp was flattened by avalanche debris swept from the headwall of the Khumbu Valley, causing many deaths among climbers and Sherpas.

A number of remote villages described in this book will have changed for ever; some have disappeared completely. And who knows how many of the Sherpas, porters and lodge keepers who add the human touch to stories in the following pages have fallen victim to the day the earth moved?

In the 1934 earthquake, some 17,000 Nepalis lost their lives. It will be months (maybe years) before the full human cost of these latest tragedies are known. But long after the horrors of 25 April and 12 May 2015 have been forgotten by the world's media, Nepal will still be coming to terms with their aftermath.

Fortunately, the Nepali people are nothing if not resilient. They will rebuild their homes and their lives, and their smiles will once again greet visiting trekkers and mountaineers with the same genuine warmth that has become their trademark. Please support them by trekking their trails, climbing their mountains to provide employment and feed the local economy.

Earnings from sales of this book will go towards supporting the work of Community Action Nepal, which has spent more than 20 years improving the living conditions of remote mountain communities of this beautiful country. So thank you for buying a copy and thereby adding to that support. *Dhanyabaad.*

Visit www.canepal.org.uk or contact Community Action Nepal,
Stewart Hill Cottage, Hesket Newmarket, Wigton, Cumbria CA7 8HX

ABOUT THE AUTHOR

Kev Reynolds has spent over 50 years walking, climbing and trekking in some of the world's greatest mountain ranges. In that time he has written over 40 guidebooks describing adventurous routes among the Alps, Pyrenees and high Himalayan regions of Nepal, which have inspired many thousands of others to follow in his footsteps. He was the contributing editor to Cicerone's *Trekking in the Himalaya*, published in 2013, a lavishly illustrated guide to 20 major treks, extending from Nanga Parbat in the extreme west to Bhutan in the far east. In the same year Cicerone published his memoir *A Walk in the Clouds* – a compilation of short stories harvested from Kev's wide-ranging mountain experiences.

When he's not away on trek or describing his journeys in books and magazines, he can be found travelling throughout the British Isles, evoking the mood and magic of the mountain world through his lectures. A member of the Alpine Club and Austrian Alpine Club, and an Honorary Life Member of the Outdoor Writers and Photographers Guild, Kev lives in rural contentment with his wife in view of what he calls 'the Kentish Alps'. Check him out at www.kevreynolds.co.uk.

ACKNOWLEDGEMENTS

Frank McCready of Sherpa Expeditions in London gave me my first opportunity to travel to Nepal, so I owe him a huge debt of gratitude, both for that trek and for its consequences. Over the years Kirken Sherpa has taken care of the logistics of numerous Himalayan treks for me. Together we've journeyed to some of the more remote regions of Nepal and shared a host of happy memories. He and various members of his staff – among them Amit, Chombe, Dorje, Jetta, Kumar, Mila, Mingma, Netra, Pemba, Phurba and Tashi (and all the unnamed porters) – made possible what at times seemed impossible or at least improbable, while in Mugu, local men Ranga, Chongdi and Sonam added much to the success of our travels. Thanks too to Alan Payne who joined me on several of the earlier treks, to my old friend Bart Jordans who knows the Himalaya better than most, to Dave and Leonie Etherington for leadership and laughter on my first Manaslu Circuit, and to all those whose company added to the joys of trekking in Nepal. They include Maggie Dilley, Martin Fry, Isabelle Lowenthal, Steve Neville, Wendy Payne, John Robertson, Clive and Frances Shelley, Sue Viccars, Janette Whittle and Ralph Wildgans. Jonathan Williams, publisher and friend, has not only been good company in the Himalaya, but agreed to produce this title under the Cicerone imprint. Special thanks to him and all his highly talented team in Milnthorpe for putting this book together, and for their continuing friendship. My editor, Hazel Clarke, has been wonderfully supportive and thoughtful in helping to shape these stories, while designer Clare Crooke created the maps and illustrations with her typical flair – it's been a joy, as ever, to work with both of them. And last but by no means least, I must thank my wife, Min, for supporting so many of my early treks in Nepal when money was tight, for sharing the dreams and then joining me for some of the best treks of all. To her and all the above, I offer my heartfelt thanks.

Kev Reynolds

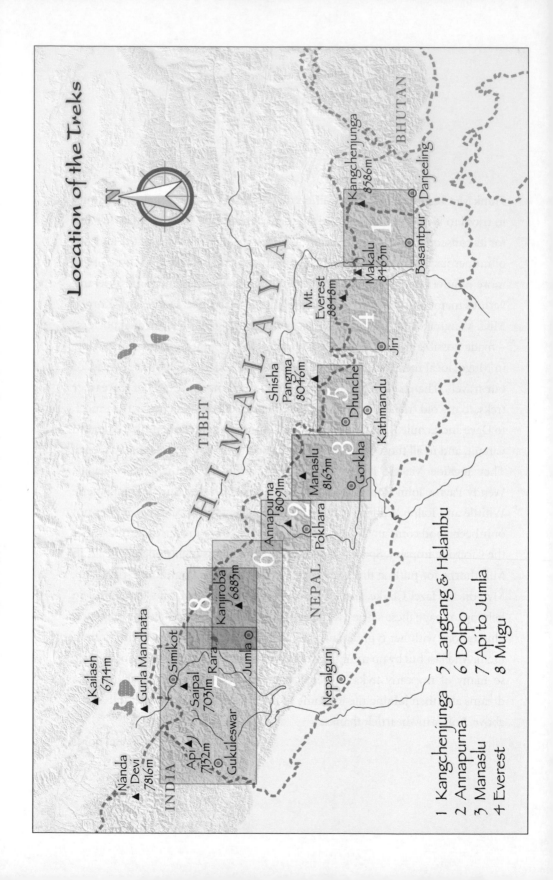

Location of the Treks

1 Kangchenjunga
2 Annapurna
3 Manaslu
4 Everest
5 Langtang & Helambu
6 Dolpo
7 Api to Jumla
8 Mugu

CONTENTS

INTRODUCTION

Like most leisure pursuits, I guess, trekking doesn't make much sense unless you've become addicted to it. I mean, it's only going for a walk, for goodness sake! You can do that just about anywhere – down the street, around the block or over a nearby hill; it's not necessary to take a month off work, draw out your savings and fly halfway across the world just to place one foot in front of the other day after day.

And yet, every year thousands of otherwise sane individuals do just that.

You see, trekking is addictive!

I knew that long before I ever went to Nepal, and more than 20 Himalayan expeditions later I have no reason to change my mind.

But how can the simple act of walking in another country for weeks on end bring so much pleasure? For it certainly can. And it does – especially in Nepal, where those steps take you into some of the most dramatic landscapes on Earth, and you become enriched along the way by a people whose friendliness and hospitality is legendary, and whose cultures have developed at a different pace and in a different direction from our own.

Yes, meeting different cultures is certainly a large part of the appeal. For it's good to be taken out of our own cosy environment, where values have been shaped into familiarity over countless generations, and sample for a few all-too-short weeks of the year a different way of living.

It's good too to be challenged physically – to be tested by the bare-earth paths that act as Himalayan highways climbing through remote valleys and over lofty passes, trading one heart-stopping view for another, gaining the only riches that count. The riches of memory that last for ever and can never be taxed.

Travel provides a fertile ground of experience from which a harvest is ready to be gathered, and trekking among distant mountains provides daily opportunities to do just that by personal contact with a world of extremes. Every laboured breath, every doubt, every hard-won upward step confronts us with the reality of Now. This moment in time is all that matters. And when we stop and look around, the rewards are there on every ragged horizon. That harvest of experience may be gathered along the trail moment by moment, day after day.

The very name of Nepal has an exotic ring to it, inspiring visions of great beauty – not just the ice-crusted mountains and tumultuous glaciers, but the valleys through which milky-blue torrents rush and roar; the wrinkled foothills with their terraces of rice and millet, buckwheat and barley. There's the scent of frangipani; bougainvillaea splashed across a hillside; gentian and orchid; forests of rhododendron and magnolia; and poinsettias two metres tall. There are houses of wattle and thatch overhung by bananas. Faces too – smiling faces in villages and on the trail; faces that look you in the eye and offer an unforgettable greeting. Prayer flags and *mani* stones; monks in claret robes blowing conch shells or clashing cymbals under the eyes of the Buddha; prayer wheels turned by water whose mantras bless all who pass. There are gods that reside on summits and in the most seductive of icy arenas, while the cry of '*Namaste*' accompanies every Nepalese journey.

Of all the journeys I've made in the Himalayan regions, the narrative that follows concentrates on just eight in Nepal. That's not to suggest for one moment that none of the other dozen or so treks was worth recording. Far from it. But the eight chosen for this book describe in chronological order my first-time experience along the most popular routes, as well as in other less-travelled regions right across the country. These eight very different treks offered a variety of challenges and experiences, all of which were immensely rewarding, in spite of taking place during two decades of unprecedented political and social change in Nepal.

In 1990, less than six months after my first visit to the country, King Birendra was forced to introduce a form of parliamentary democracy, but a combination of ineptitude and corruption followed, leading to a violent, so-called People's War being fought with the aim of ending the rule of the monarchy. Over a 10-year period, Maoist rebels gained control of rural areas by attacking army and police posts, resulting in the deaths of many hundreds of Nepalis. It was during this time of upheaval and instability that almost the entire royal family were wiped out in a drunken shooting spree by the king's own son, Crown Prince Dipendra. Birendra's surviving brother, Prince Gyanendra, took the throne, but five years later the new king's political power was curtailed by Parliament, Gyanendra relinquished the throne, the monarchy was abolished and in 2008 Nepal became a republic. Since then, however, democracy has been in a state of flux, with one government after another failing to break the cycle of mismanagement and corruption.

Surprisingly, such profound upheavals had only a limited effect on trekking and played no part in the outcome of any of the journeys described here. It was some of the other changes that were introduced during the same period that were of more significance to those of us aiming for the high mountains. One was the bulldozing of dirt roads into valleys that had previously never known a wheel; another was the development (still ongoing) of 'luxury lodges' in the most heavily trekked regions, and the establishment of basic lodge accommodation in areas where all treks in the past had of necessity relied on the support of porters carrying tents and all equipment, expedition-style.

Although these developments now affect several routes that appear in this book, they came after my first experience of them, so are not mentioned here. But the most welcome change for those who are lured by the less-travelled way has been the opening of remote districts, such as those of Manaslu, Dolpo, Mugu and others in the far west, that had formerly been classified as restricted to foreigners because their high valleys suggested easy access into forbidden Tibet. Being among the first to journey there has been a privilege to savour.

Throughout my time in the country I developed an intimacy with Nepal, one which began with a head full of dreams and turned into a down-to-earth reality as I trekked with commercial groups, organised and led private treks for friends, travelled independently using basic teahouses to sleep in, researched routes for guidebooks, and made a journey of exploration with just a Sherpa friend and a handful of porters. Experiences gained on all these travels may have revealed a less romantic vision than that which I'd imagined when I first went there, as jealousies, frustrations and blatant attempts at corruption rose to the surface, but being aware of perceived failings in others only served to remind me of my own. Trekking into the heart of the Himalaya has been an education, for I've discovered several aspects of Nepal which have changed my own reaction to it and enabled my love for the country and its people to mature. It's when love matures that it gains true value.

This, then, is a celebration of Nepal and the high Himalaya, inspired by the simple act of placing one foot in front of the other. It's not mountaineering, where a summit is the goal. No – trekking is about going for a walk, a long walk through a land of extremes. It's all about the journey, and what happens on that journey, that counts. For the pilgrim it is not only the merit that accrues on reaching the abode of the gods, but how that sacred place is gained that has value.

CHAPTER 1

Kangchenjunga

THE MOST BEAUTIFUL WALK IN THE WORLD
(1989)

A first visit to the Himalaya and the fulfilment of a dream, as I trek to the base of the world's third-highest mountain.

'Halloo! Bed-tea!'

It's almost 6 o'clock as light seeps into a November morning, our second since leaving the road-head. For several minutes I've lain here awake, comfortable in my sleeping bag listening to sounds of the new day, reluctant as yet to trade this warmth for what will probably be more of the damp mist of yesterday and the day before. That mist had denied us mountain views, save for one brief, tantalising moment when from the broad crest of the Milke Danda the veil shredded to reveal distant clouds and a hint – no more than that – of a line of Himalayan snow peaks out

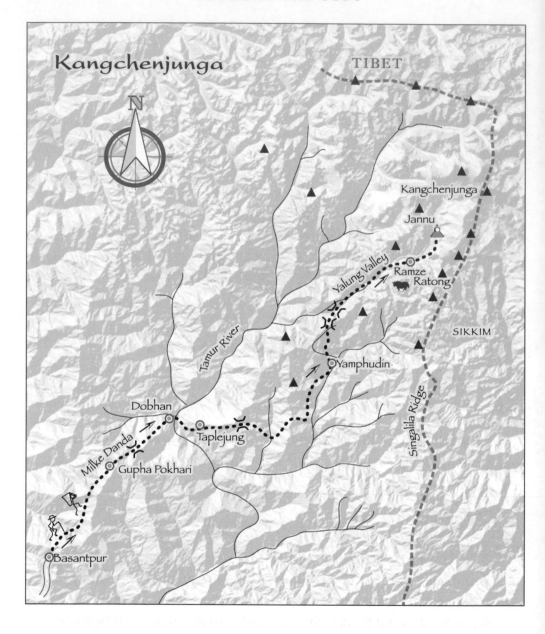

to the northwest. Then the mists closed in once more. Blinkered, we'd stumbled on, wondering.

This morning there is no wind, the tent is stilled, a vague glow brightens the fabric to tell of daybreak, and as I receive the steaming mug through the doorway, I see beyond cook-boy Indre's beaming, high-cheekboned face ('Morninggg, velly nice morning sah!') to a shallow pool trapped in a tiny scoop of a valley among the foothills. Yesterday the water seemed brackish, but now from my vantage point a dozen paces away, I can see that it's blue and sparkling, a mirror-image of the early-morning mist-free sky.

Far and away beyond the pool the rising sun pours its benevolence over summit snows. Out there, a distance of maybe 10 days' walk away, I see a vertical arctic wall shrugging the clouds – shapely, iridescent, unbelievably beautiful as its colours change with each succeeding moment.

The impact it has on me is instantaneous.

'Will you take a look at that!' I gasp at Max as I grab a fleece with one hand, boots with the other and lunge out of the tent in uncontrollable, child-like excitement, then part-stumble, part-hop my way up the slope on the right, where last night there'd been fireflies, but which this morning is diamond-studded with dew.

On gaining the top of the hill I run out of breath. Not with altitude, for we've not yet reached even 3000 metres, nor from my haste in getting here, but because all the world below to the east and north-east slumbers in ignorance of the new day beneath a gently pulsating cloud-sea. On it floats the sun. And a black-shadowed, whale-back ridge that can only be the Singalila bordering Sikkim. My eyes, a little moist (from the crisp morning air, you understand), travel along that ridge which rises steadily above the clouds until it gathers snow and what can only be hanging glaciers. There, at the far northernmost limit of the ridge, stands a vast block of ice and snow, a wall so colossal in scale that individual features can be identified even from this great distance. Although until now I've seen it only in photographs, that great bulk is unmistakable – Kangchenjunga, the world's third-highest mountain.

In response to that view a bird sings a seesaw refrain from its perch on a shrub nearby. Another joins in. Then another.

I'm inexpressibly happy, jubilant with the glory that unfolds, for stained as it is by the morning light, and gathered on the horizon in an all-embracing glance, Kangchenjunga personifies the lure of high places that haunts my dreams by night and day.

The Himalaya at last! It has taken me 30 years to get here.

Nine months ago I'd been enthusing about the appeal of trekking to a group of prospective customers for Sherpa Expeditions in London. In a large room over a pub in Earls Court I'd shown slides taken when wandering with Berber muleteers in the High Atlas Mountains of Morocco, of tackling the classic high route across Corsica, the romantic wild country of the Pyrenees, and some long treks in the Alps. Since taking the plunge as a freelance travel writer just three years before, I'd been supplementing my income with lectures and presentations at promotional events devoted to mountain travel. On this occasion the audience had been especially receptive, and after the last slide had faded from the screen I'd been bombarded with questions. Some members of the audience were inveterate trekkers, while others had yet to take their first steps, but all were united by a love of wild places and a taste for adventure. Dreamers all, I fed those dreams, then explained how to translate them into reality.

When the last of the audience had finally drifted home to dream and plan anew, director Frank McCready gathered spare sheets of promotional material while I dismantled the projection equipment. 'How is it you've never done a long-haul trip for us?' he asked.

'You've never invited me.'

'Would you?'

'Of course. Somewhere in mind?' I was winding the projection cable, looping it over the gap between thumb and forefinger, down to elbow and back again, but slowed the process as I waited for Frank to answer.

He passed me a copy of the latest brochure, which I took with my one free hand. It was open at the Himalaya section. 'You've never been to Nepal, have you? Fancy going?'

Would I fancy going to Nepal! What kind of question was that? My heartbeat quickened and I was aware of the pulse in my neck as I attempted to answer without choking on the words. 'Sure,' was all I could manage. 'Why not?'

'The far northeast of the country was out of bounds until recently,' he explained. 'The Nepalese government has just lifted restrictions, and for the first time a limited number of trekkers will be able to approach Kangchenjunga. We hope to send a group in the autumn – we've just managed to get it in the brochure. It's new, and I'm sure it would be a good route to try. We'd need someone to write about it. What d'you think?'

On the tube to Victoria it was impossible to clear the smile from my face. Others sharing the carriage must have thought me mad. I was. But my head was spinning with the prospect of going to the Himalaya at last. For 30 years I'd been climbing and trekking in a variety of mountain regions, but never the Himalaya. I'd read the books, seen the films, attended lectures – how many times had I sat in an audience enthralled by the tales of a top climber describing the ascent of some Himalayan giant, and imagined myself there! Not climbing – no, I'd lost that fantasy long ago – but trekking across the foothills, through the valleys and over high passes. That would suit my needs; just being there among those fabled mountains. Sharing promotional events with trek leaders experienced in Nepal, Bhutan, Sikkim, Tibet, Pakistan, I'd bombard them with questions, envying their travels. I'd led groups in other places, organised numerous trips to ranges elsewhere, but somehow a Himalayan opportunity had never arisen.

Maybe that omission was my own fault, that I'd never created an opportunity for myself, although friends and acquaintances with conventional jobs and a real income had managed it. Some had sent postcards and letters from exotic locations, while I'd simply drifted from one financial crisis to another and contented myself with mountains nearer home, mountains whose familiarity had become part of my workaday world. They were no second best, of that I was certain. But if you love mountains, the Himalaya will inevitably invade your thoughts and stir ambition. To me, the Himalaya had formed a major part of my dream world, while in reality those great iconic peaks remained far off, remote, aloof and unattainable. Until now.

I couldn't wait to get home to share the news. But by then it was past midnight and the family was asleep.

In the far northeast of Nepal, and straddling the border with Sikkim, Kangchenjunga is a huge massif with extensive ridges and numerous spurs. With five main summits and as many glaciers, it's considered a sacred mountain by those who live in its shadow. When the first ascent was made by a British expedition in 1955, George Band and Joe Brown honoured the beliefs of the Sikkimese people by stopping just short of the actual summit. The untrodden crown thus remained the domain of the gods, undisturbed by mere mortals. Until 1980, that is, when a Japanese team trod all over it.

Unlike many other Himalayan giants that remain blocked from distant view by intervening peaks and ridges, Kanch is clearly visible 70 kilometres away from the ridge-top town of Darjeeling, where it has become one of the sights of the eastern Himalaya. Over the years I'd met a number of men and women who'd spent time in India during the days of the British Raj, whose eyes would glaze over as they reminisced about watching the sun rise or set on that distant peak while on temporary leave from summer's oppressive heat in Calcutta. If the sight of Kangchenjunga from Darjeeling could so enthral, inspire and mesmerise non-mountain folk, I wondered what would its effect be on those of us with a passion for high places who planned to trek to its base?

In the seemingly endless months between that initial invitation in Earls Court and the date of departure for Kathmandu, I absorbed as much information as I could about Nepal in general and the approach to Kanch in particular. Truth to tell, there wasn't much written about the Nepalese approach, for nearly all expeditions to tackle the mountain since the first attempt in 1905 had begun their walk-in from Darjeeling, and had only entered Nepalese territory by crossing the Singalila Ridge near the head of the Yalung Valley, which drains the mountain's southern flank. On the one hand that paucity of information was frustrating. On the other, the sense of mystery it inspired only served to deepen its appeal.

Then I recalled Joe Tasker's *Savage Arena*, a book I'd reviewed for a magazine when it was published in 1982 at the time of the author's disappearance with Peter Boardman on Everest's Northeast Ridge. In it Joe had recounted his part in the four-man expedition to climb Kanch's Northwest Face three years earlier. Taking it from my shelf I leafed through the book and found teasing references to walking along the crest of a ridge between the valleys of the Arun and Tamur, of rhododendrons and clusters of huts, and of porters dwarfed by monstrous loads as they made their way from village to village. Only once did he mention catching sight of the mountain he'd come to climb, 'hovering white and unobtrusive in the distance so I thought it was a cloud'.

By contrast, Boardman's story of the same climb, which appeared in his *Sacred Summits*, offered more descriptions than Joe's of the approach from the then road-head at Dharan, and brought to mind something he'd told a mutual friend when he'd arrived home from the mountain. It was, he'd said, the most beautiful walk he'd ever made. Considering his vast experience on several continents, that was quite a claim, and it excited my imagination more than anything. Could I be embarked on the most beautiful walk in the world?

Max joins me on the hill overlooking the cloud-sea. He's brought my camera as well as his own. 'Here,' he says with his distinctive Belfast accent. 'I figured a new boy like you might like to take a few snaps of your first sight of the Himalaya.'

A 30-year-old bachelor with a high level of disposable income, my tent-mate comes trekking in the Himalaya twice each year and enjoys teasing me for being what he calls 'a new boy'. Mind you, he's never seen the Alps or Pyrenees, or any other European range for that matter, but in common with many other trekkers in Nepal, his only mountain experience has been here, among the highest of them all. How times change! Until very recently it was usual to serve an apprenticeship among the hills and fells of Britain before graduating to the Alps in order to build experience to face bigger, more remote challenges in the Himalaya. It was a natural progression, and if not exactly a law carved in stone, it was something to which most of us conformed. But the advent of adventure travel and cheap international flights has changed all that, and a trek in Nepal, Ladakh or Pakistan is now seen as a viable alternative to a fortnight on the Costa del Sol.

'Thanks,' I say as I take the camera from him and try to capture the essence of this moment in time. Through the lens I scan pillows of mist that froth and foam and lap like a tide against the Singalila Ridge, sharply outlined like a cardboard cut-out. I note the light which floods almost horizontally across the sea of mist, painting a skyline of mountains and pushing blue shadows westward.

We breakfast in a *bhatti*, a simple teahouse in the tiny village just up the slope from our tents. Mingma and his team have taken over the building next door for their kitchen, and ferry the food to us. There's porridge, fried eggs and slices of luke-warm toast to spread with peanut butter, honey or over-sweet Druk jam imported from Bhutan. And there's as much tea, coffee or hot chocolate as we can drink. As I eat, I can see through a hole in the wall to where a pig stands knee-deep in a trough snuffling his own breakfast, while at the same time peeing into it. 'Adds to the flavour,' says Bart, our leader. 'But don't try it on my breakfast.'

It's good to be trekking with Bart Jordans once more. Last year we'd been in the Alps together, and I'm delighted to see that his enthusiasm for mountains is as infectious as ever. Only a few days ago this tall, effervescent Dutchman with a halo of dark hair and wire-rimmed John Lennon glasses had arrived back in Kathmandu from leading a trek to Everest Base Camp, and had barely enough time for a shower before heading east to Kangchenjunga with our group. He must have slept well on the 26 hour bus ride, for since we began trekking he's been bursting with vigour that energises the rest of us.

While we eat the Sherpas collapse the tents, and our porters make up their loads and head off along the trail with small jerky steps, their towering bundles or bamboo dokos held only by hessian tumplines round their foreheads. How do they do it? These guys are only slightly built, with thin legs and either plastic flip-flops or nothing at all on their bare feet. They give no indication of having either strength or stamina – but what must their neck and leg muscles be like?

Leaving the village, our trail slants across open country with an uninterrupted view of the Himalaya ahead. There's Kanch again, demanding our attention, but as we turn a little to the northwest, we can see across the depths of the Arun Valley to Makalu, Lhotse Shar and an insignificant peak that someone says is Everest. Really? I find that hard to believe, but what do I know? Best of all is a mountain standing south of the main Himalayan watershed, with an extensive, flat-looking ridge supported by a vast wall of snow, ice and rock. It's Chamlang, a 7000 metre giant first climbed 27 years ago. Bart speculates that we should have had this panorama yesterday, had it not been for the mist. I'm just thankful we have it now.

Our trek takes us over short-cropped grassland that in the Alps would be grazed by bell-ringing cattle; the only livestock we see here are a few goats. We enter groves of rhododendron trees tall as an English oak. Between lumps of moss cladding, the pinkish bark has a rich sheen as though it's been varnished; ferns and exotic tree orchids adorn some of the trunks, tattered ropes of lichen hang from the branches, and dried leaves form a carpet beneath our boots. At the edge of one of these little woodlands the stumps of recently cut trees tell of nearby houses, and as we pass by women are sweeping the dust from their doorways. Grubby-faced children emerge with hands pressed together in the attitude of prayer: '*Namaste*,' they cry; 'I salute

the god within you.' It becomes a *mantra*, the soundtrack of our journey, as much a part of the Nepalese trekking experience as bed-tea
and distant views.

For an hour or so I walk alone, senses alert to every new experience.
This is what I've dreamed of for so long; I want to miss nothing. There
are riches to be harvested wherever I turn; I'm greedy for life.

Suddenly I'm aware of a young voice singing. Delivered in a
strong but high-pitched key, the sound is approaching fast, and when
I turn I see our 15-year-old porter we've named Speedy come trip-
ping along the trail under his 20 kilo load. Neither the weight of his
doko, nor the speed of his footwork, appears to have any impact on
his singing. I'm impressed. There's no room for him to pass just here,
so I continue until there's a broadening of the trail where the shrubbery is not so dense. There I stand back, but Speedy decides to stop
too, leans his *doko* against a convenient rock, adjusts the *namlo* on his
sweating forehead, and gives me a wide grin. His song has ended, but
I figure it would be good to have it on tape as a record of the journey,
so pull my hand-sized recorder from my pocket and give him a dem-
onstration. He speaks, and I play his voice back to him. Eyes wide
with wonder, he takes the tape recorder from me to examine. '*Ramro*,'
he says. I sing a few phrases, play them back and point to him. 'Will
you sing for me?'

He understands my request and willingly gives a rendition of the
song he'd been singing only moments before. Then we resume our
journey together. But the young lad soon draws ahead, singing a different song this time, his plastic flip-flops slapping a rhythm of their own
on the bare-earth trail, while I jog behind trying to record more of this
very special soundscape.

Together we make rapid progress along the trail, which now
slopes downhill before easing along a more open flank of the Milke
Danda. A broad valley lies far below the ridge – the same valley that
was drowned by the cloud-sea at dawn. Now I see it is patched with

trees and small villages, and on its far side hillsides are cleft with streams draining the Singalila Ridge where cloud-shadows ripple their own journeys.

After less than three hours of walking we return to the crest to gain a view onto a dip in the ridge where two lines of simple houses face one another across a paved street. To the left of the houses there's another small pond, which gives the village its name – Gupha Pokhari. 'Pokhari', Max later explains in his eagerness to educate me, means 'lake'. Beside the pond I notice the blue tarpaulin that signals our lunch stop. But it's only 10.30!

A stone-built *chautaara* stretches along the centre of the village street. Our porters have stopped here; their dokos are leaning on the wall, and their sticks – on which they take the weight of their loads when resting briefly on the trail – are hooked on the baskets. Inside two of the *bhattis* I recognise familiar faces drinking tea, peering out at nothing in particular as I wander past through a haze of wood smoke, pausing to study shops that display a few packets of biscuits, cigarettes, small bottles of the local Kukri rum and brightly coloured hair ribbons – but little else.

Life in Gupha Pokhari is unhurried. Outside one of the buildings a woman seated at a loom weaves a scarf in the November sunshine. Beside her an older woman with wrinkled face and the faintest hint of grey in her hair spins wool, while next door a young man pedals a sewing machine. On the other side of the *chautaara* a hen with a brood of yellow velcro chicks scratches the earth between stone slabs as a bare-bummed child toddles from one of the houses, squats in the street and looks in amazement at the arc of pee which comes from his tiny willy. 'Did I do all that?' he appears to ask. Rising from sleep a black dog yawns, then turns his head to nip at a flea before slumping back to sleep once more.

I turn my back on the buildings and wander across the meadow to where Mingma and the cook-boys are preparing a meal.

25

Mingma kneads a round of dough. Indre takes it from him, rolls it into flat discs which he lightly forks, then drops them one by one into a pot of boiling fat, where they rapidly swell to become what our cook calls Tibetan bread. Someone thrusts a mug of hot fruit juice at me as I slide my daypack to the ground. 'Thanks,' I say; '*Dhanyabaad.*'

Seated on the blue tarpaulin the group is beginning to gel. Some are discussing the morning's journey, while others write diaries or read a book. Max fiddles with his camera, polishing the lens with a tissue. He'll be taking no more long views today, though, for clouds are boiling out of a far valley, and one by one the mountains are being swallowed by them. Yet still the sun beams down upon us.

The group consists of seven men and two women, plus Bart the leader and Dawa the *sirdar*. And Mingma the cook, seven Sherpas and cook-boys, and 26 porters, half a dozen of whom are female – the bright-eyed Sherpanis who keep very much to themselves. This army of 45 is by far the largest I've ever trekked with, but such is the scale of the landscape that it's easy to wander alone whenever I feel the need – as I do now and then – for I'm eager to absorb as much of this country as I can without distraction.

To ensure no one is lost or left behind, there's always one Sherpa walking ahead to mark the way with an arrow scratched in the dust or on a convenient rock whenever the trail divides, and there'll be another at the back to scoop up any stragglers. A third Sherpa, an anxious-looking Tibetan, carries a Tilly lamp and keeps his eye on the porters. He'll need that lamp tonight.

Along the Milke Danda we trek the afternoon hours, at first making an easy contour of the right-hand slope, then heading onto an obvious saddle, followed by a short climb up the crest to a cluster of prayer flags hanging limply from bamboo wands. '*Om mani padme hum*' drips from them. Now we descend below the flags on a corrugated clay path that takes us in and out of rhododendron woods, through tiny villages consisting of no more than half a dozen timber-and-bamboo houses, and up once more to a view of a solid-looking wall of cumulus where the Himalaya should be.

Camp is set on a terraced meadow within an arc of woodland. Speedy is already there when we arrive, his *doko* unpacked, a song on his lips as he gathers dry wood for a fire. An overhanging rock provides shelter for the cook, who has a brew stewing in a kettle. Mugs are passed round, and as evening gathers someone points out that the clouds have gone. Above the trees Kangchenjunga hovers in the flush of alpenglow.

Darkness falls, but some of our porters have not yet arrived, and as we eat our meal by the light of a hurricane lamp, heads turn uphill at the slightest sound in the hope that the missing men are coming. An hour drifts by. Then another. Some of the group go to their tents. A bottle of whisky does the rounds, for it's cold here at almost 3000 metres, and the sky is studded with stars. Then suddenly a faint glimmer of light is detected in the black pitch of the wooded hill. Voices are heard, and half an hour later the Tibetan porter-guide with long jet-black hair braided in a pigtail arrives with the weary stragglers, for whom it's been a long day.

I beat the dawn in order to be ready to photograph Kanch as the great mountain emerges from night. Frost has painted the grass around our camp, and blanketed porters congregate wherever fires have been lit. The dawn chorus is loud with coughing, and with throats and nostrils being emptied.

Breakfast over, I'm saddened to discover that Speedy is being paid off, and am unconvinced by Dawa's explanation that he's asked to go home, for the expression on his face suggests otherwise. I fear he's been victimised as an individual who stands out from the crowd. Although the youngest of our porters by far, Speedy has been carrying an adult's load with surprising ease. What's more, he almost runs along the trail, singing as he goes. By comparison (and I accept it's an unfair one to make) the rest of the porters appear weak, lazy and slow. I also wonder whether the fact that I'd been seen recording his songs might have counted against him – a sign of favouritism, perhaps, leading to jealousy? If so, it's something I regret, so when I'm certain no one is looking, I hand him a clutch of rupee notes, which he secretes inside a fold of his shirt and makes his departure back the way we'd come.

By the time we're on our way the frost has melted, and sunbeams shaft into the forest to illuminate huge spiders' webs strung across the trail. Lianas hang almost to the ground, and grotesque tumours of moss lend some of the trees a Disneyesque appearance. All that is needed is a haunting melody to set them dancing. I sense that the forest has eyes. It also has sounds. Birds call to one another and cicadas tune up as we burst out into the eye-squinting splendour of unrestricted sunshine.

Now that we've arrived at the end of the Milke Danda's spur, the hills spill in a convex slope for 2000 metres to the Tamur Khola. For much of the way there's a vast staircase of terraces on which tiny houses are dwarfed by the immensity of the landscape. Far below a milky blue ribbon twists with no sound of its glacial fury reaching us, while on the far side of the Tamur's valley, halfway up the opposite slope, the little township of Taplejung can just be detected – once we know where to look, that is. High above it there's a small airstrip, beside which, according to Pemba, we'll make camp tomorrow night. He's happy to direct our gaze. He's been this way before with a Japanese expedition to climb Kanch's Southwest Face and is eager to be back.

But what catches and holds my attention is the sight once again of that ragged Himalayan skyline – Jannu, Kangchenjunga, Talung, Kabru and all the other 6000, 7000 and 8000 metre peaks that stretch as far as the eye can see; fairyland castles in the sky, they are, supported by clouds. What was it Joe Tasker had written? 'In the sky hovering white and unobtrusive in the distance so I thought it was a cloud…'.

I settle beside the trail letting others pass by, and am aware that this bewitching land embraces me in its warmth. Fragrances drawn from the vegetation by the morning sun are intense, yet they are so kaleidoscopic in complexity that I fail to separate them into individual scents. Instead I have to content myself with their overall effect. Sounds, too, are beyond my frail ability to recognise and define them. Exotic birds with fanciful plumage swoop from tree to bush and back up to tree again, there to warble their morning anthems while the piercing electric cadence of a million unseen cicadas builds to a deafening pitch.

Before coming to Nepal I had imagined the drama of the great peaks. To me, trekking would mean a visual feast of glacier and rock face, of marching breathless through avenues of soaring mountains, of plodding through crisp snow en route to a lofty pass, there to gaze on scenes of untamed grandeur. I'd given little consideration to the foothill country. Yet this too, I've discovered, is a wonderland, and although the snowbound horizon has its seductive allure, I'm in no hurry to reach it. Each step of the approach is full of its own unique brand of magic.

As if to emphasise that fact, all the way down to Dobhan on the banks of the Tamur Khola is a dream. Thatched houses with white and ochre walls stand beside the trail, sweetcorn cobs hang to dry beneath their eaves, garlands of marigolds over doors and glassless windows, pumpkins against a wall...children laughing...voices calling from fields of ripening millet...cocks crowing, goats bleating.

Every terrace has been put to use. On the upper hillside the rice is not yet ready for harvesting, and chuntering streams feed irrigation ditches. Dragonflies hover over them. The sun dances in flooded paddies to flash diamonds as we pass.

The path levels for 20 rare paces. Alongside it a *chautaara* has been built, some of its stones having been rubbed and polished black by generations of porters who've rested here; the upright blocks wear lichens, but the sun-baked path is littered with cigarette butts and orange peel. At the end of the *chautaara* two young girls and a boy with a dreamy look stand sentry. Silhouetted as they are against castles among clouds, I carry that vision with me.

Further down the slope we pass orange trees and green-skinned grapefruit the size of footballs. Bananas grow beside many of the houses; flame-coloured bougainvillaea and straggly poinsettias hang over the trail; I catch the scent of frangipani.

Here the rice is being harvested by women in scarlet or vivid green saris. Bent double over the waist-high crop, their fingers deftly gather clumps of stalks as a blade flashes the light. The cut rice is then laid over to dry, for water has drained from the terrace and the warm sun will soon draw out any excess moisture. Lower down the slope a bare-footed farmer is ploughing with a pair of water buffalo, turning the soil in pocket-sized terraces, yelping a command each time he reaches the terrace end, where he then hops down to the next tiny field, manhandles the plough and virtually steers the stumbling buffalo to face the opposite direction. He pauses in his work to watch me pass. I raise a hand in acknowledgement. He lets go the plough, and his hands come together. '*Namaste*,' he calls.

I continue down the trail enriched by his greeting.

There are no certainties in trekking among mountains. Here in the Himalaya I accept that any one of a number of circumstances could affect our plans – sudden snowfall or landslip, ill-health or an inability to acclimatise, the mood of our porters, availability of campsites with water, problems with route-finding... All these things (and others) make it essential to retain a flexible attitude of mind. Although we've been given an itinerary, it's merely a framework within which the trek will manoeuvre a course. We have a date by which we ought to be in Tumlingtar on the River Arun, where a charter flight is due to fly us back to Kathmandu. The rest is open to speculation, and rather than create tensions, it should provide a sense of freedom. That is certainly how I feel, and relaxing by the side of the icy Tamur below Dobhan's houses while the valley gathers darkness I'm aware of the joy of now and the essence of being. Tomorrow is of no concern until tomorrow arrives.

The river crunches and grinds rocks and boulders that lie in its path. It has its own agenda, its own history. Neither rocks nor boulders will deter its journey to the sea, for with time its ally, and with patience counted in millions of years, the river's relentless pounding will reduce those blocks of stone into grey powder. Nepal's greatest export is its mountains, for even as they grow, they're being worn down and transported via its rivers to the Bay of Bengal, along with countless tons of soil from terraces washed away by the annual monsoon rains.

Our journey has a more limited time scale. It is estimated that we will need 12 days to trek from the road-head to the south side of Kangchenjunga and another two to cross a series of passes into the valley of the Ghunsa Khola, where we will take a day's rest. Then there will be four or five days to descend back to Dobhan, followed by another four or five trekking up and along the western flank of the Milke Danda to Tumlingtar. But, as I say, this is little more than speculation, a plan written down in a London office. Reality could be very different. Reality is this moment in time, the darkness that has now filled the valley, the rush and crunch of the river, the cool silty sand between my toes, the crackle of the porters' fires and the rise and fall of laughter. I am aware of the insect chorus among unseen trees – a different sound from that of daylight hours. I see faint lights moving in the village above me, and imagine candles flickering from room to room in medieval homes. I momentarily shiver with the cool air that washes through the valley, riding the snowmelt from high, wild places, and am glad.

The 1600 metre climb from the banks of the Tamur to the Tibetan settlement of Suketar on the ridge of the Surke Danda is a steep and demanding one for porters. It's a long enough route for us trekkers carrying only daypacks, but for heavily laden men and women it is a gruelling ascent. Bright sunshine, little shade, barely a breeze and the belief that we'd be stopping earlier than we do add nothing but misery to their day, and when they finally arrive at the village long after night has fallen, their mood is sullen. I sense a poisonous blister of resentment held in check only by utter weariness. In the morning that blister must be lanced or it will burst of its own accord.

It bursts.

Breakfast is over, our gear packed and tents collapsed, yet the porters have so far not even begun to sort their loads. Nor do they give any impression of doing so. Bart is deep in discussion with Dawa by the side of the white-painted Buddhist *gompa* which overlooks our dismantled camp. Strings of brightly coloured prayer flags dance in the morning breeze to match the incongruous sight of a windsock nearby. Just behind the *bhatti*, where we'd sat for hours last night awaiting the arrival of our tents, a barbed-wire fence deters animals from straying onto a flattish meadow that serves as the airstrip for Taplejung, the township halfway down the slope towards Dobhan. By that fence groups of disgruntled porters sit hunched in circles. At a distance of a hundred paces it is clear that serious negotiations must begin soon or tempers will erupt.

Dawa walks nervously to them. Other Sherpas watch from a discreet distance, as do we. Max voices general concern: 'The next few minutes will determine whether our trek continues or not. If Dawa buggers this up, we're doomed to spend the next three weeks sitting here!'

Bart explains that last night there'd been an angry dispute between some of the porters and Dawa. They, the porters, claimed they'd been led to believe we were camping at Taplejung, not here at Suketar. (We'd taken an early lunch at Taplejung, but no porters had arrived by the time we'd set off again; and that should have been a warning.) Now Dawa is going to assert his authority and pay off four of the most troublesome men – and that will not be easy. Neither will it be easy to calm the mood of fizzing discontent.

Dawa Sherpa treads eggshells.

An eruption of angry voices breaks out. Thin men leap to their feet, all shouting, arms waving. Dawa steps back a pace or two, but is quickly surrounded. 'I'd better go,' says Bart, who hurries to the fray, followed by Pemba and Dendi.

The noise continues for several minutes, but although there's a certain amount of pushing and shoving, there is no meaningful physical violence, yet it takes the joint diplomacy of Bart and Dawa to calm the situation. Eventually loud voices subside and spaces appear where moments before there'd been a tight mass of volcanic tension. Dawa's face appears above the crowd and beckons to Mingma, who hurries to his *sirdar*'s side. A few words are exchanged, and Mingma goes off to find Dawa's rucksack in which he keeps a fat wallet of rupee notes.

A few minutes later the blister has been doctored and the tension evaporates.

'What you English would call a true compromise,' explains Bart in obvious relief. 'The porters demanded double pay for yesterday's climb. It was a bit tough for them, I'll admit, but Dawa's got them to agree to one and a half day's wages. That's pretty fair, I'd say. Mind you, if we have any more days like that, it could prove to be a costly trek.'

Porters gather their loads. Some are even laughing, while those who were paid off count their wages and set off down the hillside without a backward glance. 'The trek resumes,' cries Max, like a wagon-master eager to be on his way. 'Let's go!'

Our route across the Surke Danda is more complex than the one had been along the Milke Danda, as we descend to cross streams and rivers and climb through one village after another. For hours at a stretch we are denied mountain views, but this is of no concern, for these Middle Hills, whose summits approach 4000 metres, are rich in visual contrasts, rewarding in vegetation, and lively with wildlife. White-faced monkeys bounce among the forest trees, highly coloured birds swoop across the trail, and I see my first butterflies of the Himalaya – as big as sparrows, they seem to my wide-eyed gaze.

Day after day the trail works its route through an ever-changing landscape, and my eyes are everywhere, for I'm innocent as a child and filled with a sense of wonder. In sunshine and shadow I drift without effort – sometimes among trees and shrubs, sometimes on bare and open hillsides. Life makes no more demands than that of placing one foot in front of the other.

Today we stop early. The harvest has been taken, ploughs have turned the soil in endless terraced fields, and that soil is now baking in the full sunshine. This rucked and wrinkled land fills me with delight, and I'm glad that Dawa has chosen this spot for our tents – two to each terrace with an airy outlook as though from a balcony. Max and I are on the second terrace down from the kitchen tent, which suits us both. Our loads having been dumped above us, I climb the terraces and manhandle a couple of kitbags, and with one under each arm foolishly jump down to the small field of baked earth below. Landing awkwardly, my left foot twists beneath me and I crumple to the ground in agony. I feel physically sick as I grip my ankle, convinced it's broken. Sweat breaks out on my forehead, but I shiver all over.

'Let me feel.' The voice is John's, a member of our group with a cultured voice and an authoritative air. Until now I've not found him easy company, but in this emergency he's calm and efficient, and I recognise that whatever his background he certainly knows his first aid. His hands are gentle but probing, and he announces (with more certainty than I feel) that nothing is broken. But my ankle is swelling like a balloon. Bart calls for two bowls of water, one hot, the other cold, and after carefully removing my sock, my ankle is immersed first in one, then the other repeatedly until the hot water has turned cool. Then more is called for. I'm given pills to help reduce the swelling and ease the pain, and am carried to my tent.

Passing an uncomfortable night, I'm reminded that mountaineer Pete Boardman also damaged an ankle on his way to climb Kangchenjunga 10 years ago, and had then been carried by a relay of porters until he could walk again. Perhaps that should have given me confidence, but I fear my trek is over. 'Nonsense,' says Max. 'You'll walk. The alternative is to be buried here.'

In the morning my ankle is discoloured with bruising, and I'm given more pills to swallow. John carefully straps the wound in a crepe bandage, but when I ease my foot into the boot, I find I can only tie the lace very loosely. I'm given a stick to use and helped to stand, but as soon as I put any weight on the foot, pain shoots through my body and I feel sick again.

Pemba is now my constant companion as I hobble slowly along the trail, but a rhythm gradually develops and my pace improves, although it'll be a full week before the swelling starts to subside. On the second day I lose my balance and sprawl face down on the path, twisting the ankle once more. Every part of me throbs with pain. Pemba helps me up, and soon after I'm seated upon a rock with my foot submerged in a clear forest pool at the base of a cascade pouring over a mossy green slab. I'm dashed with spray, and the water is cold enough to make my whole leg ache, but it's sheer bliss.

Our trek takes us over ridge spurs and down to gorge-like tributaries, which we cross on suspension bridges that sway and shudder beneath us. The route is a helter-skelter, and there's barely more than a few paces of level ground anywhere along it. Attractive houses cling to impossibly steep hillsides; snow mountains tease above distant hills before hiding again for hours at a time. Passing through the village of Mamankhe we discover a couple of houses with beautifully carved balconies decorated with containers of flowers. But for the thatch on their roofs they could have been transported from the Bernese Oberland. Padding barefoot along the trail nearby, two young children return home beneath towering loads of foliage – presumably fodder for their animals. They stand back to watch us pass, but say nothing. Much later the route takes us through a cardamom plantation, after which we splash through a side stream and make camp below a sad-looking broken village.

Yamphudin is still in shock. A month ago, at the tail-end of the monsoon, the Kabeli Khola burst its banks and swept half the village away. Huge boulders and mud banks remain where no boulders or mud banks belong. Trees have been uprooted, and river-ravaged houses stand among banana groves tilted at odd angles where the land has been uplifted by the force of the water. Villagers stare at us with vacant expressions as though life has been drained from them, but a policeman appears to check our permits, and while the tents are being erected he squats on his hunkers and draws deeply on a cigarette. He tells Dawa there's an American climber with a broken leg waiting in the village for a helicopter to carry him out. Apparently he fell while crossing the ridge ahead, and since he was too heavy for his porters to carry, he had to crawl all the way down to Yamphudin. I feel the pain in my ankle and make a mental note to take extra care on our crossing tomorrow.

We discover there are two ridges to mount before we finally enter the valley that leads to the south side of Kangchenjunga. The first of these is crossed at the Dhupi Bhanjyang, below which the slope is steep, greasy and crowded with mist-hugging trees, while the second gives way at the Lamite Bhanjyang, where we catch sight of chisel-topped Jannu, Kanch's most impressive neighbour that was first climbed by a French expedition in 1962. No other snow peaks can be seen, yet we know they are there. In another day or two, perhaps, we will be among them, but first we must descend with care along the edge of two monstrous landslide scars, then through a forest of chir pine, fir and bamboo, and finally among rhododendron trees above the east bank of the river that drains Kangchenjunga's glaciers and snowfields.

There's a bird that sings first thing in the morning with a sound like that of a gate in need of oil. But not this morning. The forest is silent. A heavy frost stiffens the tent, and the only sound to be heard is the rumbling of the river. Autumn is in the air, and the last deciduous trees are patched with russet and gold. Leaves drift in lazy spirals as the day slowly warms.

Once we're on the move we rise along the true right bank of the river, exchanging broad-leaved trees for tall mossy-trunked conifers. On open meadows straggly clumps of berberis blaze scarlet.

Then all of a sudden mountains are just ahead. Well, a day or so's walk away, but seeming just ahead. White-plastered mountains, they are, with crests etched sharp against a deep blue sky. My heart makes an involuntary leap in my chest, and I realise I'm smiling. This is an alpine world, for although the summits are maybe 4000 metres higher than our part of the valley, I'm unable as yet to grasp the scale of things, and I stumble. A sharp pain shoots through my leg, for my eyes are not on the inconsistencies of the trail. They are focused on peaks unknown.

We take to the broad, stony river bed. The river is only a few paces away. We can hear its thunder and see occasional bursts of spray tossed from midstream boulders, but other than that it's lost to view. We pick our way towards the mountain wall that blocks the far end of the valley. There is no path to speak of, but our porters are ahead, the prints of their bare feet easy to follow in drifts of glacial sand between the rocks.

In the early afternoon we pull up a rise and come onto the *yak* pasture of Tseram at a little under 4000 metres. The size of a football pitch, sloping gently towards the river, it's fringed with scrub and rocks. Rhododendrons bank the lower hillside, while a fuzz of cypress trees grows a little higher. A group of porters build a fire against a huge smoke-blackened boulder that stands on the edge of the pasture. The unmistakable sound of kukri knives hacking at the branches of rhododendron trees rings clear. It is one of the alarming sounds of the Himalaya, and although I hold no knife, the guilt is as much mine as that of our porters.

Other porters arrive, dumping their lozenge-shaped loads of tents and kitbags where they stop. They wipe their brows, look around, and in a glance decide where they'll build their own fires. Moments later I notice one man sitting alone hacking at something by his feet, the curving blade of his kukri shines as he makes swift cutting movements. I'm intrigued – is he carving something? If so, what? I edge nearer and am horrified to discover he's trimming his toenails with a blade as long as his forearm. One slip and he'll be toeless.

37

On the eastern side of the valley lies a way to Sikkim over the Kang La. Some of the early expeditions used this pass on their approach to Kangchenjunga from Darjeeling. Frank Smythe crossed the Kang La in 1930 with an international expedition led by the German-Swiss geology professor GO Dyhrenfurth, and on arrival here he found a simple *yak*-herder's hut. A long building with wide eaves, one end housed the yaks, while the other was reserved for the herder and his family. According to Smythe's account, the family's bedding was a mass of dirty straw alive with fleas, and cooking was done on a fire of rhododendron wood on a stone hearth. Our porters are not the first, then, to attack the rhododendron trees of Tseram.

I'm unable to take my eyes off the head of the valley. Up there, Kabru's lofty ridge sparkles in sunshine. Next to it is shapely Ratong, with the deep saddle of the Ratong La below. Snow and ice smear every verticality, yet the valley walled by those peaks is devoid of glacier or snowfield, so far as I can tell from here, which makes the impact of that white vision the more profound. Then, as the afternoon moves towards dusk, the lowering sun turns an unnamed rock peak a little northeast of here into a glowing tower of bronze. Suddenly Kabru and Ratong lose their dominance. Clouds boil up from the lower valley, and one by one all the mountains take their leave.

One more camp and we'll be within sight of the Southwest Face of Kangchenjunga. Since leaving Basantpur at the road-head – what was it 10, 11 days ago? – every day has been filled with wonders. The lush foothills and more rugged Middle Hills have rewarded each hour, and if we were to go no further, they would have justified travelling all the way to Nepal. Even so, the prospect of coming within touching distance of those Himalayan giants denies me sleep, and I'm saddened to know that two of our group will wait here while we go on tomorrow. For several days one of our women has been suffering from diarrhoea, and the other says she's trail-weary and has run out of steam. So near, yet so far…

38

I cannot believe this day has arrived!

On three sides I'm hemmed in by mountains of exquisite beauty. Behind me the Yalung Valley descends in a series of steps. On each level a baize of autumnal grass hints at pasturing for yaks, although I've not seen any this morning. Every once in a while a diaphanous web of mist drifts up from the lower, unseen valley, but by the time it reaches this point it spins, tears and evaporates. The air has a crisp bite, yet shaded from any breeze the sun's warmth is reminiscent of a late Indian summer. On this dazzling day the light is so acute I'm forced to squint behind dark glasses.

Topping another rise I'm suddenly aware that for the past hour or so I've been walking through an ablation valley – off to the right there's a dark wall of moraine, which conceals from view the great Yalung Glacier, and to the left the pasture stops abruptly at the foot of a mountain. A hanging valley breaks the uniformity of that left-hand slope, but ahead...ahead I see a glacial lake. Shallow and ice-edged, it acts like a shining mirror. In those waters summits of rare perfection have been uprooted. Images of snow-sheathed mountains dazzle the sun; they float and shimmer upside down, while their real selves form a backdrop that until now belonged to a world of dreams.

I lower my rucksack to the ground and position myself on a convenient rock. Alone, my soul floats in a breathless silence.

The poet Robert Service once wrote that silence is man's confession of his own deafness, and I know he's right, for it's not silent here at all. Peaceful, yes. Almost devoid of sound – but not quite. There comes the whisper of a stray breeze, filtering not from the lower valley, but from ahead and across the other side of the unseen glacier where Koktang is a crystal curtain, its immaculately fluted ridge tilting shadows that outline every individual fold and ripple of its face. That breeze brings with it frostnip and the soft hum of distance.

Koktang's left-hand arête sweeps down to the U-shaped cleft of the Ratong La, through which I see mountains that belong to another country. Those snow peaks of Sikkim seem to be dwarfed by the immediate scene,

39

yet their presence adds to its glory. On the north side of the Ratong La rears the great cone of Ratong that we'd gazed on yesterday from Tseram. This acts as a buttress to the formidable block that is Kabru, whose face is crumpled with hanging glaciers, but from here I am unable to see the continuation of its summit ridge, although I know it leads to Talung and then up to Kangchenjunga itself. Kangchenjunga…just around the corner. Only just around the corner…yet I am content to wait a little longer before setting eyes on its Southwest Face. For this moment in time there's as much scenic grandeur as I can absorb.

Now I'm aware of a soft tinkling sound, so lightly suggested that it's necessary to hold my breath. There it goes again – and again – as a stream breaks free of its early glaze of ice and finds release across the pasture.

I'm not certain how long I enjoy the solitude, but eventually the peace is disturbed by a familiar sound when one porter after another comes over the bluff behind me to traipse across the *yak*-cropped grass. The first announces his presence with a cough, a hawk, and a gob of smoke-induced phlegm. The juggernauts of the Himalaya are on the move again.

Once more we camp early, this time on the uppermost *yak* pasture known as Ramze, where the successful 1955 Kangchenjunga expedition had their so-called Moraine Camp, and where their 300 porters set down six tons of food and equipment to be ferried up the Yalung Glacier to their base camp. By comparison it is empty today. Just a handful of our blue ridge tents to provide a modicum of shelter for one night only.

At an altitude of more than 4600 metres, the pasture is hemmed in by a curving black wall of moraine just short of the point where the valley makes an abrupt turn to the north. Two herders' huts stand on a slope behind our tents, and above these Boktoh scratches at the sky. With nightfall the temperature plummets, and when I brave the chill for a pee shortly after midnight everywhere is coated with frost and Boktoh glows in the light of a full moon. I stand entranced by a heaven flushed with stars, each one diamond-sharp and close enough to touch. I'm tempted to pluck two or three from the sky to carry back to the tent to use as candles.

Bed-tea is early in that frost bowl, and we breakfast on porridge long before the sun is awake. Cocooned in down we trudge round the bend of the valley towards the bulk of Kangchenjunga, which gradually appears like an impregnable fortress at its head. An avenue of snow peaks, anonymous still in shadow, draws us on. It's bitterly cold and too early for words. Day may have dawned high on Kanch, but here in the ablation valley night still holds sway. But before long, across the Yalung Glacier the great crusted ridge of cornices that links Ratong with the many summits of Kabru, and Kabru with Talung, begins to appear translucent. Beyond those mountains the sun is working its magic from a secret Sikkimese meadow where it has spent the night. I sense its rising. Then there's an explosion of light, a halo appears and ice crystals dance in the still morning air.

Kangchenjunga, to which we have been walking for so many days, now offers its Southwest Face for inspection. Broken here and there by black ribs of rock, it has a formidable presence, its glaze of ice and snow stippled by what appear from this distance to be minor cracks, but which in reality no doubt are monstrous glacial shelves. Almost 4000 metres higher than where I stand, the wall is topped by a crest of ice carved against a sky of deep intensity. A glorious mountain it truly is, but so too are those to the right and left of me, each one no less spellbinding in its beauty than Kanch itself.

Pemba grabs my arm and points up the left-hand slope. '*Bharal*,' he hisses. These are the so-called blue sheep of the Himalaya, and I stand rooted to the spot to watch as a small herd of the short-horned animals skitters across what looks like a vertical gully. A few stones rattle down. Then peace is restored.

My Sherpa friend is excited to be back in close contact with Kangchenjunga. Today it is his mountain and, full of stories of his time

41

here with the Japanese expedition, he directs my attention to individual features on the massive face. In honour of his return he's wearing a pair of red quilted trousers from that expedition as a souvenir.

We clamber onto the moraine crest and look down upon the glacier. In the Alps it would either be riven with blue-green crevasses or carpeted with snow. Here in the Himalaya we gaze upon a junkyard bearing the debris of the mountains that wall it; a chaos of rock and rubble – grey, drab and lacking appeal.

Pemba presses on, now joined by Dendi, while I follow close behind, panting with the unaccustomed altitude. I am made breathless not only by the thin air, though, but by the scene ahead, above and behind, for this is the culmination of a dream; the Himalaya at last!

At last we reach a prominent *chorten*, like a huge milestone on the moraine crest, with an uninterrupted view of Kangchenjunga as a backdrop. A cluster of bamboo wands wearing strips of printed cloth rise from the top of this pile of stones. We stand before it without words as a gust of wind snaps at the flags to disturb the prayers. A flotilla of '*Om mani padme hums*' is released to the mountain deities. Kangchenjunga, abode of the gods, absorbs them all.

Pemba and Dendi move to the other side of the *chorten*, where they deposit grains of rice and a few small-denomination rupee notes on a flat stone shelf. In unison they begin to chant their prayers, deep mumbling sounds like the hum of the universe, while broken thumbnails flick prayer beads. I stand to one side, deeply moved.

When they finish, Pemba turns to me and commands: 'Now you must pray.'

'Okay,' I respond. 'What should I pray?'

'You pray like we do. That you come back again.'

So I do.

CHAPTER 2

Annapurna

THE ANNAPURNA CIRCUS
(1991)

I trek the Annapurna Circuit with an old friend, but reach the Sanctuary alone, surrounded by 7000 metre peaks.

After trekking to Kangchenjunga I was hooked. That trek of a life-time could not be filed away in memory as a one-off; I'd have to return to the Himalaya. So before my flight home I spent two hectic days in Kathmandu visiting local agents and quizzing seasoned trek leaders. Plans took shape, but the following year writing projects diverted me to the Alps, to eastern Turkey and the Russian Caucasus. The Himalaya had to wait, but not for long…

For eight hours I'm forced to crouch almost double in the cab of a bus, a metal box above my head, knees embedded in the back of the driver's

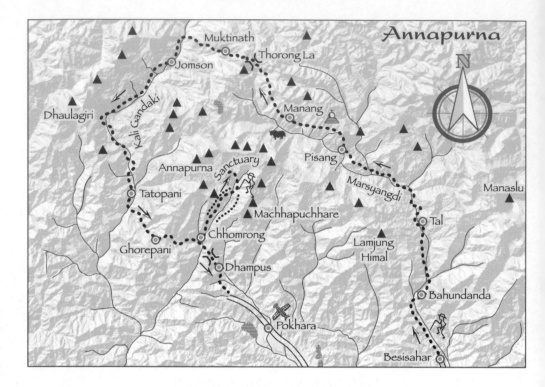

seat, so when we arrive at last at the grubby township of Dumre, between Kathmandu and Pokhara, I hobble down the street bent like Quasimodo. One glance at the open-backed truck which provides onward transport to the trail-head convinces my companion, Alan, and me that there must be an alternative. There is. We locate the driver of a jeep, negotiate a price and encourage two other travellers – one Swiss, the other American – to share the costs, and depart for the mountains in a cloud of red dust.

The 40-odd kilometres of dirt road to Besisahar consume three and a half hours, and by the time we arrive a dense film of dust covers everything – the jeep, our rucksacks, the driver, us. Our nostrils are caked, eyes sore, my head is splitting. Next time, I swear, I'll walk all the way from Kathmandu.

This is Alan Payne's first visit to Nepal. Raised in Derbyshire, but now living in Devon, where he's a planning officer, we met in the Atlas

Mountains in 1965 and have since trekked and climbed numerous times in the Alps and Pyrenees. He's fit, good company, easy-going and undemanding, and content to leave me to make decisions as to where to go and when, so when I told him of my plan to trek to Annapurna, he jumped at the opportunity to join me.

Annapurna is an obvious choice – its reputation for dramatic scenery and cultural diversity make it one of the most prized of all trekking regions. Mountains apart, the landscape varies from sub-tropical forest and lush foothill terraces in the south to frosted barren wastes on the northern side of the Himalayan divide, and from a trekkers' pass at almost 5500 metres to the deepest river valley on Earth. Within this land of extremes live an assortment of ethnic groups – Magar, Newar, Gurung, Chhetri, Brahmin, Thakali and *Bhotiya* – many of whom have abandoned traditional farming practices to become lodge- or teahouse-owners, converting the family home to accommodate foreign trekkers, thereby making it easy for independent travellers to trek here without the need to backpack heavy camping equipment and food supplies.

No wonder it's popular.

Beginning our counter-clockwise circuit we follow the Marsyangdi upstream, crossing tributaries on a variety of bridges and, in one case, wading through the water aided by a self-appointed river guide all of 10 years old. We share the trail with porters carrying crates of bottled drinks; others are laden with four metre wooden planks, sheets of corrugated iron, shiny metal trunks or dokos filled with pasta and tins of coffee. Western voices are heard in wayside *bhattis*, and some of our fellow trekkers on the early, humid stages of the route are dressed as though heading for a Mediterranean beach.

Wandering among terraces of rice and millet, we catch sight of snow peaks balanced upon clouds – Himalchuli, Ngadi Chuli and Manaslu rise from the east bank of the Marsyangdi, while hills west of the river belong to the unseen Annapurnas. So far these are just big hills, nameless hills, and we must trek for several days before we discover the mountains we've been dreaming about.

Unlike the Kangchenjunga region, every village has its lodges, and between villages teahouses ply a trade in tea and biscuits, bottles of Coke and Fanta, and bars of Cadbury's chocolate made in India. Lodges have fanciful names on brightly painted boards – Hotel Himalaya and Lodge, Hotel Mountain View, Hotel Dorchester. Despite the pretentious titles, they're just simple lodgings with smoky dining areas and bare rooms for sleeping in. Most have dormitories, while some have twin-bedded rooms furnished with wooden sleeping platforms, a thin foam mattress and a greasy pillow; sometimes there's a small table and a candle and, if we're lucky, a nail in the wall on which to hang clothes. Toilets are usually found outside in the yard – a narrow cubicle with a hole in the floor – the bathroom is just a standpipe, and when showers are advertised they turn out to be another cubicle next to the *chaarpi* with a hosepipe dribbling tepid water.

On our first day we trek as far as Bahundanda, a Brahmin village perched on a saddle on a spur of the Ngadi Lekh. Both sides of the hill are stepped with rice terraces, the trail partly shaded by trees and tall poinsettias bright with scarlet bracts. Lined with open-fronted shops, the village square is busy with locals and a few fellow trekkers studying their guidebooks and maps, and as we arrive two unkempt children shriek 'Namaste' at us as though we're deaf. A sign tacked to one of the buildings indicates the way to the police check post, where we show our permits and enter names in a register – a formality to be repeated countless times in the years ahead. The official glances at our permits, then at us. 'You trek Annapurna Circus?' he asks, and I can't decide whether he's being cynical, making a joke, or if I've simply misunderstood his question.

Tonight we share a lodge with Ray, a Canadian railroad engineer with short-cropped hair and pale grey eyes, and his daughter Linda, an attractive young woman in her mid-20s who spends her winters as a ski instructor in Japan. Over pots of tea we chat about mountains and travel and the lure of Nepal, about the day's journey and prospects for tomorrow, and the onward trail to Manang. Ray has time to kill. 'More vacation time than I know what to do with,' he says. 'Trouble is, I'm not sure I have the energy for this trekking game. Sure found today plenty tough.'

'Don't worry, Dad. I'll see you make it,' and his daughter pats him kindly on the knee.

Rising early, Alan and I leave on a trail heading north, twisting downhill through terraces of rice spread in an artistic fan, the early light playing on streams and irrigation ditches, the milky blue Marsyangdi curling round the base of the spur with white-flecked rapids as it cuts through a gorge. Our trail edges a former river bench now crowded with millet. Lemon trees line the pathway. Ahead the valley is restricted by steep hills; on the opposite bank a thin cascade hangs above the river, twitching with a breeze. We pass a solitary lodge, then curve left, descend to a suspension bridge and cross to Syange, a one-street village of shops and lodges. Geordie, Scots and Australian voices drift from a *bhatti*, but we walk through without stopping and soon find ourselves among cannabis plants. 'There'll be some grass smoked tonight,' says Alan, referring to a couple of trekkers we'd passed earlier.

Ahead the valley narrows. More waterfalls streak the rocks while the trail slants uphill and the gradient increases. The path is well made, in places carved into the rock, and is certainly a great improvement on the route described in 1950 as a series of frail wooden galleries strung across the cliffs. At the top of the rise we stop for a bowl of noodle soup at a small teahouse standing alone with views in both directions, and wonder how serious the Nepalese authorities are in their plan to extend the road from Dumre as far as Manang. The very idea spells disaster.

As we enter Jagat a squall of voices erupts from a field behind one of the houses, where a group of villagers gathers round the carcass of a recently slaughtered buffalo – a bubbling mess of steaming guts and liquid spilling into the harvest stubble. A wall-eyed man with a simple grin and kukri knife in hand has sliced open its belly, while his audience offers advice in the way it's offered all over the world by those least qualified to give it. The butcher stands bare-legged astride the carcass, his light brown skin spattered with blood. Already he and the onlookers anticipate the taste of fresh meat. It will last them for days.

When the Tibetan salt trade was in full swing, Jagat was a customs post where taxes were levied, but since 1959 cross-border trade between Nepal and Tibet has officially ended, and its reason for existence has changed. Drying racks of sweetcorn cobs now stand above fields where children chase one another in a game of tag. One child trips, sprawling head-first into the stubble. As he explodes with tears a girl I take to be his sister picks him up and swings him onto her back. She can be no more than five years old, but accepts responsibility for his welfare without question.

The valley is little more than a gorge now, the scenery wild, intimidating, and the way ahead apparently blocked by boulders that swallow the river. But when we top another steep rise, before us lies a broad, flat plateau, on the far side of which the toy-like houses of Tal are dwarfed by soaring mountains, as alluring as Shangri-La. This is Buddhist country, and as if to emphasise the fact peace settles over us. A crow barks as it circles overhead, making only a brief intrusion. In the breeze comes the far-off boom of a waterfall, but the breeze is inconsistent, the sound falters, then shuts off completely. Peace settles once more.

Tal's wide street is lined with shops and lodges, and with ponies tethered to a rail the place has a Wild West appearance – externally, at least – but once we book into a lodge all that changes. We're back in a medieval world that attempts to ape the 20th century.

A bright-faced woman in a wrap-around *chuba* entices me across the street to study the bangles, earrings and pocket-sized *mani* stones on display in her tiny sentry-box of a shop. Her hair is coal black and glossy and hangs halfway down her back. Teasing me for my grey beard she calls me '*Baje*', so I show her photographs of my wife and daughters and assure her I can wait a while before becoming a grandfather. Calling softly behind her, a beautiful little girl presents herself. She's gorgeous, like her mother, and smiling sweetly returns my '*Namaste*'.

In Pisang, a spartan village of stone-walled houses at well over 3000 metres, there's a long *mani* wall fitted with a row of prayer wheels, each stone in the wall carved with the Buddhist *mantra* '*Om mani padme hum*' ('Hail to the jewel in the lotus'). Cylindrical prayer wheels are likewise etched with manis, and as each wheel is spun it scatters the prayers contained within it, '*Om mani padme hum*'. Strips of cloth bearing the *mani* imprint hang from long wooden poles, and as we pass through archways, known as kanis, a gallery of Buddhas fades in the shadows of time. The faith lingers on...'*Om mani padme hum*'.

Here in the Himalayan rain shadow the Buddha's timeless prayer is like an electrical charge – unseen, unheard, but felt in every stirring breeze.

Our journey adopts a deeper meaning. It's more than a walk through an ever-changing landscape – a pilgrimage, perhaps? There's a cultural intensity as we slip into a very different world that works on our emotions. Alan senses the change too. Having known each other for so long, we have no need to articulate what we feel about the places we explore. Often we'll wander at our own pace with thoughts undisturbed. Only later will a word or phrase be spoken that conjures a moment in time or a place spirited from memory.

This morning Alan wakes with a streaming cold and a hint of fever. 'The dry air will be good for it,' he says. 'But I'll see about hiring a porter for a couple of days.' Within minutes we are joined by a neat-looking Magar with a quiet smile and a name that sounds like 'Mahdri'. He has no English, and the few Nepali words Alan and I have gathered make for very limited conversation, but smiles count as much as conversation on this winding trail.

It's cold in our Pisang lodge when evening falls, but the table where we sit eating *daal bhaat* is located over a shallow pit in which a brazier

49

of hot coals warms us while we eat. Mahdri squats beside the cooking fire with the *didi*, his hands held in the smoke, fingers splayed, but a Danish couple in their early 30s who share our table complain about the cold. In a thick Icelandic sweater the woman looks mournful and gives an involuntary shudder. 'Boy,' she says in near-perfect English. 'If this is autumn, how bad is it in winter?'

'Why don't you put some more clothes on?' I ask.

'I'm wearing everything I have.'

'Really? No down jacket?'

She shakes her head. 'We did not know it would be cold like this. We have never been to 3000 metres before.'

I wonder then how far they intend to go, but the boyfriend answers my unspoken question. 'We want to cross the Thorong La,' he says. 'Will it be cold like this?'

Almost 2000 metres higher than Pisang, the Thorong La is the pass which leads to the Kali Gandaki. 'No,' I say. 'It'll be much, much colder than this.'

Seen from our lodge Upper Pisang is like a series of swallows' nests high above the river. On this crisp November morning a cocoon of blue-grey smoke embraces the village, each house wearing a prayer flag that hangs limply against its pole. Having slogged up the path to it, we pause to catch our breath and appreciate the sight of Annapurna II across the valley, its summit crest blistered by the afterglow of sunrise. The main trail to Manang remains below, but an alternative path heading northwest wins us a view through the valley where organ pipes of rock have been sand-blasted by the dry winds of high Asia. Mahdri is just ahead, a grey turtle with the faded blue shell of Alan's rucksack concealing all but his legs. Together we wander among juniper and pine trees above a small green tarn, then slope down to another *mani* wall, cross a stream and come to a fork in the trail.

With a vague twitch of his head Mahdri gives directions. 'Hongde' (indicating to the left), 'Ghyaru, Ngawal' (uphill). The nasal sounds of 'Ghyaru' and 'Ngawal' hang in the air like an adjunct to *'Om mani padme hum'*. In this land of other-worldly encounters Alan and I are attracted by these sounds. So uphill it is.

It's a steep climb, and wheezing with his head-cold Alan suffers, but all the effort is forgotten as Ghyaru gathers us into a long-distant past. This ancient village of flat-roofed houses crowds the hillside with an outlook onto a wall of glacial mountains – Lamjung Himal, Gangapurna and the north face of Annapurnas II and III. Notched tree trunks serve as ladders up which locals climb to their living quarters, while yaks are stabled on the ground floor. Once again, prayer flags adorn every rooftop, and now the air is stirring they gently slap against their poles.

Mahdri suggests a tea stop, takes us into a walled enclosure, then up a ladder, where he removes the rucksack and ducks through a low door-way to be swallowed by the darkness of the room beyond. Following, we're struck by a cloud of acrid smoke, and it's clear that whoever is in this room is burning dried *yak* dung. 'This should clear your sinuses,' I murmur to Alan.

As we grow accustomed to the gloom we're directed by the man of the house to make ourselves comfortable. He appears to be old, his face rutted with high altitude wind and sun, a woollen hat pulled tightly over scalp and ears, his teeth broken where his lips part in a wordless smile of greeting. There are no seats so we use the floor, sitting cross-legged on a rug in front of the fire that burns on a stone-slab grate. A blackened pot of *tsampa* is being stirred, and moments later the clay-like substance is offered first to Mahdri, then to us. I decline, as does Alan, but Mahdri accepts without visible sign of gratitude, as is often the way in this land where acceptance of a gift adds *karma* of the giver. He who gives should be grateful. The man of the house laughs at me, aware no doubt that the tan-coloured goo is not to a Westerner's liking, but nonetheless scrapes a lump from the pot with a stick and holds it across the fire. Our eyes meet. He nods. I accept the offering, take the lump with my fingers and pop it into my mouth. It tastes just as it looks… The old man laughs again, turns to Alan and asks in pantomime fashion if he is father and I the grandfather. Since there's only six months' difference in our ages, Alan appreciates the joke more than I do.

One tiny slit-like window allows light to enter and some of the smoke to leave. A faint blue beam angles from window to floor, picking out the gentle swirl of smoke and dancing dust fairies. The bare walls are black and shining with the soot of who knows how many years of *yak*-dung fires; the only furnishings are the rugs on which we sit and a pair of long, thick cushions against the wall beneath the window.

Rolling the *tsampa* into a ball with one hand, Mahdri tosses it into his mouth. He does this many times until the bowl is empty, then runs his fingers round the edge to collect any spare food before licking his fingers clean. The old man passes him a metal jug, which he holds above his tilted head and pours water into his mouth. Not a drop is spilled, and none touches his lips. Above the crackling of the fire I hear the gulping sounds as Mahdri swallows.

'It's easy to die of altitude sickness. Anyone can do it! Trekkers do it every year. Not the same trekkers, of course – they only do it once. Once each, that is.' The newly qualified German doctor, with an enviable command of English, is enjoying himself. No doubt it's the same spiel he uses every day, but it's effective, and his audience takes note.

We're sitting in the roofless outdoor lecture room at the health post run by the Himalayan Rescue Association (HRA) in Manang, where every afternoon during the trekking season one of two volunteer doctors based here gives a presentation on how to avoid altitude sickness. While the subject is serious, the lecture is entertaining. It has to be in order to keep the audience's attention. But more than that, it's informative and, no doubt, life saving for some of those present, for the Annapurna Circus attracts plenty of visitors with little or no mountain experience – let alone high-altitude experience. These include world travellers who last month were on the beach in Goa, next month will be drifting through Thailand, but this month are 'doing Nepal'. And that means a week or so in Kathmandu followed by a quick trek round Annapurna. Many are ill equipped and, like the Danish couple in Pisang, have no idea what to expect.

Recognising this the doctor stresses the importance of drinking plenty of liquids, of gaining altitude in slow and easy stages, and of keeping alert for warning signs in yourself and your companions. He's graphic in his description of death from pulmonary and cerebral oedema, and makes his audience sit up by telling them, 'It can strike even here in Manang. You don't have to go all the way to the Thorong La to die.' Warning of the cold and high winds up at the pass, he gives several instances of trekkers and their porters setting out for the La never to make it. 'All because they were not prepared, were in too much of a hurry, were too proud to turn back, or – in the case of the porters – they did not know what was happening to them. Remember', he says, prodding the air with emphasis, 'you can die through stupidity if you like. That is your choice. But if you have porters with you, you are responsible for their safety. Their lives are as important as yours.' He pauses for effect, then says, 'Actually, from where I'm standing, I'd say *more* important than some of you.'

We all laugh, but wonder who he's getting at.

Manang is bustling. At just over 3500 metres, it's sensible for anyone planning to cross the Thorong La to spend at least two nights at this altitude to help the process of acclimatisation. That's why there are twice as many trekkers congregating here than in any other village along the trail. Not only independent teahouse trekkers, like us, but organised groups too, with their porters, Sherpas and sirdars. Two groups are camped on the edge of the village, but there are even tents pitched on the flat roofs of some of the houses.

There must be at least 200 houses in Manang. A maze of narrow alleys twists between them, opening to a square with a row of prayer wheels and a heart-stopping view of the Annapurnas across the valley. The Tibetan influence is strong in the features of the Manangis.

Tough and worldly-wise, I doubt anyone ever beat them to a bargain, but we find them friendly and hospitable, and although the food served in our lodge may not always be what we order, it helps keep the cold at bay.

It *is* cold too. Wandering alone up-valley I visit a neighbouring village where *yak* crossbreeds plough the frozen fields. Winter is in the air. It comes drifting from Annapurnas II and IV as snow plumes are torn from their ridges. It comes from Gangapurna's glacier, whose icefall tips to a half-frozen lake. And it comes in blusters of wind tasting of snow, yet the sky remains blue and almost cloudless.

Passing a row of well-worn prayer wheels, a metallic clack-clack accompanies each of the prayers as I spin their release. Above a *chorten*, prayer flags are stripped into tatters by the wind, and because of that wind I go no further, but crouch in the lee of the *chorten* and listen to the cracking of the flags, thankful to be in view of the Himalaya once more. Heaven, I tell myself, is a crowd of snow mountains and no demands to climb them.

Back in Manang I find Alan drinking hot chocolate behind steamed windows in the dining room of the Yak Lodge, most of whose tables are occupied by trekkers wearing down jackets. Seated opposite him are the Canadians Ray and Linda, with whom we'd shared a lodge in Bahundanda. They arrived an hour ago, having stayed last night a short way down-valley. Ray is wearing a week's stubble and an incomplete smile. His eyes speak of concern, and when his daughter leaves to visit the *chaarpi*, he confides in us. 'She's kinda sick. I dunno what it is, but she's not right. Keeps telling me not to worry, but I know that kid, and she's just not healthy. There's no way she's gonna make it over the La until she's got herself fit.'

'Is it the altitude?'

'Nope. At least, I don't think so. Got pains; I can see that, but she says nothin'. Spends a lot of time visitin' the *chaarpi* – in fact she probably knows more about the *chaarpis* of Nepal than anyone alive!'

'Have you been to the health post?'

'Health post?' asks Ray. 'Where's that?'

'Just across the way. Two doctors are based there. Why don't you get Linda to go for a check if you're that concerned?'

The Canadian's eyes brighten. 'Hey now, that's like good news.'

Half an hour later father and daughter wander across to the HRA post. They're gone for quite a while, and Alan and I are on our third mugs of hot chocolate by the time they return. Linda's face is still pasty, heavy bags beneath her eyes, her nose glowing with the cold. She smiles a weak smile and pads off to visit the *chaarpi* again. Her father scrapes the bench, sits beside me and sighs with relief. 'We're going down!' Alan's eyes briefly meet mine and an eyebrow goes up. We wait, for it's not our place to pry, after all we hardly know the man, but he wants to share the news.

'Kidney infection. The German doctor says there's no way she should go any higher.' Ray scratches at his week-old beard, then wipes his nose with the back of his engineer's hand. 'Maybe there's a flight we can take from Hongde that'll get us back to Kathmandu soonest. She's supposed to be in Japan for the ski season, so we'll need to get her right. I guess we'll head out in the morning.'

In Bahundanda Ray doubted his ability to get over the Thorong La, but Linda was going to look after him. In trekking, nothing is certain.

Tonight the chill invades our cell at the Annapurna Hotel. Awake before midnight, I lie listening to the wind while trying to find the courage to get out of my sleeping bag, pull on boots and go for a pee. When at last I do, it's to find snow falling – big flakes, the size of goose down. It's still falling as dawn light filters from unseen mountains, and what we can see of Manang reminds me of Christmas. But instead of reindeer, two hefty yaks lie outside our lodge with fresh snow piling round them. No one is going anywhere in this.

Feeling delicate Alan is off his breakfast, but I'm okay and have a double helping of porridge, an omelette, *chapatti* and several cups of tea. Alan sips his tea and wonders aloud if Mahdri is home yet. When we'd arrived late in the afternoon the day before yesterday, Alan had paid him off. 'Sure,' I say. 'He'll have been home in no time; downhill with a following wind and no rucksack to slow his pace.'

It had been our plan to go up to Letdar today, move on to Thorong Phedi tomorrow and cross the La the day after, but this snow has put paid to that. Happily we have time to sit and wait, but this morning there's tension in the dining room. A number of our fellow trekkers have set themselves tight schedules and are frustrated by a day's forced inactivity; others voice concern that the Thorong La will be impassable for several days, even if the snow stops now, for if it's snowing like this here, what's it like 2000 metres up?

We visit the Canadians at the Yak Lodge, where Linda remains in her room, snug in her sleeping bag. Ray is hunched beside the stove, cramped between down-wrapped trekkers. 'There's no way we're going down to Hongde in this,' he says. 'We'll wait a day or two and see what the weather brings.'

Braga is the next village down the trail from Manang. Built in tiers against steep outcrops in a shallow amphitheatre of crags, in the snow it looks like a multi-layered wedding cake in danger of collapse. When we'd passed below it a couple of days ago it had attracted our attention, desert brown against rust-coloured rocks, but we'd been unwilling to stop then as the afternoon was fading and Manang beckoned. Now, with time to explore, we shuffle our way through neglected drifts up to the *gompa* at the top of the village. The caretaker appears, rattling a bunch of ancient keys, and lets us in.

Innocent of Buddhist culture, I can only feel a reverence I do not understand in this dusty place of nine hundred Himalayan winters, lit as it is by butter lamps with a faltering orange glow. My wandering eyes drift across racks of rectangular manuscripts – scriptures borne down the ages by followers of the Buddha, whose words took shape hundreds of years before Christ began his own ministry. I'm aware of how little I know.

More than a hundred terracotta statues appear as my eyes grow accustomed to the moody light; there are coloured banners hanging from the ceiling, a gong, a drum and smaller instruments used in times of prayer. A large bronze Buddha watches every movement until the caretaker directs us to an upper building where yet more Buddhas gather dust, and in an ante-room we find a collection of archaic knives, swords and rusted muskets, then return to the lower room where silk scarves are placed around our necks with a blessing.

We'll need that blessing when the snow stops, if we're to cross the Thorong La.

The stroll back to Manang is through a stark monochrome landscape. The wind has dropped, but heavy clouds fill the valley and empty their contents of damp white flakes. When we call at the Yak to see how Linda is, the room is crowded with more than 50 trekkers as today's acclima-tisation lecture has been transferred here from the HRA building, so we return to the Annapurna to find some French trekkers who'd left yesterday, bound for Letdar. They tell us conditions are very bad up there, which is why they've returned, and we speculate that it must be much worse above that. Since it could be days before there's sufficient improvement to allow a crossing of the pass, the atmosphere is charged with what-ifs and if-onlys.

But next morning all that has changed, the snowfall has ended and remnant clouds scatter to reveal a canopy of deepest blue. Stepping out of the lodge I'm almost blinded by the intensity of light. Flashing crys-tals of ice prance in the air, the valley is bewitched and I'm excited by its rebirth.

Alan, on the other hand, is still feeling rough. During the night he'd been outside vomiting and now huddles in his sleeping bag as waves of nausea sweep over him. It looks as though Manang will have the pleasure of our company a little longer, so I take him a mug of black tea, which he glances at and gags. 'I've decided to go over the road for a consultation,' he mumbles. 'I feel like death.' I help him to his feet and watch as he shuffles through the snow. He looks old and doddery, yet trekking is supposed to be a healthy pursuit.

Seated outside the lodge with another pot of tea, I watch as Sherpas collapse a snow-coated tent on the roof of a neighbouring building. As they shake the snow from it, one of their group emerges from the dining room below and receives the full bounty on his head and shoulders. One of the Sherpas sees this and dodges back out of sight. He and I burst into laughter. The snowbound trekker is not amused.

Alan returns, head low, shoulders hunched. 'A virus,' he says. 'It could be with me for days.' He slumps on the bench beside me, holding his head as though it weighs more than his shoulders can manage on their own. 'It's no good; I'll have to go down.'

I say nothing, but think much. We're not yet halfway round the Circuit, but if he's really sick there's no way he can contemplate crossing a pass at almost 5500 metres, so I understand his decision. But what do *I* do? Do I leave him to his own devices and continue on my own – or go down with him to make sure he's okay? He knows what I'm thinking and appreciates my dilemma. 'Sorry,' he says. 'But I can't see any alternative.'

Then a compromise comes to mind. 'If I could get down to Hongde,' he says, 'it might be possible to fly out from there. But not today. I've got no energy.' So I offer to go down-valley for him to enquire if any flights are scheduled in the next few days. If so I'll get him a ticket. As I understand it, Hongde is supposed to have a flight on Thursdays – weather permitting, that is. Today is Tuesday.

It's a glorious walk without a rucksack. The deep snow squeaks beneath my boots, and wherever I turn a world of pristine beauty greets me. On my right the Annapurnas form an enormous bank of snow and ice; ahead and on the left Pisang Peak sends out spurs that cast blue shadows against dazzling white, and throughout the valley multi-layered cushions of snow are piled upon chortens and half-concealed *mani* walls. It's heaped upon drystone walls and flat-roofed houses, and on the posts either side of a cantilever bridge spanning the Marsyangdi. Rafts of snow drift downstream, shrinking in size as they go. When I come to pine trees, each branch wears a basket.

'No flight Thursday,' says the RNAC official at Hongde. 'If no more snow, next flight maybe one week. If more snow, next flight could be three, four weeks. Maybe not till spring.'

I find a *bhatti* and sit inside with two handsome *Bhotiya* women. Sisters, they are, chatting as one washes dishes and the other makes noodle soup for me. There's so much garlic in the soup it almost blisters my lips. The cook-sister sees my eyes water and laughs. 'Good for cold,' she tells me.

I give Alan the news as soon as I get back to Manang in the early afternoon. 'No flights, thanks to the snow. As I see it you have three choices. One, you die here. Two, you walk down to Besisahar and have your body shaken to bits on the truck to Dumre. Or three, you get better and cross the Thorong La with me.'

He still looks decidedly unhealthy and weak, but half an hour after my return, while I'm enjoying a tin of pineapple chunks bought at a local shop, he staggers to the back of the lodge and spends several minutes being violently sick into the snow. When at last he reappears he wears a smile. 'That's cleared the system,' he says. 'I'm going for some tea.'

With that I assume the trek is on once more.

In Letdar we manage to locate a two-bedded stone cell for our accommodation in an unfinished building. It's cold as death inside the room at over 4000 metres, so we sit at a table outside with a tremendous view down-valley to mountains of the Annapurna Himal that have grown even higher in the aftermath of the snowstorm. Just a few extra-steep bands of rock remain exposed. All else is caked with snow – high ridges corniced with layers of unimagined depth above a soundless avalanche that pours down the face of Gangapurna.

While our socks dry in the sunshine, our faces burn with reflected heat and snow-glare. Alan is happy now but, weak from his days of sickness, he's arranged for a local man to carry his rucksack to Muktinath. Our man from Manang looks tough as a *yak*. Clad in winter-proof clothing and size 12 expedition boots, he has few words, and as yet we've not managed to discover his name, for in response to our attempts to converse, we're offered a few grunts only and dark eyes that refuse to meet ours.

The dining area of our so-called lodge has no roof. As night falls we sit in what appears to be an inner courtyard with a starry sky in place of a ceiling, ankle-deep in snow – adding new meaning to 'alfresco' as we fight a way into plates of *daal bhaat*. The primus stove which serves as the cooking range is only a couple of paces behind us, and the food is hot and steaming when scooped onto plates, but by the time it reaches our table – seconds only – it's just luke warm. Luke-warm rice quickly solidifies and is difficult to swallow.

It takes only a couple of hours to reach Thorong Phedi, at the foot of the pass, where soaring cliffs form an amphitheatre round a bed of snow-carpeted meadowland. Alan and I sit with our backs against the lodge and gaze up at the steep slope that leads to the Thorong La. It looks as formidable as the North Face of the Eiger, and a very unhappy Dutch woman confirms that it feels like it. She'd set off for the pass early this morning, but halfway there was affected by the altitude and had to be brought down by her friend. Now she clutches her head in misery and wonders whether she'll make it tomorrow. I tell her she should descend further, but she and her friend refuse to listen.

Since the Thorong La is the high point of the Annapurna Circuit, tension among our fellow trekkers vibrates like the build-up to an electrical storm. Almost everyone feels the altitude, and none can be certain how they'll be affected by tomorrow's climb of almost 1000 metres. Some have grown irritable, others have gone to lie down, while yet more sit in the sunshine and grow fearful of tomorrow. No doubt the words of the HRA doctor at Manang ring in their ears.

As soon as the sun dips behind the mountains the temperature drops like a stone. Shadows bring frost, and in moments the scene is transformed as everyone rushes indoors, where orders for hot drinks are shouted across the room. Appetites are diminished by the altitude, yet mine remains as strong as ever, so I tuck into a large plate of boiled potatoes almost explosive with chilli sauce, then retire to bed. It's only 6 o'clock, but I'm one of the last to go.

Alan and I share a dormitory with two Germans, three Americans, a group of airmen serving with the RAF, and a young married couple from Sheffield with whom we'd spent several hours at Dhaka airport on the way to Kathmandu. As for the airmen, one of them tackled the Circuit two years ago and was so impressed that he couldn't wait to repeat the experience. 'The Thorong La? A tough day, but wow – what a crossing!'

At 4.30 we breakfast on porridge and three cups of tea each, fill our bottles, then step out into the pre-dawn grey at 5.15. The thermometer reads minus 16 and my feet soon lose feeling – how do the porters cope, I wonder? Dawn will flood the hills in another 30 minutes or so, but for now the route is picked out by the head-torches of trekkers who've beaten us to it. But we're in no hurry; this is not a race; so Alan and I settle to our own steady rhythm with the porter from Manang kicking in behind. Ahead of us a string of heavily laden men zigzags slowly under loads belonging to a group; we leapfrog a shape losing his breakfast in the snow; and a little later, just before the sky brightens, we pass a couple standing face to face, one sobbing and clutching her head, the other no doubt battling with indecision. I'm thankful just to feel old, and am aware of the privilege of tackling the route on this day of all days.

Night makes way for the briefest transition to a morning of sparkling brilliance. Around us moraine ribs hang on to their snows, while ice gleams and flashes minute diamonds from cliffs that capture the first sunlight.

Hour succeeds hour, and figures in the landscape are no longer bunched – some have fallen by the wayside, heading back to Phedi in misery and disappointment. Some are just slower than others and trudge their own journeys through their own secret worlds. Each of us deals with the effort, the cold and the altitude in our own very personal way, shrinking within to find a barrier of comfort to deaden the reality.

But I'm relieved to find I'm enjoying myself. My toes have come back to life, my head is not even muzzy. Okay, I'm short of energy and puffing like a steam engine, but I haven't come here to run, and even in the snowdrifts, where the trail is a series of holes instead of a well-trodden groove, I pick the way cheerfully enough. Whatever the route may be under snow-free conditions, today it meanders from one false col to another as steep slopes converge, bringing us not to new valleys but into hollows and snowdrifts between mountains. Behind us the Annapurnas are slipping away, soon to be vanquished by minor ridges and mountain folds. Then the slope ahead eases, and mountains to right and left give way to create an impression of space as the pass beckons.

At a little after 9 o'clock Alan and I stand misty-eyed by the 5415 metre summit cairn among the wind-disturbed prayers of high places. 'Om mani padme hum' swirls silently around us. Even our man from Manang is smiling as he stands between Alan and me while a trekker with a German group takes our photograph before starting her descent. I'm jubilant, and on this day of gifts I wander away for a few minutes and, finding myself alone, turn slowly in a full circle to embrace the scene and whisper words of gratitude.

There are no Annapurnas to gaze upon, but in the northwest an arid, dun-coloured landscape tells of the Kingdom of Mustang. There's romance in that vision – a vertical desert dusted with snow, Tibet beyond its borders and the hidden land of Dolpo forming a buffer on the far side of mountains without names. The Thorong La not only rewards our presence, it taunts with forbidden horizons.

The descent to Muktinath proves more tiring than the climb to the pass. On this west-facing slope there's less snow than on the route from Phedi. Two days of sunshine have melted open patches, but the melt has frozen again and a treacherous sheen of ice makes every step a challenge. Half an hour below the pass we come upon the German woman who'd taken our photograph on the Thorong La. Just 15 minutes ago she fell and broke her right leg, which now juts misshapen with an ugly bulge midway between knee and foot. Friends fuss around her offering comfort, while the group leader and his *sirdar* make a rudimentary stretcher from trekking poles and items of clothing. They're competent and unflustered, and when we offer assistance they assure us that everything is in hand, so we continue down the slope, moraine ribs spilling towards the valley, ice reflecting the sun, stones projecting through retreating snowfields. Alan and I both fall several times. Not so our man from Manang. He remains on his feet, big boots digging grooves in the slope behind us.

Now with a clear view into the Kali Gandaki, the harvest fields of Kagbeni can be seen, as can the graceful cone of Dhaulagiri. Pausing for a moment, I collect its simple beauty and commit the scene to memory.

At the foot of the moraines we reach grass and stop for a cup of tea at a *bhatti* that looks less like a building than a ruin. Apart from the cairn on the pass, it's the first man-made structure we've seen since leaving Thorong Phedi. A Sherpa from the German group is here arranging for the *bhatti*-owner's pony to carry the woman with the broken leg down to Jomsom. From there she should be able to get a flight out to Pokhara in the next two or three days.

Our porter suddenly comes alive, for the *bhatti*-owner and his wife have with them a short *Bhotiya* woman who's clearly a friend of old. She and our man from Manang huddle together in animated conversation. She giggles like a teenager on her first date, and I worry that we might have difficulty encouraging him to leave with us. None of it. When we're ready to go, he rises too, but now there's a spring in his step. I suspect I know where he'll be spending the night. And with whom.

An hour later we reach Muktinath. Set in a grove of poplars and a walled enclosure, sacred temples and 108 water spouts mark the culmination of a famous pilgrimage followed by generations of Hindus – for after Pashupatinath this is the most revered Hindu site in Nepal. Buddhists are drawn here too, for the footprints of the eighth-century saint Guru Rimpoche are said to be embedded in stone nearby. Yet in our weary state the site attracts little interest. Our knees ache, toes are sore, and the prospect of unlimited drinks, a plate of food and a bed spurs us on. Thankfully we have no need to go far, so Alan hands a clutch of notes to his porter for his three-day journey with us, and moments later our man from Manang is striding back the way we've come. He has a date.

Standing naked on the flat roof of the lodge at a little under 4000 metres, I feel somewhat bemused. Having spent an hour celebrating our safe passage of the Thorong La with bottles of Star beer that proved potent on empty stomachs, I'd asked the lodge-keeper for some hot water. 'You want shower?' he asked.

'You have a shower?'

'Velry good shower!' he assured me.

Anticipation is a marvellous thing. A single word transports me into a fantasy of steam and soap, clean hair, pink glowing flesh, and an end to the accumulated dirt of mountain Nepal. As I'm led upstairs and out to the rooftop overlooking the village, Dhaulagiri hangs over the valley to the southwest, a symmetrical mountain of purest white against the azure of an unclouded sky.

'Mister, you wait here. I fetch shower.'

Waiting in the late afternoon sunshine with only a small towel round my waist, a frantic sweep of small grey birds brushes past – a rush of feathers come from nowhere and are gone in an instant.

Seen from the Milke Danda, a cloud-sea fills the valleys of northeast Nepal as far as the Singalila Ridge, beyond which lies Sikkim (Chapter 1)

Far beyond the Tamur's valley, the Kangchenjunga massif forms a backdrop to life in the foothills (Chapter 1)

A typical wayside bhatti, or teahouse, hundreds of which serve travellers right across Nepal (Chapter 1)

At last! After 30 years of mountain activity I've finally made it to the Himalaya – the world's third highest mountain towers behind me (Chapter 1)

The stately cone of Ratong is part of a long crest of peaks extending from Kangchenjunga that carries the Nepal–Sikkim border (Chapter 1)

The Southwest Face of Kangchenjunga, by which it was first climbed in 1955 (Chapter 1)

Setting up camp on the yak pasture of Tseram (Chapter 1)

(Opposite) After crossing the Thorong La, Alan Payne overlooks the timeless village of Jharkot (Chapter 2)

With Annapurna South as a backdrop, weary trekkers capture the magic of the Sanctuary (Chapter 2)

After a dump of snow, the way from Manang to Letdar on the Annapurna Circuit is transformed (Chapter 2)

Though still recognisable from Annapurna Base Camp, Machhapuchhare (far right) has lost its solitary status as guardian of the Sanctuary (Chapter 2)

Our first camp on the Manaslu trek (Chapter 3) looks north across a pastoral land to the arctic wall of the Himalaya

In the rain shadow of the Himalaya, the valley of the Jhong Khola below Muktinath is like a high-altitude desert (Chapter 2)

Sharing a book of photographs with a young friend from Samagaon
(Chapter 3)

From their home above the Buri Gandaki, village children watch the world go by (Chapter 3)

The juggernauts of Nepal make their way along the lower valley of the Buri Gandaki (Chapter 3)

The lodge-keeper returns with a red plastic bucket of water, a jug and an enamel bowl. 'Shower!' he says with pride.

Having been psyched up to enjoy my first overall wash since Kathmandu, I'm not prepared for disappointment, so drop the towel anyway and, standing in the bowl one foot at a time, pour jugs of water over my head. What had seemed tepid in the bucket is now close to freezing, and I shiver uncontrollably. But although it may not be the most luxurious shower of my life, I've never had one with a better outlook, with an unrestricted view of massed snow peaks sharp against the Himalayan sky gathering the first colours of evening. It's also the highest and most exposed bathroom of my life, so I dry myself as best I can and dress quickly before ice forms on my extremities.

The valley below Muktinath is one of which dreams are made. Totally different from anything we'd seen along the Marsyangdi, a seemingly barren land is contorted into a series of folds, gullies and terraces. This northern side of the Himalayan divide could not seem more remote if it were on the far side of the moon, and as we approach the ancient village of Jharkot, I'm enchanted by everything I see – a line of peach trees, a half-frozen stream, a small pond, the snowy west wall of the Kali Gandaki, and Jharkot itself. As I glance through a *kani*, the Himalayan time-machine cranks me back at least 500 years. I can taste the dust and clay of Asia upon my tongue, smell warm dust and clay in my nostrils, and trail my fingers against the wall of one of the houses, scraping the wind-baked dust and clay of a world marooned from the late 20th century. A small child with dirt-spiked hair and a tan-coloured tunic pads along the alleyway. 'N'maste,' he grins. 'Gimme one pen!'

Below Jharkot our path sidles among a few bare poplars and fruit trees, and through crusts of ice where a stream crosses and recrosses the trail. Snow patches spatter the hillside, while the hanging valley becomes yet more arid in appearance. Dhaulagiri rises as though on an elevator behind a spur of Tukuche Peak, a vast yacht whose sails are stretched to capture winds we cannot feel down here. To our right, across the Jhong

Khola's gorge, caves are pitted among strangely eroded crags sculpted by frost, wind and water over countless millennia.

Kagbeni is an oasis. We see a hint of the village with its patch-work fields and row of willows gathered at the confluence of the Jhong Khola and Kali Gandaki. It's as far north as foreigners are allowed to travel, although last night we heard rumours that restrictions would soon be lifted and, for payment of a large fee in Kathmandu, a special permit would allow trekkers to enter long-forbidden Mustang. If this is true, we're too late and without sufficient funds to take advantage. Ah, Mustang… Another dream for another day.

Sidling through its valley, the Kali Gandaki is a series of streams that reunite here and there. At a little under 3000 metres, in a land-locked country in the heart of Asia, 800 kilometres from the nearest sea, we walk on the bed of a one-time ocean. Among the stones and glacial silt we discover ammonites – coiled, fossilised creatures that once inhabited that sea until its bed was raised to become India. And the Himalaya was born. As the Himalaya continues to grow, the Kali Gandaki leaks away from the Tibetan plateau, undeterred from its southbound course by the highest mountains on earth. Nibbling at the growing land mass, the river carves a passage until, a day's walk downstream from here, it breaches the wall between Annapurna and Dhaulagiri to create the world's deepest river valley – more than 5500 metres below the summits.

No wonder the wind sweeps up-valley with enough force to carry small stones in its teeth!

The sound of 'Sergeant Pepper's Lonely Hearts Club Band' is an incongruous intrusion. Decades ago I twice saw the Beatles in concert and still enjoy their records. But not here. Western music in a Nepalese lodge at the foot of the Annapurnas is not one of the reasons I came to the Himalaya. Trekking among these mountains is not simply a multi-day walk in the hills, it's a way of experiencing other cultures, of testing one's own values, of learning how other people live, listening to their beliefs, and sharing for a moment in time an existence unknown in our technological society. At best, trekking is a multi-layered experience that leads to an enrichment of the soul. I'm an eager sponge, anxious to miss nothing. 'Sergeant Pepper' does not belong here. Or does it?

It's the best lodge we've been in by far. Although still simple, the rooms are reasonably clean, and the couple in charge are efficient; a framed certificate at the entrance announces that the owner attended a course in lodge management. Some of the walls bear a wash of mottled paint, and threadbare curtains hang at the windows, but this is five-star luxury compared with many lodges we stayed at on the other side of the pass. There's even an indoor shower in a cubicle with a door! On the far side of the Thorong La Nepali fare was still more or less par for the course. Here, the menu boasts a range of Western-style meals. We've entered a land of pizza and apple pie.

The Thakalis are famed hotel-keepers, but then they've had lots of practice, for the Kali Gandaki is a valley of both trade and pilgrimage. For hundreds of years Hindu pilgrims from as far away as southern India have made the arduous journey to worship at the shrines of Muktinath, and traders to and from Tibet were passing through the valley with their pack animals centuries before the West had even heard of Nepal. So our circuit of the mountains has entered yet another phase. Not only is accommodation of a higher standard and the food less ethnic this side of the La, but the trail itself has more traffic and is not so demanding. For well over a week we were gaining altitude day after day towards the Thorong La. Now we're heading downhill away from the raw cold of the high country, down towards a more equable climate. The challenge of the Thorong La no longer hangs over us.

Leaving Jomsom we cross to the right bank of the river and once again have our permits checked at the police post. It's a busy little town, with government buildings, a hospital, a military base and an airstrip, but I'm glad to be on the way out. Not that I'm anxious to end the trek, for we still have much to see and to do, but Jomsom reminds me of the outside world with its bureaucracy and sagging power lines reminiscent of a Third World shanty. Besides, this is a day to be out and moving.

There is no wind, and the sun spreads fingers of warmth over the eastern mountains, marking individual features on our side of the valley as stepping stones on the journey. Willows without leaves wear orange haloes in their entwined topmost branches where birds twitter at the November sky; neatly walled fields are turned by the plough, and the barking cries of a farmer come to us as we pad the trail. Passing a small watermill built across a tributary stream, we wander through a *kani* to find ourselves in Marpha – and regret not having stayed here last night. White-painted buildings, paved street, attractive lodges and shops, and a view of mountains across the valley make this the finest village we've yet visited. So choosing a lodge at random we enter, order drinks and treat ourselves to chocolate brownies. (So much for my scorn for Western influence in the high Himalaya!)

Beyond Marpha rows of apple, apricot, peach and walnut trees give rise to a burst of admiration for the folk who live here, for in this land of extremes, this ever-rising land of avalanche and earthquake, human existence itself is a triumph. That fruit can grow in this semi-desert is a miracle. The valley seduces us with wonder.

Further on, the once-prosperous village of Tukuche is set in an open meadow where, before the Chinese invasion of Tibet, traders would gather to exchange Tibetan rock salt for Nepalese grain. What scenes would have been enacted here in centuries past! *Yak* trains with wild-looking Tibetans meeting strings of pack-ponies and mules from the lush south – two very different cultures coming together in this meadow in the mountains, overlooked by Dhaulagiri in the west and outliers of the Annapurnas in the east. I imagine the rise and fall of haggling voices, the occasional bellow of a *yak*, the jangle of bell-laden harnesses. But today there's only a pair of crows bouncing across the grass and the shadow of a lammergeyer circling overhead.

Our day is unplanned. We drift as each whim demands and find ourselves crossing numerous streams flowing from a small side valley at the foot of Tukuche Peak, with the notorious Kali Gandaki wind now gusting in our faces. Khobang is protected from that wind, its houses built close together for mutual protection, while the main street serves as a tunnel with doorways opening from it. One shows an inner courtyard smelling of livestock.

South of the village the valley is distinctly alpine, the trail a switchback among stands of chir pine, with huge mountains crowding nearby as we enter the deepest gorge on Earth and descend into an amphitheatre dominated by Dhaulagiri, whose face is plastered with hanging glaciers. There is no bridge across the torrent, but as it's been divided and sub-divided by gravel beds into a series of braidings, we scout up and down for the easiest crossings, pole-vaulting the deepest streams. Once across we locate the continuing path that leads to a suspension bridge high above the Kali Gandaki. It sways with each step we take.

In the late afternoon we enter another geographical, climatic and cultural zone. A new world lies before us, and for a brief moment I feel a sense of loss. I love the wild aridity of that northern side of the Himalaya, with its Buddhist values and sometimes sterile wastelands, and wonder how long it will be before I can tread such places again. Then almost as soon as the moment comes, it leaves, and I'm excited by prospects of warm nights and abundant vegetation.

We settle to a lodge in Kalopani after gaining a surprise view of Annapurna pink-tinged with the alpenglow. It's comfortable and busy with a cosmopolitan crowd of trekkers, most of whom are making their way up-valley. Two dark-haired, dark-eyed Israeli sisters whose white, close-fitting teeshirts leave little to the imagination concentrate their attention on a pair of climbers from the US, who return that concentration without difficulty. After Alan and I turn in, we discover that in the room next to ours, and separated only by a plank-thick dividing wall, a passionate night is being enjoyed by all four. Almost deafened by their gasps and groans, by the time morning dawns I'm exhausted. How they'll continue up-valley after all that exercise, I've no idea.

Having passed through the great Himalayan divide our trek enters a new phase. Dhaulagiri no longer dominates. Instead its numerous spurs and ridges push southward as the valley's right-hand wall, while the Annapurnas reveal themselves when our trail crosses to the west bank. Several times we cross and recross the river, descending, climbing and descending again. The temperature rises, perspiration runs freely and we stop frequently at wayside *bhattis* to knock back bottled drinks cooled in buckets of water. Houses are no longer flat-roofed and stone-slabbed, but steeply pitched as proof that the monsoon drenches this side of the mountains, and as we lose more height some wear thatch.

Between Ghasa and Dana the route has been swept by monstrous landslips, and as our trail fights to stay high above the Kali Gandaki, in places it's both wildly exposed and potentially dangerous. Descending again we find ourselves among rhododendrons and poinsettias, whose shining leaves are laced with intricate webs and huge spiders silhouetted against the blue. Annapurna thrusts her snows where clouds would otherwise sail high winds, but down here there is no wind, and our manky shirts are soaked with sweat. Pressing ourselves against the hillside to allow a heavily laden porter to pass, my heart goes out to him. He smells of wood smoke and unwashed clothes, but to my mind he is one of the unsung heroes of Nepal.

After a night in Dana we wander on to Tatopani for a second breakfast. The lodges are crowded with trekking groups for whom this marks the extent of their journey into the hills – a short foothill trek from Pokhara to Ghorepani, the wonder of sunrise on Dhaulagiri captured from Poon Hill, then down to the hot springs and chocolate gateaux of Tatopani before turning back. By comparison our journey seems to have lasted for ever.

All trekkers in Nepal know of Ghorepani and Poon Hill, for of the many thousands drawn to the Annapurna region each year, I'd imagine only a small percentage fail to visit this famed ridge-top. The savage deforestation of rhododendron woods is one result of its popularity; the growth of lodge accommodation astride the pass is another. Neither Alan nor I are enchanted by it, yet we stay all the same. We arrive early while views are clear, but by midday clouds are swirling and there's a damp chill in the air.

I wander alone through ghosted woods where limbless trees stand forlorn to await the inevitable axe. Where birds were screeching on the northern approaches, here on the ridge there are few sounds of life. Bare trunks are blackened by the damp mists. It's a sorrowful place, so I return to our lodge to sulk over a pot of lemon tea. Once again Alan is feeling unwell. Was it something he ate last night or is it the haunting melancholy of this place affecting his digestive system as well as our general mood? There's little laughter in the lodges, and all gathered here seem morose. It's as though everyone has grown trail-weary – even those in the early stages of their trek.

Nevertheless we rise early and tramp up the ridge to Poon Hill in darkness. There is no mist now, but in the hour before dawn there's a natural chill and we've taken to wearing down jackets again as we wait for sunrise. Dhaulagiri is moody in the grey early light, and a film of cloud far below hides the Kali Gandaki's valley, but as beams of sunshine at last flash across the topmost ridges of the Annapurnas, so Dhaulagiri draws breath and blushes from head to toe. Trekkers gasp, and the dawn chorus is composed of the rattle of two dozen camera shutters.

Feeling jaded and under the weather, back in Ghorepani Alan decides to go down to Pokhara with a couple of other trekkers from our lodge. It'll take them two days. But I yearn for the Annapurna Sanctuary – to see into the heart of that fabled amphitheatre, to be embraced once more by big mountains wearing glaciers – so we say our farewells and I'm gone before he finishes packing.

71

As a freelance writer, much of my time among mountains is spent alone, and I've come to enjoy the challenge that solitary trekking attracts. Yet I recall stories of travellers disappearing in this particular corner of Nepal, tales of banditry and mugging, with a small criminal element picking on single trekkers along popular trails. The thought is disturbing, but I've made my decision and am well on my way, so I push it to the back of my mind, determined to avoid the paranoia of an over-worked imagination, and make a vow to enjoy every moment. And I do.

Alone with a forest trail sneaking among rhododendrons that have so far escaped the Ghorepani axe, I adjust to the fact that there's no one with me. The pace is entirely my own, I can indulge myself shamelessly and, aware that my step has quickened, I scamper along the ridge heading east. Sounds of the forest burst around me, and occasional views to Machhapuchhare set my pulse racing with excitement.

The route is convoluted, with plenty of ups and downs and changes of direction, in forest for at least half the day. Before leaving I was told it takes nine hours to reach Chhomrong, but I may stop before then. At this moment there are no decisions to make, and won't be until there's a trail junction – there are neither signposts nor waymarks, nor arrows marked by a friendly Sherpa to suggest which way to go. And since the map leaves much to be desired, route directions must come by word of mouth. But first, find someone to ask.

With the trail to myself, I'm happy beyond words. Gone is the gloom of Ghorepani, and after the almost constant procession of trekkers, porters and local traders met along the Kali Gandaki, the solitude is refreshing. Sharing the trail with butterflies I enjoy the sound of a monkey laughing, of birdsong and stream, of dried leaves and snapping twigs beneath my boots.

Stopping for lunch of soup and fried potatoes at a *bhatti* in Tadopani, the fish-tail peak teases through the window, but the dining room walls are covered with newspapers and magazines from around the world left by previous trekkers, and it's unnerving to find Margaret

Thatcher's face glaring at me from a two-year-old *Daily Telegraph*, so I move to another table and turn my back.

On the way again a flight of paved steps leads to another rhododendron forest, emerging later above the deep valley of the Khumnu Khola, whose far side has been exquisitely terraced. However, its charm is lost when I realise that is where my trail goes – a steep descent to a suspension bridge over the river followed by a brutal ascent to regain lost height. Clouds gather overhead and the heat is oppressive. The trail twists to and fro and sweat runs freely, but at last I come to a deserted building on a broad terrace, where the path cuts away to the right. Pausing for breath on a drystone wall, I'm serenaded by a mynah bird in a nearby tree, and when I take off again I do so with renewed energy.

Hours drift by, and the route resumes its undulating course. Although there are few houses, the abundance of terraced fields says much for the labours of Nepali hill folk. But where do they come from? Where do they live? These fields are not planted by accident, and the crops of rice and millet are almost ready, so where are the men and women who must soon gather the harvest? There are no clear answers, but as I speculate, so the trail divides. One branch rises, the other slopes downhill, and it's not obvious which is the onward route to Chhomrong. There are no houses in view, except far away on the opposite side of the valley, and I've seen no one to speak to since leaving Tadopani.

I study both paths, wandering up and down looking for boot prints that would suggest where trekkers have gone in the past. But there are no signs, and I'm perplexed. Then I hear a distant voice, and gazing across a vast bay of terraces, spy a Gurung farmer standing waist deep in a field of millet. He's looking my way and waving his arm. Then I recognise what he's calling. 'Upside! Upside!' I shout back, '*Dhanyabaad*' – thank you – and head off up the trail.

A paved stairway links the two sections of Chhomrong, the many hundreds of steps being well made and bordered for much of the way by a flat-topped wall. From the many lodges that line the route I choose one in the upper part of the village which should, I imagine, look directly at Machhapuchhare through a large plate-glass window. When I arrive there are no views and rain is soon falling as a fine drizzle, but my immediate needs are taken care of – a clean room, unlimited tea and the promise of a shower with water heated by a solar panel. The nine-hour route from Ghorepani took me seven, including time off for lunch under Margaret Thatcher's gaze, and I feel a trifle pooped. But after the shower and several pots of tea, exhaustion turns to simple weariness – the kind of weariness you know will be gone after a good night's sleep.

The lodge is busy, so I share a table with a family from Brussels – father, mother and two teenage girls with yellow hair and deep-set eyes the colour of violets. They've been into the Sanctuary with a local guide and porters from Pokhara, and the mother is gushing with enthusiasm for the scenery. 'But it is so cold,' says one of the daughters, interrupting. 'Mama, tell the man how it is cold!'

'Cold,' says Mama. Father agrees. 'It *really* is cold!'

I'm prepared for the dry cold of the Sanctuary, but at the moment the drizzle has brought a damp chill to Chhomrong. Even in the crowded warmth of this room I sense the gloom outside, and later, when night has fallen, the drizzle turns to a heavy downpour while I lie in my sleeping bag deafened by rain hammering on the corrugated tin roof.

By breakfast the rain has stopped, but clouds are still suspended low and grey, and there's not even a hint of a view towards the Sanctuary. Chhomrong hangs on the hillside at the entrance to the Modi Khola's gorge, and to enter the Sanctuary involves a trek through that gorge before passing between the gateposts formed by Machhapuchhare on one side and Hiunchuli on the other – both 6000 metre peaks of impressive stature. Or so I'm led to believe. Were it not for the architecture and the steepness of the stairway outside the lodge, I could be on the Thames Estuary in bleakest January.

At the check post halfway down the steps I meet Stefan, a tall Dutchman in his mid-20s. He too is on his way into the Sanctuary, so we travel together. But he's eager to talk and he walks fast with long strides, which soon reminds me that I'm twice his age and my knees have taken a beating from 30-odd mountain years. If I try to match his pace I'll never make it. With better light conditions I'd use the age-old ploy of stopping to take photographs, but there's little to aim a camera at this morning. Clouds swirl in gusts of wind, waterfalls thunder, and where rivers meet nature is in turmoil. The light is flat, and I know at a glance that photography will not work. Not today, so I suggest he goes ahead, but he insists he's in no hurry. 'We will go together,' he tells me as though he's doing me a favour. 'I will walk slower.' And he does. For maybe 10 minutes.

The trail is narrow and muddy. Water lies in puddles, and minor streams flow everywhere. There are steep ascents and sudden descents, patches of rhododendron and dense bamboo thickets, and no views. There are probably no views even when the clouds have lifted and blue sky frames the highest peaks. Here in the gorge, with rampant vegetation and steep mountain walls to right and left, the atmosphere is almost claustrophobic. For much of the time the trail is only one trekker wide, and I grow used to the sight of Stefan's rucksack disappearing through the bamboo, slowing only when forced to by others on the trail. Barefooted porters push towards us, their toes finding purchase in the cold mud, their bulky loads covered with sheets of polythene – a waterproof token against the next downpour.

Stefan is waiting for me at Bamboo Lodge. 'I ordered tea for you. Is that okay?'

'Thanks,' I say, trying to appreciate his thoughtfulness, but already I regret the loss of yesterday's solitude.

When we're about to set off again we're delayed by the arrival of a porter carrying a Norwegian woman in a specially adapted *doko*. We help the porter set down his load, and when the woman eases herself from it, she explains that the steep descents on wet ground have damaged her knees to the extent that she can now barely walk except on the level.

'There is no such thing as level ground in Nepal,' remarks my Dutch companion, and my own knees suddenly begin to ache.

Heavy rain beats upon the roof of Himalaya Hotel, a very simple lodge, as basic as some of those in which Alan and I stayed on the way up the Marsyangdi. But it's reasonably dry inside, with space to lie down and plenty of food and drink on offer. That's as much as I need. Tomorrow I should be in the Sanctuary and, anticipating this, recall the words of the family from Brussels: 'It *really* is cold!' The cold I can take. I just hope it's dry and clear.

Frost is on the ground at sunrise. Where puddles and sluggish streams lie exposed, they're covered with ice. It's a sharp, crisp morning, so sharp and crisp it almost burns the throat. Ears and fingers tingle, and steam accompanies every breath. But what a morning to be alive!

Continuing up-valley the way demands care, for ice sheaths the rain-sodden trail and there are many steep sections. Because of the rain I wonder how much snow fell yesterday on the mountains – it's impossible to tell down here. After heavy snowfall there's avalanche danger just beyond Hinku Cave, a vast overhanging boulder formerly used as a bivouac site by the shepherds who originally forced this route. A simple lodge is tucked under the cave now, but it's closed today with a big padlock at the door. Beyond it the trail descends to cross a ravine choked with mounds of old discoloured snow pitted with rocks.

Half an hour from Hinku Cave the valley is less constricted, the vegetation more alpine. Abrupt walls act as guardians to the Sanctuary, towering on either side, while the triangular, snow-patched Gangapurna, which I'd last gazed upon from Letdar on the far side of the Thorong La, gradually eases into view directly ahead, framed by those gaunt rock walls. Once again I feel a bubble of excitement and anticipation. Stefan feels it too, and suddenly takes off like a greyhound unleashed. 'See you later,' he calls over his shoulder, and I'm happy to see him go.

Although generations of shepherds had been grazing their animals in the rough pastures of the Sanctuary, it was not until 1956 that the first Westerner managed to penetrate this huge glacial basin formed by the encircling ridges of the Annapurnas. Jimmy Roberts, then an officer in the Gurkhas and a seasoned mountaineer, was on reconnaissance a year ahead of an expedition to attempt Machhapuchhare. It was he who named this cauldron the Sanctuary. And it's a fitting name, for Gurungs consider it sacred, and in order to placate the gods that dwell there Roberts had to deposit 50 eggs at a small shrine along the way.

Passing through the rocky gates of the Sanctuary, I cross a stream which runs at the foot of a steep moraine bluff and once again enter the abode of the gods.

Bursting above me to the right, so steep and close as to have its true identity foreshortened, Machhapuchhare throws shadows of frost. Thanks to the intruding moraines and close proximity of the mountains, views are restricted, but I've been prepared for this, and know I have at least another 400 metres to climb before the full splendour is revealed. Beyond the bluff more lodges occupy a site used by the British expedition that climbed Machhapuchhare to within 50 metres of the summit. Since then the mountain has been kept sacrosanct, thanks again to Jimmy Roberts, who persuaded the Nepalese government that this, of all sacred peaks, should remain unclimbed for all time.

Views are better now. Hiunchuli, Annapurnas I and III, and Gangapurna, as well as Machhapuchhare, rim the spinning horizon. I'm standing once more at over 3500 metres and feel light-headed. Or is it a sense of wonder that takes me out of myself? With a deep breath I begin the slow ascent of moraine grooves and runnels of an ablation trough in which the tents of an expedition from South Korea are clustered. Ahead Annapurna South is being drawn to its full height, its northern ridge curving round via the Fang to Annapurna I, the highest of them all. Annapurna, named for the goddess of Hindu mythology, and first of the 8000ers to be climbed, is almost close enough to touch.

At 4130 metres I've reached my goal. The squat, stone-built lodges of Annapurna Base Camp are hunched below the final moraine barrier. A short distance away stand the dome tents of another expedition, with a wall consisting of snow cubes which, when melted, will be used for drinking water. A string of coloured flags thrashes the icy wind as, venturing beyond the lodges, tents and blocks of snow, I clamber onto the moraine crest, muffled in down while wind-induced tears speckle my glasses. There I stand on the frontiers of a vertical world.

An almost complete circle of mountains, many in excess of 7000 metres, thrust their ice-flutings and yellow buttresses towards the black-blue heavens. There's only one break in this near-perfect ring – the narrow cleft between Hiunchuli and Machhapuchhare through which the ice-melt of numerous glaciers escapes as the Modi Khola.

With its wind-stacked cornices Annapurna South is a mountain of singular beauty. In some respects it's more impressive even than Annapurna I, with which it is linked, although the South Face of that 8000 metre giant is so immense that my first impression is one of disbelief that anyone should contemplate climbing it, let alone succeed in the endeavour. For a fleeting moment I recall seeing a 35mm colour slide of this very wall projected onto a cinema-sized screen in Croydon a few months after Don Whillans and Dougal Haston broke through to the summit, with the measured tones of Chris Bonington's commentary sounding so professional by comparison with Haston's shy, mumbling Scottish brogue.

That projected image has become reality, but instead of the warmth of a South London lecture theatre, I stand breathless in 4000 metre chill as the bright early winter sunshine bathes the face. Even in sunlight it makes no concessions, for a billowing cloud of snow and ice erupts from it, hovers for a moment, then rolls slowly before gathering speed towards the lower glaciers. Somewhere near the foot of that huge face, Ian Clough lost his life in the final hours of the 1970 expedition when a serac broke free and engulfed him in a similar avalanche. My hope is that what I've just witnessed was harmless, and that no climbers were within reach.

Beyond Annapurna the Sanctuary wall continues to Khangshar Kang and Tarke Kang, confused by minor summits. Tent Peak is one. Then comes the lovely Gangapurna – another Hindu goddess, immaculate today in a gown of purest white. From her lofty headpiece the amphitheatre spreads to Annapurna III, before sending the horseshoe southward to the pinnacle of Gandharba Chuli, then up to Machhapuchhare. The fish-tail peak is impossible to ignore. Broad at its base, two ridges taper upward to a fine needle-sharp point, from which the tail-fin summit crest angles away from where I stand.

The mountain architect has achieved perfection.

But clouds are swelling now, and far below the cauldron has disappeared as the tide rises. There is no stopping it. Frothing and foaming, airstreams pump through the Modi Khola's gorge to inflate the wash of cloud, and one by one mountains are banished.

Alone again, I'm growing weary. Last night the lodge was full and I had no option but to sleep on a table. No wonder I'm tired today; bodily, mentally tired. On the bridge below Chhomrong I pause to dream into the raging torrent of the Chhomrong Khola and feel unaccountably giddy. The river swirls in pools and eddies, crashing over boulders with a pulsating rhythm, and my head spins. I have no energy, and the steps leading from the lower village to the upper one seem endless; a vertical ladder climbing towards the clouds. Time and again I stop to gaze on Machhapuchhare. The fish-tail seems more graceful than ever from this angle; cornflower blue, with black-shadowed walls of the gorge providing the perfect foreground. But the bloody steps go on and on…

Just below the lodge where I'd stayed on the way in, I can go no further. My legs are like jelly. I'm lathered in sweat and all my strength has gone. So I dump my rucksack, crawl onto the slab-topped wall and lie flat out, dead to the world. I've no idea how long I'm like this, but am suddenly brought awake by a Nepali voice.

'Old man tired?'

Through half-opened eyes I see a lad of about 15 peering at me with obvious concern. A woman I take to be his mother stands a little to one side. Our eyes meet and she smiles an understanding smile.

'Old man very tired.' There's no use denying it. I'm exhausted.

'Which lodge you?'

'That one.' I point to the white building not 50 paces away. Fifty paces, but they're all uphill.

The lad shoulders my rucksack, helps me off the wall, and chases up the steps. His mother nods her head and walks slowly with me, one step at a time.

At the lodge I ask the boy his name. 'Sondru Gurung,' he tells me.

'Sondru, how would you like to carry my rucksack to Pokhara?'

'Me? Pokhara?' He looks to his mother, then back at me.

'I need to be in Pokhara in two days' time.'

'Two days no possible.'

'Sure it's possible, strong man like you.'

'Chhomrong Pokhara three days fast. You old man go slow. We go four days.'

I shake my head. 'Two days to Pokhara. Easy.'

We haggle over days, although in my present condition this must seem an academic exercise, for I'm in no fit state to go anywhere until I'm properly rested. He senses this and argues with more logic than I can muster to rebuff, but I'm adamant that I must be in Pokhara in two days' time. Then I decide to offer him a straight fee. That way it will be to his advantage to make the journey in the shortest possible time. Of course, he dismisses my offer as being totally unreasonable, but I know it's a good one, and sooner or later we will strike a deal. It comes sooner rather than later, and he agrees to meet me here at seven in the morning.

Now all I need is plenty of liquids, a good meal and about 10 hours of undisturbed sleep. I manage six, but am content.

At 7.30 Sondru appears. 'Pokhara mister. We go, yes?'

'We go.'

I've not been a day without my rucksack since Manang, and the transformation is beyond belief. It feels as though I'm flying. Gone is yesterday's exhaustion, and in its place there's fresh energy and a new enthusiasm for the trail. At first Sondru walks slowly, with undisguised concern for the old man – is he afraid he'll be saddled with a corpse? But he soon learns that there's been a resurrection as I skip down the near-vertical path to New Bridge. With no weight on my shoulders my legs are working, my head clear, lungs pumping well. I've been reborn. Like my Dutch companion on the way to the Sanctuary, Sondru wants to talk, but this time I have breath to spare, and today I'm spurred by relief.

'How many member, you?' I guess he means how many in my group.

'Two,' I tell him, holding aloft two fingers. 'My friend waits for me in Pokhara.'

'Two member group, where you go?'

'Manang, Thorong La, Muktinath. Then Ghorepani, Chhomrong, Sanctuary.'

'You go Thorong La? Two member no porter? Father very strong!'

So now I'm not just an old man, I'm Father – how I've gone up in the world! Later, when we stop at wayside *bhattis*, I'm aware that Sondru is bragging about it to other Nepalis. I'm also aware that he's the only one who's remotely impressed.

From New Bridge we gaze back at Annapurna South and Hiunchuli, both of whose summits are more than 5000 metres above us. On those ice-tipped crowns a high wind tears loose snow into plumes that look like clouds. Down here by the river cicadas challenge the water's roar, and away from its cool channel the November air is full of summer.

We head down-valley alongside the river among rhododendrons and huge boulders, then climb among hibiscus flowers to Landrung. Without my rucksack the ascent is hardly noticed. Sondru simply ignores the fact that the slope angles uphill. Chatting with barely a

81

pause for breath, his step retains its spring, and I suspect he's testing me. When he knows the woman at a teahouse in Landrung, we stop for a drink. Perched high above the river, with terraced fields above and below, the village has narrow paved streets and clear views across the valley to Ghandrung, another handsome Gurung village. I gaze back along the Modi Khola's valley to the Annapurnas, whose individual peaks are reluctant to take their leave. Me too, but it's not just the big mountains I'll be leaving behind – it's all of this. All of it! Waiting for Sondru to finish his drink, I take a seat in the shade against the ochre walls of the house, listening to the rush of Nepali voices, the snort of a buffalo tethered in a nearby field, the background buzz of cicadas, the distant rumble of the river carried by a stray breeze...and come to recognise the special relationship that has developed between me and this land. In that recognition I know the meaning of contentment.

Sunlight paints each leaf, each straw in the thatch of neighbourhood houses. Hens scratch at the dry clay soil, a red-billed magpie lands on the grass across the way, does a couple of hops, stabs at something unseen by me, then takes off with a squawk. Narrow fields of rice, and the brilliant yellow of mustard, spread in a fantail below, terrace walls engraving the contours of a wrinkled land. Across the valley the harvest has been taken, and bare earth adds grey, tan, coffee-brown and even russet to the palette of morning colours. In a week's time I'll be home with my wife and daughters, and I have a yearning for them right now. But I want them *here*, to share this moment. I want them to know the colours and fragrances of foothill Nepal, to view the distant mountains with their arctic splendour revealed. How can I possibly take this to them? There are no words to capture such a kaleidoscope of other-worldliness. Language is an impotent substitute for experience.

Our journey devours hills. The weight of my rucksack is of no concern to Sondru. At 15 he has strength and energy to spare, and we're friends. Sure, when we stop at *bhattis* he's eager for Coke and biscuits, while I'm content with tea – he could not afford bottled drinks, so takes advantage of my pocket full of rupees, and I don't blame him. We laugh a lot; he finds excuses to call me 'Father', and when the trail is broad enough to walk two abreast I notice the sly way he extends his stride to increase the pace. It's another challenge I'm happy to meet.

Through forests loud with birdsong and lush with hart's-tongue fern I welcome the shade, but by the time we return to sunshine I welcome that too. It's another day to rejoice over. But as we descend from the Deorali Pass a sense of unease washes over me. Nothing has been said, but I have an eerie feeling as though eyes are studying us, yet I see no one. I have goose-bumps and shiver in the warm sunshine. Then Sondru speaks. 'This place very bad. People no good. You with me, Father. No alone.'

Below the untidy village of Pothana the trail brings us to the upper part of Dhampus. It's mid-afternoon and Sondru is trying to steer me towards a lodge in the main part of the village. 'Hotels very good.' But I'm unimpressed, and Dhampus fails to inspire with prospects of either food or lodging. 'How far Pokhara?' I ask.

'Too far, Father. Very very.'

Then we meet a couple of Americans, and while their guide speaks with Sondru, I enquire where they've come from today. 'Pokhara,' they tell me. 'Taxi to Phedi and an hour uphill from there.'

'That's it, Sondru. We go Pokhara. Now!'

At first he cannot believe I'm serious. Then the message sinks in. He throws back his head and laughs aloud. 'Oh, Father, you strong man!' Checking my watch he issues a challenge. 'Pokhara, we go!', and with a brief adjustment of the rucksack he takes off, cantering along the trail yelping with delight. I chase after him, and side by side we jog out of Dhampus and across the fields beyond. When the trail narrows along earthen causeways I tuck behind; then we descend steeply, laughing with the crazy joy of speed at the end of a long day. At the foot of the slope we stumble onto a road – the first since leaving Besisahar, a lifetime away. I look at Sondru's laughing face. Beads of sweat tumble from his brow. 'Hey! Father we good, strong. We go Pokhara one day Chhomrong!'

Three battered, dust-covered taxis are parked in the shade. Their drivers approach, touting for business. I ask Sondru if he wants to return home now or continue to Pokhara. The bright lights of town obviously beckon. Besides, he'll have money to spend. 'Pokhara me,' he says.

As the car bounces and weaves through the dust clouds, weariness once more drifts over me. But I'm happy with that. As for Sondru, he keeps tapping my leg and laughing. 'Chhomrong Pokhara – one day. Ha!'

CHAPTER 3

Manaslu

ONE IN FOUR HUNDRED
(1992)

*On trek through forbidding gorges to the raw beauty of high
mountains close to the border with Tibet.*

There's a ridge above Gorkha, in central Nepal, with one of the finest views I know. Framed by trees, terraced fields can be seen spilling into narrow river valleys squeezed by converging foothills. In an orderly matrix of rice, millet, barley and buckwheat, this fertile land also produces oranges, bananas, apples and lemons. At the end of summer, when the monsoon has wrung itself dry, colours are vivid and the fields shimmer in the newly laundered air, while houses, several hours' walk away, seem almost close enough to touch. All this is little more than foreground, though, for above and beyond the terraced hills, and sometimes separated from them by a filmy line of mist, stretches the Himalayan wall – Annapurnas to the northwest;

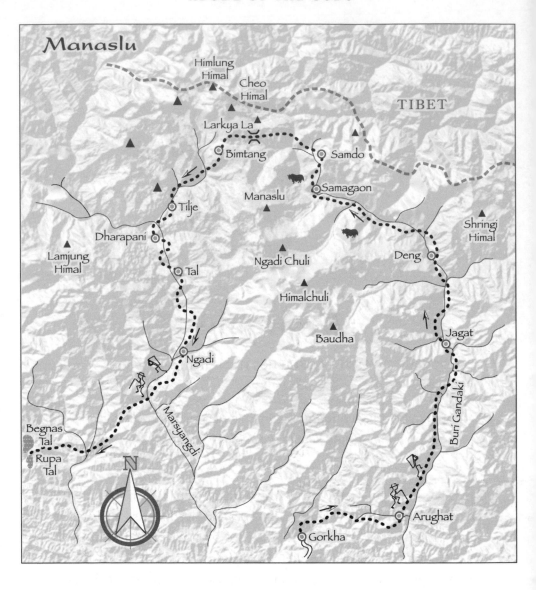

Ganesh Himal to the northeast. But directly ahead, tantalising in its creamy sawtooth outline, it's the Manaslu range that excites more than any other – Ngadi Chuli, Himalchuli, Baudha. There is no Manaslu. That twin-peaked seducer, despite being the world's eighth highest mountain, keeps its secrets hidden.

We pitch our tents upon a bare terrace below the ridge. There's a farm-house nearby, woodland behind and a view to the north almost identical to that from the crest 100 metres or so above us. On the outer edge of our camp one of the crew uses an ice axe to dig a hole for the latrine as a pure white cockerel with scarlet comb takes advantage and spikes an uncovered worm with his beak. A young girl wanders along the trail waving a stick at half a dozen goats. Her mind is distracted; she stops, turns to face our mess tent where I stand with drink in hand, rubs a bare foot against her other leg so she's balanced like a heron, and tilts her head as though listening to something far off. Our eyes meet. I offer her 'Namaste'. Her hands automatically come together as if in prayer, but instead of returning my greeting she blushes and scurries away, shouting at the goats.

It was just a year ago that Alan Payne and I trekked the Annapurnas a few valleys west of here, sharing the trails, lodges and teahouses with countless others from Europe, Australia, Israel and North America. Despite being very different from the earlier trek to Kangchenjunga my first visit to Nepal – the Annapurna experience proved to be just as memorable. It deepened my love for the country and the warmth of its people, and underscored a determination to return.

Now I can hardly believe my luck. As with Kangchenjunga three years ago, the Nepalese government has recently lifted trekking restrictions north of Gorkha, and the group I've been invited to accompany as a journalist on a circuit of the Manaslu Himal is one of the very first to respond. Just 400 permits have been allocated, and we're among the privileged few. As I say, I can hardly believe my luck.

Nearly 40 years ago, and long before commercial trekking took off in Nepal, David Snellgrove, a scholar of Tibetan culture and religion, found his way down through the valley of the Buri Gandaki between the Manaslu and Ganesh peaks, and described having to wade waist deep through raging tributaries; he told of narrow wooden cat-walks pegged against the rocks, and of single-pole bridges across which shepherds carried their sheep one by one. His was a journey of epic proportions, and some of his tales, published in *Himalayan Pilgrimage*, which I found in a Kathmandu bookshop, remain with me now. His descriptions of the valley we'll soon be trekking through feed my appetite for the days ahead and add a tingle of trepidation.

We're a cosmopolitan group – four Americans, an Australian brother and sister, a Dutchman and his English wife on their honeymoon, our leader, Dave Etherington, with his girlfriend, Leonie, and me. Plus *sirdar*, liaison officer, several Sherpas and an army of porters and Sherpanis to carry the loads for us. There are no lodges and very few teahouses, so the full complement of tents, food and cooking equipment must be taken; hence we are a team of 40 or more, including porters to carry food for porters.

Dave has been here twice before on climbing expeditions – an aspirant mountain guide and instructor at Glenmore Lodge in Scotland, he has a light touch to his leadership, and within a very short time has gained the confidence and respect of us all. This evening, before the sun vanishes behind the western hills and while its glow still stains the sky, he unfolds a dyeline map on the ground and outlines the route for us.

Making a counter-clockwise tour, we'll begin by heading roughly eastward to Arughat Bazaar in the valley of the Buri Gandaki, then strike north alongside the river, working our way upstream for eight or nine days, cutting through the Himalayan wall until we arrive at Samdo, our highest village, inhabited by Tibetan refugees. Once acclimatised we will turn westward, cross the Larkya La at over 5000 metres, and descend to the Marsyangdi to join the trail of the Annapurna Circuit at Dharapani. Against a tide of independent trekkers, we'll wander down-valley for two or three days before breaking away to the west for a cross-country trek to the lake of Begnas Tal near Pokhara, and a flight back to Kathmandu.

'At least, that's the plan,' says Dave. 'But when in Nepal, anything can happen.'

I'm out of my sleeping bag long before bed-tea, stepping into the morning dew, ears alert to sounds of the new day. There's a glow coming from the kitchen tent, the urgent hiss of a primus, the low chatter of Nepali voices. A lone bird in the forest beats the dawn with his territorial cry as I stroll past the farmhouse and smell wood smoke. Nearby there's a paved area with water coughing from a bamboo pipe. Ducking my head beneath it, my breath is caught by the sudden chill, and I make a mental note not to repeat that mistake again.

Beshkumar appears beside me, a mug of tea in his hand. '*Chai, Baje?*'

'*Dhanyabaad!*'

'Good place,' says the man who is to be our guide. 'You like?'

'Yes,' I say. 'I like.' And at that very moment the horizon turns pink with the rising of the sun. What is there not to like?

It takes two easy days of trekking to reach Arughat Bazaar. Two days along bare-earth paths between thatched villages, wandering beneath net-like spiders' webs, alongside hedges of grey cactus, above rice terraces and past groves of banana, orange and lime trees. We see pumpkins on the roofs of outhouses, canna lilies and lantern like hibiscus flowers in neat garden plots. Pipal and banyan trees spill their generous shade over paved chautaaras, their aerial roots hanging rope-like above the porters who gather to rest their loads and watch the world go by. One village has a school, and when we pass at least 30 children scramble onto walls and giggle at the white-skinned strangers drizzling sweat. A farmer comes along the trail with a two-day-old calf slung across his shoulders, its bulging eyes puzzled by the world it has entered. A buffalo with dribbling nose and bony hips drops steaming piles of dung on the path, and I have to alter my stride to avoid it as we approach a group of houses where two young Chhetri women in scarlet saris wash their long black hair beneath a standpipe and watch me pass, upside down.

Today the harmonies of life in the foothill country are as they were (I imagine) hundreds of years ago, but when we come across the scar of a vehicle-sized track that's been bulldozed over the hills, I sense we're on the cusp of change.

A two-hour lunch is taken on a recently harvested terrace with a view that stretches from Annapurna III to the Ganesh Himal. It's hot in the sun, so three of us opt for the shade of a nearby tree and pick at the tinned pilchards, fried potatoes, coleslaw and leathery *chapatti* served to us with mugs of steaming juice. A tall, thin woman emerges from a nearby field. Wearing a red-and-black scarf round her head, a faded blouse and green wrap-around ankle-length skirt, with a sickle fitted inside a cotton cummerbund at her waist, she pads bare-footed across the terrace to the edge of the blue tarpaulin on which the rest of the group are sitting and studies their food without any sign of embarrassment. Dave offers her a *chapatti*. She takes it but makes no attempt to eat. Instead, she absently folds it two or three times, before padding back to her field.

We camp for the night in a hollow below the trail. There are neither mountains nor houses in view, but within minutes of arrival we're visited by a pair of travelling musicians – he with a home-made instrument like a child-sized violin that he scrapes with a bow, cello-fashion; she beating a rhythm on a tubular drum. For an hour they play and sing to us; Nepali folk songs they are, repetitious in melody and with endless verses that compete with the cicadas, but in these early days of innocence the group finds them enchanting. The setting is perfect, the songs and the singers are part of the Nepalese experience, so the buskers are rewarded with a clutch of rupee notes, after which they vanish without a sound as shadows slide into the hills. I spend the night on top of my sleeping bag, and once more am outside long before dawn.

An hour after breakfast we cross a saddle that gives a brief view of Ganesh peaks and tuck behind flat-footed Beshkumar as he plunges down the slope on a narrow trail almost choked with vegetation. As we lose height so the trail finds a tiny stream to follow; at first little more than a spillage of water, within 20 minutes it has grown with a character all its own. We cross and recross countless times, and before reaching the bed of the valley it has been swollen by so many tributaries that we now need semi-submerged rocks and an occasional make-do bridge to help us over without getting wet feet. Along the way we meet groups of local men and brightly dressed women with nose jewellery, some of whom carry umbrellas as protection from the sun; we hear them long before we see them, for the women chatter like monkeys with shrill, hysterical voices that pierce even the densest screen of bamboo.

Beshkumar weaves a route among rocks and boulders, then returns to the stream that is now almost a river. Consulting the map, I see it is called the Moti Khola, and it leads us to Arughat Bazaar.

According to Dave this is the only village of any size we'll meet on our trek. Boasting electricity, Arughat Bazaar offers two or three simple hotels and a large number of shops whose goods spill into the street. There's a bank with a shotgun-toting guard, and a police check post where our permits are registered by Lal, our liaison officer. A teahouse selling dusty bottles of chilled Coke and Fanta is too tempting to resist, and while I stand outside clutching my drink I fall into conversation with a local man who has a reasonable command of English. He tells me that three days ago Bill Clinton won the US presidential election, and when I pass this news to the Americans in our group, one of the women from Los Angeles is so distressed she's almost in tears.

Camp is to be outside a small village some way upstream. As it's not far I let the others go ahead so I can walk alone for the last hour or so. The way is obvious, winding between fields of rice, millet and mustard, the ripe crops creating a subtle palette below hills of dark green forest. Some fields have already been harvested, and in one of them two young boys invite me to take their photograph as they manoeuvre a plough across a bare terrace, dragged by a pair of buffalo. Among a group of houses I photograph another eight-year-old, who proudly displays his tiny infant sister and practises the few words of English he's learnt at school. I savour each moment. The drama of high mountains can wait.

Our riverside camp has the persistent soundtrack of rocks crunching one against another, and when I rise at dawn the tents are drenched with mist. Until the sun's warmth can do its work, the valley is haunted by strange figures that drift in the grey light, only their lower limbs visible, as head and torso have been removed by the damp rack of fog that hangs at waist height. Most disturbing of all is the group of hooded trolls that emerges, hunched against the chill, preceded by a chorus of coughing and hawking. As they draw near I recognise some of our porters wrapped in the heavy brown garment known as the *bokkhu*, which serves as both blanket and cape and is used for protection by the valley's honey gatherers when they scale the cliffs to raid pendulous bees' nests.

By 10 o'clock the mist has gone, the heads and torsos of our crew are reunited with their legs, and the air is hot and sticky. There is no sky. The walls of the valley are connected by a smear of cloud that acts as a ceiling, trapping the heat. The trail makes no demands, yet for some unaccountable reason my knees ache and I'm lacking energy. Perhaps it's the heat.

In the afternoon we enter the valley's lower gorge to discover a string of waterfalls dusting the cliffs on both sides of the river. The path climbs and descends in quick succession; it takes us into the spray of one of the cascades, crosses a side stream on a two-log bridge and plunges down to the stony river-bed where the air is much cooler – for, being funnelled through the gorge, it carries the chill of snowmelt and glacier. With that change of temperature my energy is restored.

For several days the valley draws us on. We traipse across exposed banks of grey sand as though on a beach. We squeeze through jungles of plants that draw blood from exposed arms; we scale cliffs via paths drilled from the rock, in places supported or buttressed by retaining walls of timber and stone that lead to airy belvederes, and we cross bridges of questionable stability that creak and sway high above rapids. The porters, of course, take it all in their stride, despite the size of their loads.

In this gorge there is no monotony. The devious nature of the trail, the bold architecture of the landscape, and the light all guarantee it – especially the light, which changes by the hour and depends for its strength on the valley's direction. In this arthritic piece of geography the gorge twists this way and that, alternating sunlight and shadow, white light or blue, dense or filtered, a broad flood of light or a thin sliver beamed through a chink in the Himalaya's armoury.

For a while our path is little more than a ledge, but when it slopes down towards the river, a flock of two or three hundred sheep files up the path towards us, heading south away from the oncoming winter. Some of the rams have large curling horns, and there are a few goats too. At the head of the file a wild-looking shepherd carries a stave; on his back a *doko* rattles with pots and pans. In the middle of the flock another shepherd has a *doko* almost overflowing with lambs bleating for milk, while at the rear a third shepherd has a sling in his hand and a new-born lamb under his arm, which the mother ewe desperately tries to reach with her extended tongue.

We cross landslides, see plenty of signs of rockfall, and come upon groups of houses in the most unexpected places. Terraced fields fill open spaces where the gorge slackens its hold and the valley opens to a wash of sunlight. On the approach to one tiny village we walk through an avenue of poinsettias three metres tall, and stop at a teahouse for biscuits and mugs of sweet lemon tea. Our cook buys a chicken for the evening meal, much to the horror of Mandy and Alba from California, both of whom are vegetarian. To make matters worse, throughout the afternoon Alba insists on cradling it in her arms like a pet, thereby deepening her affection for the doomed hen that will only add to her distress when it's served up in a curry tonight.

I love these early days on trek when the unknown becomes familiar, when a relationship with the crew is cemented – greeting our porters with 'Hiya!' when we pass on the trail and receiving a grin of recognition in return. I'm in my element wandering among the foothills, the Middle Hills, and the gorge that drives a route right through the Himalayan barrier. We're so close to the huge mountains that we cannot see them, except for a brief glimpse through a side valley, such as that which offered us Shringi Himal. Some of the group were so full of chatter they missed it completely.

One morning we round a bend in a narrow section of gorge to discover a gush of steaming water. 'Tatopani,' says Beshkumar with a touch of pride in his voice. 'Hot water. You can wash if you like.' It's not at all like the Tatopani I'd visited on the Annapurna Circuit. That Tatopani had a pool of bubbling water large enough for perhaps a dozen people to bathe in, and its popularity with trekkers was such that a settlement of lodges and teahouses had been built to exploit it. Here on the banks of the Buri Gandaki there are no buildings, just a solitary spout in a stone surround.

Shortly after leaving the hot spring a suspension bridge takes us across to the east bank of the river, where a flight of stone steps angles steeply up the slope towards a beckoning V of light. Tall cannabis plants crowd the trail, and when it divides Beshkumar grabs a stone and scrapes an arrow in the lower of the two path options. Now we pick our way along another ledge before swooping down towards the river once more, losing all the height we'd just gained. Across the valley silver threads mark the course of waterfalls against ochre-coloured slabs, but below us the river thrashes bungalow-sized boulders with giant blue humbug stripes.

Up again on more stone slabs, we emerge from shadows to sunshine. The temperature is several degrees higher than it was moments ago, and the distant voice of the river is drowned by a massed choir of insects in full joyous celebration of our arrival.

Some days we have the scent of pine in our nostrils, sometimes it's cannabis, sometimes mint, vanilla or wild thyme; later I imagine it will be the crisp smell of frosted ground or even snow and ice. Every day is special, and whichever way I turn there's something to capture my attention. I'm eager to miss nothing. On trek to Kangchenjunga one of the group walked most days wearing earphones so he could listen to music. Each to his own, I guess, but I could never understand why he would do that; he could enjoy his music at home, while the Himalaya is full of sounds that only belong here, can only be heard here – they are surely as much a part of the trekking experience as the sight of the highest mountains on Earth. Why not soak them in? I won't even bring a novel to read at night in my tent, for that would take me to a different place. I want nothing to confuse the magic of this moment in time. Being here. Now.

Perhaps I'm obsessive.

It's the night of the full moon when we arrive at Deng and pitch our tents in a meadow below its string of stone-built houses. We ran out of thatch a couple of days ago, and most of the buildings we see now have roofs covered with pine shingles or stone slabs. There are prayer flags, too, and *mani* stones beside the trail, and a neat *chorten* when we came through Jagat – when was that? Yesterday? We're still in the gorge and making a lot of height gain and loss each day, but we've still not reached 2000 metres, although nights are chilly. Tonight, for example. After we've eaten our meal and the rest of the group have gone to their tents, I need my down jacket as I wander away from camp to perch upon a boulder beyond the village and wait for the moonrise. There'll be a frost tonight, that's for sure.

Down-valley a silvery glow reveals Ganesh IV, a 7000 metre peak first climbed by a Japanese expedition in 1978. Up-valley an ethereal light shows Shringi Himal towards the Tibetan border. We've seen it several times recently, but never for more than a few brief moments. Now it's revealed as the unseen moon climbs rapidly behind the eastern mountains. Shafts of white light tell of its advance, and moments before the great disc pulls itself over the valley's rim I'm joined by Bob.

'Got up for a pee', he admits, 'and saw what was happening. Didn't wanna miss this.' He leans against the boulder as the moon in all its glory sails above the ridge and fills the valley with its goodness.

'Gee, what a sight!' gasps the man from Boston with permanent stubble on his chin. 'The best yet.'

This is his third Himalayan trek too. The oldest of the group, Bob is in his late 50s, a well-travelled man with slow, thoughtful speech, and his enthusiastic response to the rising of the moon both surprises and delights me with its spontaneity.

Our map is not the finest example of cartography I've come across, and with contours at intervals of 100 metres it leaves much to the imagination. But it's good enough for us. After all, we hardly need it to navigate by, for the route is mostly obvious, and we also have Beshkumar as our guide, so when the trail is depicted on the map as following the left bank of the river, while reality has it on the opposite side, I simply use a bold pen to mark my sheet with the route we take. I just hope it's accurate enough to identify some of the mountains we'll pass on our journey. So far these have been few, but I sense that is about to change.

The gorge slackens its hold on the valley. On the way to Ghap we cross a tributary on a suspension bridge to catch sight of big snow-spattered peaks that block its head. Then they're gone again, all hint of the Himalaya being vanquished by crowded mountains of rock and forest. Yet Ghap rewards in other ways. Below the village there's a water-driven prayer wheel, a decorated entrance *kani*, and a *mani* wall consisting of the most elaborately carved stones I've yet seen. An outdoor art gallery, it is, with stone after stone depicting Buddhist saints; exquisite figures and religious symbols etched in slate. Phurba says they're the work of men from Bih. 'Where's that?' I ask. He waves his hand dismissively. 'That way some place,' and moves off along the trail. Not long after, we enter pine forest with khaki tatters of lichen and moss-covered rocks, then cross the Buri Gandaki once more by a shaky cantilever bridge spanning a narrow rock arch, through which the river thunders and foams in an explosion of sound.

Beyond Namru autumn has arrived. Frost is on the ground and scarlet- and gold-coloured leaves spiral from deciduous trees, but some way up-valley fields of barley have yet to be harvested, and waves ripple through them with every passing breeze. A skein of blue smoke drifts across the houses of Ligaon; it seeps through the shingle roofs and flavours the air with the smell of cooking. Then we cross a tributary with a hint of the Manaslu Himal at its head, rise up a slope to an entrance *kani*, and less than an hour later come to Sho. Outlined by drystone walls, the fields here have all been harvested, and on the way through the village I notice small yards beside some of the houses covered with drying grain or fearsome red chillies.

Suddenly Manaslu North bursts into view ahead, and I feel the blood throbbing in my temples as I focus my camera on a lofty apparition outlined against the Himalayan blue. The foreground is a patchwork of yellow and brown – yellow of barley, brown of stubble. Men, women and children too are working in the fields, their voices piercing the air. A haystack with two feet comes down the trail and I squeeze against a wall to let it pass. All around us the rhythmical beat of threshing is joined by a chorus of crows and human voices. But for the altitude and a backdrop of mountains, my great-great-grandfather could have been part of this harvest scene; it's almost as old and universal as humanity. Yet again I know what a privilege it is to be here. Now.

The gates of Paradise are flung open at Lho when we camp at 3000 metres in view of Manaslu at last. I doubt if anything could improve on the outlook from the village or its neighbouring fields, but when the sun sinks into twilight, the view fades and an icy wind springs up. Now we have other priorities beyond simply gazing at mountains; we need thermals, a layer of fleece and down jackets as we huddle in the mess tent and pick at our food. The two Californian women cannot believe how cold it is, and are visibly concerned that we still have another 2000 metres and more to climb before we descend to warmer temperatures. Ted and Sally from Australia are more worldly-wise, but they also feel the cold here. We all do, but later, alone in my tent and with a decent sleeping bag, I'm cosy enough, yet in the night I develop a cough that goes on for so long and is so violent that a sharp pain erupts in my chest and I spend the remaining hours of darkness in agony.

The 500 metres of ascent to Ramanan Kharka (now known as Syala) are purgatory, for each intake of breath is like the twist of a knife, and I drop far behind the others. One of our Sherpas stays with me and offers to carry my daypack. I resist his offer and instead use my extra-slow pace to celebrate the glorious landscape we're wandering through. But when we enter woodland and views disappear I become absorbed in self-pity that only lifts when we reach the grazing land of the *kharka*, with its three or four houses and simple *gompa*, and a direct view of Manaslu, Manaslu North, Naike Peak and Ngadi Chuli that fill the horizon above an old haunted forest. Eased by paracetamol, the pain is almost forgotten as I gaze up and up at a scene of rare perfection; the best of the Himalaya, it appears, captured in a single glance.

Overnight even the mountains glitter with stars, and shortly before 6 o'clock dawn's first light burns on Manaslu's twin summits before draining gold onto its snowfields and glaciers. With one eye on the yaks whose meadow we share, I steady my camera on a tree stump and, with fingers wooden with cold, capture a scene that will stay with me for ever.

Beyond the *kharka* a broad, open pasture sliced by the much-reduced Buri Gandaki draws us on. Through it a row of large white chortens can be seen marching up-valley towards the village of Samagaon. Dozens of yaks and Tibetan ponies graze the short-cropped grass, but my attention is irresistibly drawn to the mighty wall of snow and ice that soars

over everything. Manaslu dominates the scene. A graceful, immaculately dressed peak, I understand the urge to climb it. But I also appreciate its significance to the folk who live in its shadow. Manaslu is not just
a mountain with an 8000 metre summit for an ego prize, but a religious
symbol, a home of the gods. Forty years ago, after a massive avalanche
destroyed the Pungyen Monastery and killed all 18 of its occupants,
members of a Japanese expedition were blamed for the devastation.
Their trespass on Manaslu's flank was believed to have upset the gods,
and villagers were so angry that when another team of mountaineers
from Japan arrived with Manaslu their aim, they were driven away in
fear for their lives.

Today the gods – and the people of Samagaon – are in a more benev-
olent mood, and we wander undisturbed through the village, whose
many sturdy houses and piles of *mani* stones lie in a sheltered scoop
out of the wind. Continuing up a slope among bushes and stunted juniper trees we reach the *gompa*, with its gold-topped pagoda style roof
reflecting the sunlight.

Not much more than two hours from last night's camp we pitch tents
on another *kharka* edged with berberis and juniper and backed by a
moraine wall. The sun is full upon us, and out of the wind it's a welcoming site. While lunch is prepared I take my notebook and, seated
on the grass, try in vain to capture in words the magic of this place
for future reference. Once again I can hardly believe my luck in being
here.

Suddenly I'm aware of another presence as a shadow falls across
the page. Gentle pressure is being applied to my shoulder to disrupt
my writing, and when I look up the quizzical face of a 10-year-old
boy who had arrived as silently as a breeze peers down on me. 'Hello,'
I say. '*Namaste!*' He grins, flashing his teeth, his wind-chapped cheeks
squeezing his eyes, but says nothing in response to my greeting. So I
close my journal and exchange it for a soft-covered book full of glossy

photographs of the Himalaya, and open it at the section devoted to Manaslu. The boy's jaw drops as he recognises his village in one picture, and stabbing it with a grubby finger he then proceeds to give me a commentary on every photograph in the book, whether the subject is familiar or not. Then we fall into conversation – he in his language; I in mine. Neither understands words spoken by the other, yet that ignorance is no obstacle to our relationship. For 10 minutes, on a *yak* pasture at about 3600 metres, we become friends.

The beauty of the place is such that I'm restless to see more, so four of us wander up to an icy lake at the foot of the Manaslu Glacier, where a savage scene greets us – green water littered by ice floes; the dirty snout of the glacier towering perilously over the lake; the frozen cascade of the icefall; and, above that, huge slabs of rock that disappear into cloud. From our vantage point on a moraine tip we spy several yaks below, and when I slide down to the lake's edge I'm astonished to find two of them mating while standing knee-deep in the freezing water. Any creature that can manage such a feat in a glacial lake has my admiration!

Several members of the group have developed head colds and a variety of other ailments; one was vomiting earlier and has taken to his sleeping bag, while another has a painful ear infection that upsets her balance. Our newly wed Dutchman has stomach cramps and eggy burps – classic signs of giardia – and he's given a blast of tiniba, which we hope will flush the bug from his system. As a result the mess tent reminds me of a GP's waiting room, but at least the pain in my chest has eased, and I feel rejuvenated when I get up twice after midnight and each time spend a few minutes gazing at the night sky. The frost both inside as well as outside the tent should kill any germs, or so I tell myself, but to make sure I keep my first-aid pack handy – just in case.

We make a slow hike to Samdo. It's only two hours away, but it takes all morning to get there, and as soon as the tents go up at least half the group vanishes from view. It's a pity, because the outlook down-valley to the cluster of now familiar snow- and ice-coated peaks is truly spectacular. But I guess if you're feeling out of sorts, scenery is inclined to lose its appeal. Soaring above our camp, which shares the levelled moraine on which the village is built, Pang Phuchi is every bit as dramatic as most of the Manaslu range, its north flank topped by ice flutings, while behind it a hanging valley gives access to Tibet, where the villagers originated.

Samdo consists of perhaps 30 or more two-storey stone-built houses huddled in a group at the foot of a towering hill whose lower slopes are peppered with scrub. Livestock are stabled on the ground floor, with the family's living space directly above it, and because there are no chimneys in any of the dwellings, all doorways and windows are crusted with smoke-blackened timbers. This afternoon, in a walled enclosure between two of the buildings, a family is threshing straw with long-handled bamboo flails. When I approach with my camera, the woman I take to be the mother calls out to me, her voice crackling as she invites me into the compound, where I squat against a wall and study the rhythmic movement of the flails, the rising clouds of chaff and individual heads of barley that spring from the threshing floor to catch the sunlight. Mother is teamed with son, and father with daughter, and in turns they raise, then bring down the flails with perfect timing; each pair works in unison, with the whole exercise forming part of a choreographed ritual that owes its origins to centuries past.

Using pantomime I ask whether I can take part, and the teenage son then offers me his flail. In exchange I give him my down jacket to wear, hang my camera round his neck, and join the rest of the family for the next 20 minutes. As a novice from another land I have neither their natural rhythm nor the essential knack of giving the flail a slight twist at the top of its arc before bringing it down on the barley, but despite my clumsiness I revel in the experience. Meanwhile, in a reversal of roles the boy aims my camera and takes photographs of me, his parents and sister, and who knows what else, until there is no film left.

With prayer flags slapping their poles, a November afternoon in Samdo becomes engraved on my memory.

Allowing time to recover for those of our group who are unwell, Dave suggests we spend three nights here. I'm happy with that, and on our first rest day scramble up the hill above Samdo with Dave, Leonie and big Gordon from the US. Above a belt of scrub a very steep slope climbs to a summit cairn at 4600 metres, about 800 metres above the village, and as we gain height so the panorama expands to include chisel-summited Larkya Peak and the glacier saddle of the Larkya La, which we must cross in the next few days. The outing tests our level of fitness and acclimatisation, and I'm relieved to discover that, apart from a shortage of breath, there's not even a hint of headache. And the views make all the effort worthwhile.

Two days later we're camped behind a solitary stone hut at around 4450 metres in readiness for our crossing of the Larkya La. The cook has taken over the hut for his kitchen, while this afternoon our porters are huddled in a group outside; some play cards while others sleep among a mound of blankets. In bright sunshine and out of the wind it's a pleasant site with a great view back to Pang Phuchi above Samdo, but we all know that as soon as the sun goes down this will be a feverishly cold place.

When we arrived we were appalled to find a litter of polythene, food containers and used toilet paper scattered across the grass. It could only have been left by a previous trekking or mountaineering party, and since we're among the first to be granted access here, I fear for the future. Red-faced with frustration (or is it barely concealed anger?) Dave asks for volunteers, and several of us take plastic bags and make a sweep of the area, then with the aid of kerosene have a bonfire and curse those who went before us.

Hearing voices and a clatter of stones, I turn towards a moraine ramp that leads to the pass, where a large caravan of laden yaks can be seen descending towards us. Among them are several Tibetan herders who say they've come from Manang, but they barely pause and continue on their way, and within a few minutes have disappeared from view.

This evening bowls of steaming garlic soup bring tears to our eyes and a semblance of warmth to the mess tent, while frost patterns the canvas and hardens the ground to stone. Our meal is a carbohydrate boost in readiness for a long day tomorrow – Sherpa stew, potatoes, rice and macaroni – but appetites are poor at these altitudes, and only Dave and I manage second helpings. 'Drink up,' he urges everyone with kettle in hand. 'You need plenty of liquids, and if you don't get up for a pee at least three times tonight, you've not been drinking enough.'

By 7 o'clock the camp is quiet, and the only light comes from the kitchen. Outside, the temperature drops to minus 15, but – wearing almost everything except boots in my sleeping bag – I'm cosy enough. Yet I don't think I sleep at all, for my mind is too active, too full of anticipation and bursting with memories, and each time I creep out to wash a patch of frosted grass and gaze at the stars, I'm aware of others doing likewise.

Funny way to spend a holiday…

We breakfast shortly after 4 o'clock and are away just after five. The stars are bright as midnight, it's bitterly cold, and the sharp incision of air that's sucked into my lungs comes out as steam which turns to ice on beard and moustache; the hairs inside my nostrils are brittle as birch twigs and shoulders ache from being hunched against the chill. Yet this is a day to rejoice over; once again I'm aware of the privilege of being here. Today.

We're treading where yesterday's yaks came down, their smell lingering in the ablation valley, and when light slowly steals into the sky and head-torches are dispensed with, low piles of frost-crusted dung serve as waymarks. That first light turns a black shape north of the pass into a bronze monolith, as all around us mountains – and the spaces between them – are revealed one by one. I rejoice in the wild scene – the banks of snow, ice clusters, the inhospitable rubble tips, rocks and boulders, and semi-frozen lakes that lie below the trail; and in the great peaks thrust out of the frozen ground – those to the south form a protective barrier behind which Manaslu is concealed, while those to the north hide Tibet's remote spaces.

There's nothing difficult about the route, it's simply the act of putting one foot in front of the other and having enough puff to keep repeating the action, and by 10 o'clock we're on the pass, gathered round the cairn with its wind-bleached prayer flags at 5135 metres, relieved and excited to be here. There's barely a breeze, the sun is still climbing, and we have time to enjoy the views, which are particularly fine when looking back along the glacier to Pang Phuchi. Sadly clouds obscure the westward view, and when we set off along a corridor between walling mountains, a sudden wind funnels into our faces, making eyes water and blurring vision. Clouds disappear, but the icy blast is unwelcome as we begin to descend old moraine ribs and step gingerly over runnels of water ice. Then we turn out of the wind and gaze across a vast glacial cirque to outliers of the Annapurna range. It's a sensational view, and I'm pulled up short by it.

We stop for an early lunch among a litter of grey rocks where a brew is already on the go. Someone has discovered a spring of clear water, and porters are dumping their loads with grunts of relief. We eat together as a family – porters, Sherpas, liaison officer and trekkers, all bound by a common need. We share boiled eggs and chapattis spread with peanut butter, savoury biscuits and apples that have survived rough handling all the way from Gorkha. Quenching thirst is our main priority, though. The cold dry air sucks moisture from every breath, and we can't get enough of the hot juice poured into our mugs.

With a huge wall crowding above us, Dave points out the summits of Cheo Himal, Himlung Himal, Nemjung and Kang Guru, adding a litany of melodic names to the landscape. Mountains of peerless quality play games with wisps of cloud whichever way we turn, and it matters not one jot that their names mean little or nothing to most of us; their ridges, summit domes, snowfields and glaciers represent (for me at least) the raw majesty of the Himalaya. I could ask for nothing more.

Bimtang is an historic place, long used as a trading ground for Nepalese rice, grain, cloth and cigarettes, which were exchanged for loads of salt and wool brought over the high passes from Tibet by *yak* caravans. When he was here in 1950 mountaineer Bill Tilman was told by the man in charge that during a short season more than 3000 animal loads would be weighed in. Today that trade has finished, although a few low stone buildings, once used by those traders, are grouped near our tents on the edge of a meadow as level as a bowling green and several times the size of a football pitch. Behind the buildings a long moraine wall separates us from a glacier spilling down from the frontier peaks, while to the south-east Manaslu and the graceful tower of Phungi grab my attention when I go up onto the moraine crest to survey the scene. With the pass behind us, and all safely down in camp, I make a mental list of the blessings of this day of days.

Despite the effort of yesterday's pass crossing, I manage only four hours' sleep, and long before daybreak spend what's left of the night writing notes by the light of my head-torch, sleeping bag pulled up to my chin, frost flakes glistening on the tent fabric. Every few minutes it's necessary to plunge my writing hand between my thighs to restore life to frozen fingers before I'm able to hold the pen to scribble a few more sentences. I'm sure it cannot be as cold as our camp on the other side of the Larkya La, but it certainly feels like it.

When I hear a movement outside the tent, followed by the whisper of voices and the pumping of a primus, I realise the kitchen crew have begun their work. First up in the morning, they spend their days on the go, fetching water, preparing meals, clearing away, washing pots and pans in near-freezing water, carrying loads…and yet they're always the last to settle down at night. What heroes they are! I'm full of admiration, but slide deeper into my sleeping bag and wait for someone to bring me bed-tea.

Today we'll descend towards the Marsyangdi – down to teahouses, lodges and shops. Down towards warmth. The prospect of warm nights is something to look forward to, but I know I shall miss the close proximity of rock face and glacier, the untamed grandeur and the challenge of high places. And yes, I shall miss the sharp bite of frost and the beauty of a starlit Himalayan sky. But I won't miss the necessity to crawl outside the tent three times during the night.

Breakfast gives a close view of 6000 and 7000 metre mountains dazzling in the morning light. In camp the air is still, but a high wind strips plumes of snow from summit crests, creating a vortex of cloud that tells a different story to that of Bimtang's calm, but by the time we're ready to leave, that wind-disturbed snow has vanished, leaving mountains clearly etched and outlined by the deep November bluc.

Beyond the moraine wall we slither down to the Dudh Khola, cross the milky glacial torrent on a wooden bridge, and before long enter an enchanted forest – the first for many a long day. It is enchanted too – a mixed forest of pine, birch, oak and rhododendron trees, many of which are draped with the wispy lichen known as Spanish moss. Moss covers rocks and boulders that lie in hummocks; it thickens the trunks of trees hundreds of years old, and dense clumps transform fallen branches into grotesque shapes. We make our way through shafts of sunlight, treading the leaf-mould of forgotten autumns. No one speaks. The forest is silent as a cathedral after dark. To break that silence would be an act of sacrilege; even the Sherpas are struck dumb.

In the forest there's a huge granite boulder with a drystone wall, behind which is a cave large enough to accommodate half a dozen people. The roof and inner walls are smoke-blackened, and I imagine porters, *yak* herders and traders sleeping here. I rather fancy doing so myself, but it's too early for that and we have several hours to go before we can consider stopping for the night.

Two hours or so after leaving Bimtang we arrive at a pasture from which the group of icy peaks is seen for the last time – or at least, it's the last view of Manaslu and its neighbours we'll have from fairly close proximity. Knowing this I'm reluctant to leave, and find an excuse to delay my departure until everyone else has disappeared, then slowly make my way down-valley, only to find Nima is waiting for me where the trail enters forest once more. Just for a moment I feel guilty. But only for a moment.

Here a straggle of wild clematis clings to low-growing trees and shrubs, and fingers of light focus on the brilliant red spears of a plant that appears now and then beside the trail. Then I notice a clump of trumpet gentians on a bank above the river. Stopping to admire them, I discover more; dozens of brilliant blue heads in search of the sun. We'd seen gentians yesterday sprinkled along the moraine wall on our descent to Bimtang, but those gentians were much smaller than these. No less beautiful, of course, but less showy than these granddaddy flowers with trumpet heads all turned in anticipation of the sun's appearance.

Crossing a side stream I'm directed up a bank onto a meadow where lunch is waiting – fried spam with beans and coleslaw, Tibetan bread and fried potatoes, followed by tinned cherries and enough tea to bathe in. Comfortably full, I take out my notebook to record the morning while it's still fresh, but the sun's warmth is soporific, and the next thing I know I'm being woken by Leonie tickling my neck with a blade of grass.

Losing altitude, we pass the first walled fields we've seen for several days. They've not been worked in ages, and just beyond them we're forced down to the edge of the river to avoid a landslip. Once we've scrambled back up the slope, we find ourselves on a switchback course as dark, menacing clouds gather ahead. I grow pensive, yet their threat fails to materialise, and half an hour later the sun returns and the valley opens to give a hint of the distant Marsyangdi. Shortly after, three young children emerge from a field carrying dokos of barley. The oldest boy tells me he is 13 and is eager to practise his English lessons.

'Hello sir. Which country you from? How old are you? What is your name? My name is…' The name is spoken so fast that I have to ask him to repeat it, but he's on a roll now and doesn't want to be interrupted. 'Where are you going? Is this your first time in Nepal? Is this your wife?'

Leonie laughs. 'Don't be daft. He's old enough to be my dad!'

We end the day at Tilje, a village of stone-and-timber houses, some with outhouses of woven bamboo, in which the paved street is used as a strutting ground for chickens, ducks and geese. Children stand and giggle as we file past to find our tents being erected in a crowded orchard of apple trees devoid of either fruit or leaves. Grabbing my towel I go down to the river, kneel on a rock and dunk my head. While we were eating lunch earlier today this water was being ejected from a glacier, and the cold is such a shock to the system that in an instant my head is aching. Will I never learn?

When darkness falls I stroll into the village and try to imagine the routines of family life in this valley. How different are those routines when compared to ours at home? Here, activity is largely dictated by daylight and people turn in early; at home unlimited power enables both business and social life to continue long into the night. Technology is creeping into the hills of Nepal, and it can't be far from Tilje, but until it arrives to transform and change communities for all time, life here will be not much different from that experienced by numerous generations past. Behind windows and doorways outlined by the dance of candlelight, all sounds are subdued. There's the low murmur of voices in conversation, the chitter of children tired and ready for bed, the scratching of a dog, heavy feet climbing wooden stairs. I catch the smell of dry timber, the dust of grain, wood smoke and cooking oil that's been used once too often, and watch as a cat runs down the street in front of me, then swerves to the right to enter a house through an open door. I picture mice beneath tables.

After Bimtang it's not cold down here, but a cool breeze huffs through the valley as a reminder of what we've left behind. Suddenly my mood shifts and I'm filled with melancholy.

A new day, a different world. We've left the valley of the Dudh Khola, turned our backs on Manaslu and joined the Annapurna Circus. It really is a different world. For 18 days we more or less had the trail to ourselves, but now we meet scores of other trekkers every hour. Until now most of the villages we passed through showed no Western influence; here in the Marsyangdi Valley lodges, shops and teahouses display some form of advertising, with names in English, and goods for sale made by multi-national companies, their brands recognised throughout the world. If we hear a radio it's more likely to be playing a Western pop song than Nepali or Indian music. Around Manaslu Western litter was a rarity; when we found any we were affronted, so we'd remove and burn it where possible. Here litter is taken for granted. It's ubiquitous, as bad as in our towns and cities at home.

And yet…the magic of Nepal is as intoxicating as ever, and I rejoice at the new day's promise. Last night's sudden fit of melancholy did not last, and I was out again before dawn, eager to greet the sunrise with a chorus of birds in the apple trees and cocks crowing in the village street. All of it is worth celebrating. Especially this moment in time – it won't come again, so savour, value and treasure the magic while it lasts.

Out of Tilje we cross the river and walk down-valley into sunlight. Vegetation beside the trail is lush, the greenery vibrant, alive with insects, while the Dudh Khola is busy moulding and smoothing rocks into curious shapes, exposing striped veins in a range of colours. At Thonje the river joins the Marsyangdi, which we cross by a long suspension bridge into Dharapani, and a connection with my past.

A year ago Alan and I had bowls of noodle soup here before moving on to Bagarchhap. I remember the paved street and a crowd of porters trying to force their way past a stubborn cow with its nose buried deep in a plastic bucket, and I recall the police post and the bored expression on the face of the official who checked our permits. But that was then, this is now, and Dave collects our permits before heading for the same police post while the group indulges in an orgy of shopping for bars of chocolate, rolls of Kodak film (in date? I doubt it), and bottles of Coke and Fanta. Having seen nothing like this since Arughat Bazaar, we're bemused by choice.

Bob was here 10 years ago and finds it difficult to adjust to the way Dharapani has grown. He scratches his head and furrows his brow. 'I just don't get it,' he mumbles. 'This was just a teensy place; now it's a city!' It's the only city I know that has just one street, but I understand what he's getting at. Change can be difficult to accept, but who are we to criticise the Nepalese for meeting the needs of ever increasing numbers of visitors? After all, we are part of that growing number.

It's easy walking down-valley on a clear trail, but all the trekkers coming our way take some getting used to. A year ago I was part of that traffic, and realise I'm for ever recalling incidents, faces and even conversations from that trek, reliving that journey when I should be fully involved with Now.

We cross and recross the Marsyangdi on a series of suspension bridges, some more bouncy than others, and with a strong wind blowing we stop for lunch in a lone teahouse high above the river, the woman of the house taking little notice of us as she squats beside the fire with an infant suckling at her breast.

I'm full of smiles when we enter Tal. It's good to be back in this Wild West township, and I make a point of calling at the tiny jewellery shop of the lovely Tibetan lady I spent time with last year. She seems as pleased to see me as I am to meet her again, and after exchanging our 'Namastes' she takes both my hands in hers and we touch foreheads in greeting. She asks after my wife and daughters (what a memory she has!), then invites me into her house, where we drink a glass of tea together. In turn I ask about her daughter, the one I met, and she scolds me for not remembering she has three girls, all of whom are away at boarding school in Kathmandu.

'You must be a very rich lady,' I tell her. 'So I don't need to buy anything from you today.'

With that she laughs and retorts, 'No. With three girls at school I need you to spend many, many rupees.'

Before we part, I buy earrings and bracelets for my daughters and promise to bring my wife to see her next time.

Heading out of Tal alone, I scurry along the remembered trail that rises slightly at the southern end of the little plain before swooping down the stony path that twists against the left-hand side of the gorge, where I soon catch the rest of the group. Dave tells me we'll be camping tonight in Jagat and takes a bet on our time of arrival. He says 4.30; I reckon 4 o'clock. We arrive at the village entrance, where Beshkumar is waiting for us, at 4.40.

'You owe me a beer,' says Dave.

It's warm at about 1300 metres, and as darkness falls we wait for dinner with cicadas seething around us. The tents have been erected in a small terraced meadow behind a lodge, and our kitchen crew has taken over one of the outhouses. Throughout the village giant boulders remind me of the scene last year when Alan and I arrived to discover a newly slaughtered buffalo being dismembered, but I keep the memory to myself. The vegetarians in our group couldn't handle the vivid pictures I still have in mind.

Dinner is served by candlelight, and when we've eaten Nawa places a jug of *chang* on the table, then takes a kettle of the home-brew to our porters, who are soon singing round a hurricane lamp. A chorus of now-familiar voices joins the song of the cicadas and the distant rush of the river. Shadows are thrown against a boulder, and on the far side of the valley, high above the river, an orange glow suggests there's a house lost in the black anonymity of night.

Another day on the Annapurna trail takes us down to a camp beside the Ngadi Khola, where I sense that some of the group are growing trail-weary. It's almost three weeks since we left Gorkha, and very few of our group have trekked as long as this before and now daydream about a bed with clean sheets and old familiar meals. Fantasies centre on food and drinks unobtainable in the Himalaya; conversations divert to favourite films and music. It's the familiarity of home they crave, while I'm caught between a love of wife, family and friends at home and the deeply satisfying act of wandering day after day through landscapes of great beauty. The simplicity of life on trek is not something I'll ever take for granted, nor be eager to end. I know that from experience.

Away shortly after seven, we pass through the village of Ngadi and continue between rice fields still in shadow, and when I pause to look back my eyes pick out Manaslu, Ngadi Chuli and Himalchuli once more hanging in the sky above a foreground of wooded hills. Morning is full of sunshine when we reach Bhulbhule and cross the Marsyangdi for the last time on a suspension bridge in a state of disrepair – some of the wooden slats are missing; others are either rotten or broken, so the river surging several metres beneath our boots threatens with every step. Yet no one complains, and we move on with barely a comment as we meet the first wave of trekkers coming up-valley from Besisahar. How fresh and innocent they look!

At Khudi, a bridge of bamboo poles takes us over the Khudi Khola, and moments later we take our leave of the Annapurna trail. With that the nature of our journey changes, and Beshkumar assures us we will only meet locals along the way now, as we're off the beaten track so far as trekkers are concerned.

'Look for arrow sign,' he urges. 'Path not easy to find.'

It's good to have Beshkumar as our guide; he has an eye for the country and an unerring memory for trails, and although today's route is a complex one he never falters. At every path junction he automatically signs the right direction with an arrow scraped in the clay.

Moving through the land at a comfortable pace we slip in and out of shadow, drifting among poinsettias and umbrella-leaved banana plants, passing fields now bare of rice or millet, but with circular hayricks, around which dusty-backed buffalo trample straw. There are houses with walls painted orange and white, children clutching exercise books on their way to school, a farmer leading his cattle to a neighbouring field while his wife pads along the top of a drystone wall yapping instructions like a two-legged terrier. Crickets leap away from our boots; squadrons of birds swoop and dive in an orchestrated feeding frenzy; innocent clouds drift on oceans of autumn air.

How good it is to be back in a land that owes nothing to the West! Our days of Coke and chocolate on the Annapurna trail had their benefits, it's true. But these first few hours spent trekking through traditional Nepalese farmland are revitalising. Once again I'm excited as a child at Christmas.

The path narrows as Beshkumar guides us over terraces and alongside a stream, which we then cross on stepping stones to discover the blue tarpaulin marking our lunch spot below a clump of bamboo. It's only 10.30, but time is irrelevant. We have shade, water, a view to distant snow peaks, and a kettle of hot juice to share. There are no complaints, we're content to rest here and be fed in due course, especially as before long we're entertained by a flock of goats grazing nearby under the watch of two young girls. Later there are sheep and buffalo, their herders pausing to study us, and we them. Then an old lady with a wizened face creased into a life history of deep-tanned leather appears before us. Leaning her weight on a long pole, it's obvious she's in a state of mental confusion. Her eyes are misty and seem not to focus; her mind wanders; her voice mutters incoherent sounds. A stream of dribble hangs from her chin and my heart goes out to her. Does she have dementia? If so, I speculate that she could be better off here than some of the elderly we in 'civilised' Britain shut away in over-heated care homes smelling of urine.

Passing through a village with Manaslu as a distant backdrop, I find this afternoon's trek something of a trial. The way is relentlessly steep, and whether we're in shade or out in the full sun, I shrivel in the heat. This is November, for goodness sake! Beshkumar barely glows, but I leak through every pore. My shirt is stuck to my back with sweat. And when we go through woodland and emerge to a brief clearing, familiar mountains taunt with a view of snowfield and glacier and a memory of frosted nights.

Continuing through forest the gradient is maintained, while my gasping breath is accompanied by the screeching calls of numerous birds. But at last trees run out and we find ourselves above the village of Baglungpani on a broad ridge of grass as smooth as a stockbroker's lawn. This is where we'll camp, and I cannot imagine a better site for one of our last nights on trek, for we automatically look out to a heart-stopping panorama consisting of Machhapuchhare, Annapurna II, Lamjung Himal, Manaslu, Ngadi Chuli, Himalchuli and Baudha crispy white beyond a sea of blue foothills and hinted valleys.

Tents up, we stand facing the mountains, voices subdued as the sun fades in the west. The temperature settles, a soft breeze ruffles leaves; I imagine prayer flags shaking out their mantras in the Buri Gandaki.

For some reason I barely sleep at all, so it's no hardship to be up and out of my sleeping bag long before dawn. As this is to be our last full day on trek I've been charged with the responsibility for making sure no one misses sunrise, so I patrol the camp with an eye on the eastern horizon, gauging how long it will take for that soft glow to explode with the blood red of daybreak. Just before six I go to each tent in turn and rouse my fellow trekkers, with two of the cook-boys following behind with bed-tea. By the time the sun makes its appearance, cameras are ready to capture the moment. It's a moment worth keeping, but it's gone almost before we know it, and the morning sky loses its vibrant stain.

Breakfast in the open gives a view that diverts attention from the food on the table. Our Sherpas dismantle camp around us and porters head off with barely a glance at the mountains that will no doubt haunt my dreams in the weeks and months ahead. Then we're off too, Beshkumar reliable as ever, guiding us down the edge of a forest before a 30 minute climb brings us onto another ridge, this one south of last night's campsite. A trail invites us along the crest overlooking valleys partly hidden by mists draped over rivers. Birds sing, and as warmth increases and last night's dew disappears, insects add their voices.

Right now mixed emotions are at play in the group, where an atmosphere part-tension, part-excitement has built up. Anticipating an end to our journey tomorrow, there are some for whom that end is too far off. They'd like to finish today; their fantasies of food and other comforts have been allowed too much freedom, and as a result they're not enjoying the route Beshkumar takes us on. 'Can't we take a short-cut? Surely there's an easier way than this?' Others keep their thoughts to themselves, but lengthen their stride as if that will shorten the trek by an hour or two. Yet today is no less worthy of celebration than any other since we got off the bus in Gorkha three weeks ago.

Searching for a way across the Midim Khola, a two-log bridge demands a sense of balance, for the river is wide here, and the bridge spans two midstream rock piles around which the water surges. Later we make two more crossings, but now the river has been fed by side streams, the water is deeper and with a powerful current, and no bridges exist. There's nothing for it but to wade through. Some of the Sherpanis are anxious, but try not to show it. Being shorter than the rest, they will be waist-deep in the water, so we form a human chain and help them across. Once in the river they shriek with nervous laughter, much to the amusement of the other porters and Sherpas who guide them to safety.

115

Our group becomes strung out along the valley, and I walk alone for a while. In no hurry, I lose myself in each moment that passes. Having lost contact with the mountains, the air is now thick and clammy and sweat runs freely. Suddenly my legs are heavy, so I pause in the shade of a banana plantation and watch as a flock of small finch-like birds dart from leaf to leaf as though engaged in a game of follow-my-leader. There's a group of houses nearby with a low bench-seat outside. As there's no one around I sit and take a deep breath, drawing the warm taste of Nepal into my lungs. The valley stretches ahead, framed by low hills, and in this late harvest season there's plenty of activity going on. In fields of stubble punctuated by domed hayricks, the 'thrap thrap' sounds of threshing can be heard; buffalo drag wooden ploughs to turn the soil; low piles of manure wait to be spread.

This is a land at ease with itself, at peace with itself. And I with it. I need to be nowhere else.

CHAPTER 4

Everest

BECAUSE IT'S THERE
(1993)

*Yaks and yetis on the long walk from the foothills to the highest
of the high Himalaya.*

R iding the thermals on outstretched wings the eagle drifts above the
wooded valley, moving in and out of the updraught with a twitch of
feathers barely perceived from the trail. Panting heavily I lean my rucksack on a raised wooden bench provided for porters' loads and envy that
effortless grace. My chest is tight, eyes red and swollen, and each time I
cough it feels as though my throat is being shredded.

The eagle knows nothing of this. Hovering now, its head is tilted.
With the aid of binoculars I detect a slight adjustment to the angle of
the legs that checks its movement against the rising current of air, the

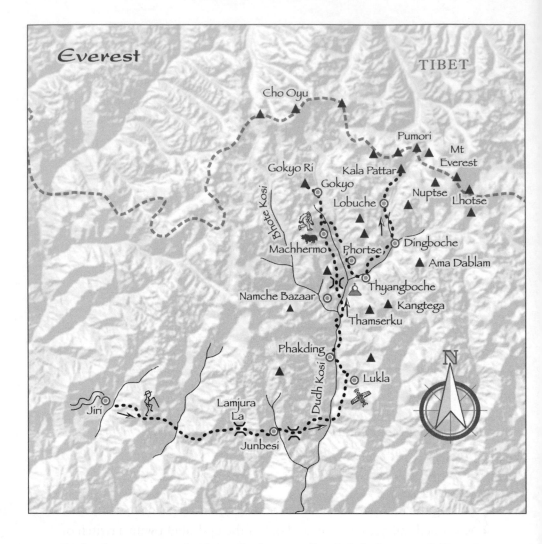

dark plumage smudged in shadow until a brief change of direction flashes sunlight on the sandy bar in its tail.

For three days I've battled a chest infection and suffered as we crossed two ridge crests in succession. A couple of days ago I began a course of antibiotics, but they've not yet kicked in and I still feel wretched. Every breath rattles and I'm feverish with sweat, but the sun is warm on my face, the sky cloudless and the grace of that eagle holds me in awe. No matter what, I know it's a privilege to be here.

Trekking around Annapurna had shown me that simple lodge accommodation makes planning a journey in some Himalayan regions no more complicated than a hut-to-hut tour in the Alps, and it didn't take much to persuade Alan Payne to join me for another two-man teahouse trek, this time towards Everest. Once again he's stretching his leave entitlement to the limit, while I can justify time away as research for another guidebook.

Knowing that foothills can be as exciting and rewarding as the high mountains, we've chosen not to shortcut our trek by flying to Lukla, which would save about seven days of time and effort, but to begin at the foothill village of Jiri, reached by a bum-numbing 12 hour road journey from Kathmandu.

Cutting across the grain of the land, our route is the ultimate switchback, for as all rivers flow roughly southwards from the Himalaya to the plains of India, our eastbound trail endures an unrelenting series of ups and downs, crossing a series of ridges and deep valleys before reaching the Dudh Kosi river. Only then will our route turn north towards Everest. We've hardly started, but I wonder if I'll make it.

The treadmill resumes. Alan shrinks in size as the distance between us increases, yet he stops now and then to offer encouragement as I'm overtaken by porters with enormous loads. Bare-footed, their broad toes spread to improve their grip in the steepest places, and when a local wanders past, he looks at me with pity and says, 'Problem soon pinniss.'

The trail is banked with gentians open to the sun. Hundreds of them cluster among rocks and at the base of rhododendron trees, their pale trumpet flowers adding two shades of blue to the lime-green lichens, the stippled shadows of leaves, the pink or silver bark of upright trunks, khaki mosses and tall grasses with ivory seed heads.

'You no good mister?' A concerned Nepali peers at me, brow furrowed.

'No good today,' I tell him, rubbing my chest and coughing uncontrollably.

'High no good,' he says. 'Junbesi low – more good.' Clearly he thinks it's the altitude, and I have neither the breath nor inclination to disagree.

At Heathrow I'd felt the start of a cold, and the moistureless atmosphere of a long-haul flight made things worse. By the time we'd reached Kathmandu my nose was streaming, but I'd figured that once we started walking I'd feel better. I was wrong, for spasms of coughing leave me weak as an infant. Hypochondria is the name of the game in trekkers' lodges, for sooner or later conversations invariably turn to health topics, and the more remote the lodge the more focused such topics become. I try to concentrate on the trail, the hills, the vegetation, the isolated houses with their neat thatch; I tell myself to ignore the burning chest pain and listen instead to the thrum of distance and feed on it. There's pleasure to be had in that alone, the whispers of a land calling, calling.

To my relief the trail eases. Ahead stand two simple lodges, the last before the Lamjura La. Alan waits for me there while I sip sugared tea and nibble a Mars bar in anticipation of an energy boost. The pass is only half an hour beyond, then it'll be downhill all the way to Junbesi, where we plan to spend the night. Just half an hour to the pass, but it looks a lot closer.

It takes me a full hour to get there.

The Lamjura La is a broad, grassy saddle adorned with prayer flags, *mani* stones and heaps of rocks left by devout locals. Himalayan snow peaks remain elusive but, knowing we'll see them in due course, I content myself with having reached this high point, the highest until we leave Namche Bazaar in about a week's time. Once more gentians star the grass, but below the ridge the rhododendron woods have been so savagely hacked I'm reminded of the deforestation at Ghorepani.

Crossing the La we enter Solu district and descend an eroded trail cut into deep channels by teams of pack-horses that for generations have traded across the pass. Since leaving Jiri we've come across several of these, their harness bells jangling to warn of approach, their wide loads forcing us off the trail, the distinctive smell of old leather, warm horse-hair and manure lingering long after they've gone. But on our descent from the Lamjura La there are no more horses; we have the path to ourselves until, emerging from forest, we discover a rough meadow with a group of Americans gathered there whom we've met several times in the past few days.

'Hey you guys,' says the leader, with his Californian good looks and colour-coordinated gear. 'You haven't seen our doctor by any chance?'

'The Mexican woman?'

'Yeah. She's gone missin'.'

Gone missing? 'We saw her some time ago on the far side of the pass,' says Alan. 'I assumed one of you was with her.'

Two days ago she'd told us this was her first ever trek and that she was finding it tough. Now we learn she's been left on her own. The group leader looks embarrassed, as he should. And agitated. 'Damn!' he says, and aims a gob of spit across the path. 'I guess I better go look see.' He takes off up the trail, calling over his shoulder, 'Thanks you guys,' and is gone.

Rather him than me.

Ang Chokpa's lodge in the heart of Junbesi is all I could ask for – except that our room is on the top floor of a three-storey building, and climbing those stairs was almost the last straw when we arrived. But the stairs, banisters and pine-panelled bedroom remind me of a Victorian inn discovered in a lost valley of the Alps. There's even an indoor flush toilet, a large wood-burning stove in the dining room, and a terrace outside bordered with flower beds. As an introduction to Sherpa country, it could hardly be improved upon.

Junbesi is prosperous. Behind a wall just across the way stands a school serving 300 children. It's one of the first to be built by Ed Hillary's Himalayan Trust, and you don't have to be in the place long before you're aware of the degree of affection with which Hillary is still held. Being the first man to climb Everest proved to be a springboard from which he launched a number of schools and health posts to benefit the Sherpa community. Others have followed his example, for Junbesi has a library given by an American visitor, and down by the bridge over the Junbesi Khola a leat diverts water from the river into a stone-built mill. By day it grinds flour, but towards evening it powers a small generator – enough to give a few bulbs' worth of electric light to most of the village houses. This simple but efficient hydro scheme was donated by a visitor from Holland, who happens to be staying in our lodge tonight.

After a good night's sleep I feel a little better, but we decide to stay another day. Junbesi is not a place to leave in a hurry, so we take a leisurely breakfast on the terrace with the laughter of children at play sounding from the far side of the school wall. But for the fact that there's no hint of motor traffic, with eyes closed we could be in an English village during term time.

Less than two hours up-valley an important *gompa* houses more than a hundred monks and nuns, and it so happens that today the head *lama* is due back from an extended tour. The village is buzzing with anticipation, and men, women and children with broad, flat faces and the typical Mongolian features of the Sherpa race gather expectantly at every vantage point to greet a chestnut pony bearing the holy man dressed in a simple claret robe. There's not much of his face showing, for he wears sunglasses, and his nose and mouth are protected by a yellow dust mask. On his head a skull cap matches the colour of his robe, but his right arm is bare and white, and when not holding the reins it signs a benediction. Two monks walk ahead, others follow behind, one of whom spins a hand-held prayer wheel. The devout stand with hands pressed together, namaste fashion, heads bobbing as the *Rimpoche* passes by.

Leaving Junbesi I have more energy than when we arrived, and my chest is not quite so raw now. What's more, the trail is the best so far, rising at first among blue pine, then through a sparse forest of holly oak and rhododendron. The morning sun shafts through, its warmth amplifying the birdsong, making me glad to be out and active instead of hacking and wheezing in Ang Chokpa's lodge. The trail contours above farms whose fields are being ploughed by buffalo. Way down-valley to the south Phaplu airstrip can be seen, while back in the west our route from the Lamjura La can be made out.

'Does it remind you of somewhere special?' I ask. Alan grins. 'Yeah! The Estos.' For a moment we're transported to the Spanish Pyrenees and that magical valley under the Posets massif.

A young boy squats beside the trail with a few small green oranges for sale. '*Suntala?*' he asks, offering one with outstretched hand and a big, pleading smile that's so hard to resist that we buy all nine for two rupees each. But a few minutes later we pass a farmhouse where larger oranges – oranges that look much more appetizing than those we've just bought – are on offer at the same price.

Again our judgement is awry for we're tempted to pause at a wayside *bhatti* just short of a prominent spur. We've been walking for about an hour and a half, but stop for cups of tea and a few so-called glucose biscuits, and when we set off again we've only been gone another five minutes when we arrive at the proudly named Everest View Hotel. This is where we should have stopped, for it's built on that spur which offers a heart-stopping line of mountains spread before us – Everest, Lhotse, Thamserku, Kusum Kangguru, Kangtega, Mera Peak and Makalu. It's our first sighting of Everest, and as we try to absorb the scene we're joined by twin sisters from Munich and their boyfriends. Six cameras record the moment.

That view draws us on as the trail continues its belvedere course. But Everest and its neighbours are lost when we're forced to descend in long windings to a suspension bridge over the Beni Khola, whose glacier-melt drains a basin formed by the mountain home of a Sherpa deity. There are gods everywhere in this mystical land. We wander among spirits, largely ignorant of their presence.

Once across the river we head uphill to Ringmo, set among orchards of apple, peach and apricot, and when we stop at a teahouse we're offered home-made cider to drink. Knowing we have a ridge to cross and another two hours or more of trekking ahead, we settle for tea instead; tea, and noodle soup and chapattis for lunch.

Sharing our table, a good-looking French couple in their 30s introduce themselves as Lionel and Françoise. In accents of lyrical beauty they explain that for seven months of the year they work in their restaurant near Perpignan without taking a day off in order to spend the remaining five months trekking and travelling. They radiate a glow, their eyes dance and emanate a rare sense of well-being, of mutual love that is not exclusive, but inclusive, of those around them. Alan and I are immediately drawn to them. But they are gone with 'Au revoirs' before our chapattis have been digested.

Less than an hour after leaving Ringmo we top the ridge at the Tragsindho La, an untidy pass at a little over 3000 metres. The sky has clouded and there are no views; a cool wind gusts from the northeast and dries our sweat in moments. The pass does little to inspire; the large white *stupa* and poles flying dozens of faded prayer flags are not enough to distract our attention from the grime and litter, and we hasten away without stopping. There's nothing here to detain us; our destination is Manidingma, a name sufficient in itself to conjure dreams.

At first glance Manidingma appears to be a welcoming place, with its broad paved street lined with stone-built houses and trekkers' lodges. But it fails to meet our expectations, and for the first time on this trek disappointment weighs us down. By comparison with Junbesi it's a scruffy place, with an atmosphere of weary resignation, as if those who live here have been dealt a bum card. Other trekkers sense it too, and general discontent adds to the gloom. Why the village should be so dreary, I cannot explain, for its setting is good, the surrounding fields productive. It's on a well-established trade route, and with the advent of trekking there are lots of opportunities for enterprise. If the good people of Junbesi are able to exploit such opportunities to their own – and their visitors' – benefit, the residents of Manidingma ought to be able to do likewise. They should be thriving. But there's no sign of enterprise, and our lodge is the worst of the trek so far, with smoky rooms and thick dust coating everything we touch; hygiene standards are abysmal, and the *chaarpi* out back is a horror story. After just one visit I hope to be blessed with constipation and a well-behaved bladder overnight, and in the morning we leave without breakfast, planning to stop at a *bhatti* along the way.

It's a fabulous morning, one of those dazzling November days that Nepal manages to perfection. In shadows the trail is tipped with a light frost, but just ahead grasses, shrubs and low-growing trees are warmed by the early sun. In the middle distance, thrusting above blue-slanting ridge spurs that fold down to the Dudh Kosi, the jagged summit crest of Kusum Kangguru scratches at the sky.

We're drawn into a spectacular landscape of multi-coloured fields, whose terraces spill down to a silver thread of river. The fertility rewards our hungry eyes, and smiles come readily. Cicadas are brought to life, rehearsing their raucous tones as the dew dries on them, while cocks crow from the yard of every lonely house along the way. Cobs of sweetcorn dry in stilted racks. There are bananas and lemons hanging over the trail as the morning breeze ruffles long-stalked millet. We perch upon a rock to eat an orange in lieu of breakfast, and suck in the warmth of the new day. Although my chest still hurts when taking deep draughts of air on an uphill trail, the antibiotics are working and I feel like a man reborn.

We're joined by two Nepali children aged about 12 or 13, who stop to speak to us. 'Good morning sir,' says the boy. 'What is the time?'

'It's 8.15,' I tell him. 'A quarter past eight.'

'Thank you, sir.' His English is immaculate. Clearly they are bright kids, clean and smart and confident without being precocious. 'You are from England?'

'That's right.'

'And you are going to Namche Bazaar? Perhaps Kala Pattar?'

'That's the plan. How about you?'

The boy looks at his sister, who wears a light blue blouse and navy skirt. 'We are going home to Lukla, sir. We have been to school in Kathmandu, but now is holiday time.'

They have no baggage apart from a small duffle bag hanging from the boy's shoulder. Both well groomed, they give no indication that they've come far. 'Yesterday we flew to Phaplu, and slept in Tragsindho last night. It is better, I think, to fly to Phaplu than take the bus to Jiri.'

'Why not fly to Lukla, if that's where you live?'

'Too many trekkers this week,' says the girl. 'No tickets left for us, but Phaplu is okay. It is also good to walk some of the way. We have friends to visit.'

The four of us wander down the trail together, and when we come to a *bhatti* just before the bridge which spans the Dudh Kosi, we invite them to stop with us for cups of tea. 'Thank you, but we should keep walking. We want to be with our parents this evening.'

It's only later that I realise just how much ground they have to cover before they reach Lukla, and am thankful that we have the freedom to stop where and when we like.

The Dudh Kosi drains all the Khumbu mountains. Glacier blue and flecked with whitecaps, it brings the chill of distant snowfields with a blast of air several degrees cooler than that of a few paces uphill. The eastward trend of our journey is over, for our trek now turns to the north along the valley's east slope, where the first village we arrive at is Jubing. Although we're in Sherpa country, this little settlement is inhabited by Rai hill-folk. Around it the land bursts with goodness. Crops are almost ready for harvesting, and small plots of vegetables and flower beds beside many of the houses have been tended with care. It's a bright, clean and cheerful village running with streams – one of which drives a mill, while others are funnelled through bamboo pipes. Garlands of marigolds are strung beneath the eaves of several homes, and '*Namaste*' hangs in the air.

Although it's only midday we decide to go no further than Kharikhola, a bazaar village populated by a mixture of Rai, Sherpa and Magar. The French couple, Lionel and Françoise, are also here, so we check in at the same lodge run by a stocky *Sherpani* with a bright, open face and newly laundered clothes. 'Well-cum,' she says, showing us to a room with a view over the valley. The window has a wide sill with a pot of flowers upon it; there are sheets on the beds and a bamboo mat on the floor.

'One night, 20 rupee,' she beams through rows of white teeth that have never known a filling. As she speaks her nose wrinkles, and creases spread from the corners of her eyes. Her long black hair is swept behind her ears to reveal turquoise studs; there are turquoise rings on two fingers and chunky bangles on her wrist.

'First time Nepal?' she asks.

'Second,' Alan tells her.

'Ah, two times. You like?' Then turns to me.

I nod. 'Me too.' In fact, I like more than I say.

We lunch on egg-fried rice and beer, then wander outside with our two French friends. The sound of a sewing machine purrs through the open doorway of a neighbouring house, and passing by we notice a tailor bent over his work. He glances up at the sound of our voices, but barely registers our presence before adjusting a length of grey material and guiding it beneath the blur of a needle. We sidestep a *Sherpani* carrying an unwieldy sack of potatoes, and her striped apron and *chuba* (traditional wear of the Khumbu women) assure us we're well on the way to our goal.

Three days later, and having bypassed Lukla, we arrive in the Sherpa capital of Namche Bazaar. It's Saturday, and the weekly market is in full swing, with traders from the low country jostling and haggling among wild-faced *Bhotiya* with matted hair and sheepskin coats who've crossed the Nangpa La from Tibet. The way into the village is virtually blocked by a chaotic but good-natured crowd, and the crisp mountain air is filled with sound – a cacophonous babble of voices, the tapping of dirty fingernails on pocket calculators, the rustling of cloth and wool, the clicking of beads, and the snorting of yaks. Weights clatter on scales. There's the sound of grain and rice being poured from sack to sack, and the smell of smoke-grimed skin, old leather and kerosene. There are piles of *yak*-wool sweaters and blankets, lengths of rope, Tibetan boots and sheepskins. There are strings of dried meat, oranges, bananas and bundles of green vegetables spread upon drystone walls. Eyes of traders beseech the clamouring crowd, while gossip is exchanged free of charge.

For several days we'd passed and been passed by farmers carrying loaded dokos up the trail towards Namche, and we recognise some of them now. One or two seem rather shy, unsure of themselves in the high pitch of this great social event, while the Tibetans exude world-weary confidence. Sherpas and Sherpanis are the middle-men and women who never miss a trick. Making their calculations, they shuffle notes like card sharps in a game of poker and deftly secrete their earnings in an inner coat pocket or the fold of a *chuba*. Transactions are made with flashing eyes and bursts of laughter, and we delay our search for a lodge to soak in the experience.

The village is built in a steep-backed horseshoe of hills high above the confluence of the Dudh Kosi and Bhote Kosi rivers, at the foot of the sacred mountain of Khumbila, guardian not only of Namche Bazaar but of two higher villages, Khumjung and Khunde. This guardian deity is sometimes depicted in Buddhist paintings as a white-faced saint riding a white horse. White for purity. White for the snow that plasters the mountains. Even Namche's long stone houses are painted white. With pastel-coloured roofs they face away from the bowl towards Kwangde, a mountain daubed with snow and draped at mid-height by a white chiffon cloud. It's a backdrop to a living theatre, and arrival here has brought Alan and me a profound sense of satisfaction, for no student of mountaineering history could fail to recognise the importance of this Sherpa township as a major milestone on the route to Everest. With some of the highest mountains of all just around the corner, Namche is on the very boundaries of the Promised Land.

We find a cosy lodge in the heart of the village but, having ordered lunch, discover it's overrun by cats. Being asthmatic, Alan has an allergy to them and hastens off to find an alternative, so when we've eaten we transfer to a cat-free, two-storey lodge above the main village, with views onto the many houses spread in tiers below. Tents are being pitched in dusty enclosures; we watch dogs, yaks and *yak* crossbreeds sniffing around them, and are thankful to be where we are. Our lodge is busy, but not crowded. It's comfortable enough and the choice of meals is impressive, so we'll be here at least two days for acclimatisation purposes. I'm virtually cough-free at last and with an enthusiasm for the days ahead that I'm just able to contain. But only just.

This morning we rise early, eager to stretch our legs and capture views we know are waiting just up and over the ridge beyond the lodge. A double helping of porridge stokes the fires as we peer at Kwangde on the far side of the Bhote Kosi's valley, its topmost snows flushed with reflected sunrise. Outside the lodge, however, we turn our backs on Kwangde and take a rising trail over Namche's rim, passing both an army post and the headquarters of the Sagarmatha National Park, with Thamserku and Kangtega displaying their ice-fluted ramparts on the opposite bank of the Dudh Kosi. Overnight frost is melting fast as we turn a bend to be confronted by a familiar view we've never seen before – other than in books, magazines, lectures and films, that is. The valley, black with morning shadow, focuses our attention to its far wall – an exquisite mountain wall washed with light that sweeps across its face from a tributary valley flanked by the instantly recognisable Ama Dablam, whose chiselled features are almost as well known as those of the Matterhorn. Seeing it in reality takes my breath away, but Ama Dablam and its forerunners, Kangtega and Thamserku, serve only to direct our vision to the Lhotse–Nuptse wall, that huge barrier over which a cone of black rock announces the presence of Mount Everest.

There are moments in life so profound that they remain indelibly printed on the open page of memory. This is one of them. The mountains, the incredibly deep blue sky, the black-shadowed valley with its rumble of unseen river, Ama Dablam in profile, the racing of blood through my veins... Unforgettable.

That view remains with us throughout the morning as we visit Khumjung, largest of the Khumbu villages, overlooking a maze of walled fields, bare at the winter-end of harvest. We go to Khunde, home of the first health post built by Ed Hillary, then return to Khumjung's *gompa*, among a stand of trees, before ambling down the slope to a heap of *mani* stones and a white *chorten* with limp prayer flags hanging at each corner. The *chorten*, *mani* stones and prayer flags have been put there by devout Buddhists to honour the spirits. '*Om mani padme hum*' seems to emanate from the very earth we tread, the air we breathe, the views we gaze upon.

I sense a rare spiritual dimension to the valley through which we travel. The cynic may dismiss this as mere nature worship. It is not. I share the Buddhist's strength of appreciation of each mountain, valley, tree, rock, stream and river, but the spirituality that encompasses these things is also above and beyond them. It's a recognition of man's temporary place here, of the impermanence of all things, the knowledge that in that very impermanence there's a duty of care. All forms of life are worthy of respect, while the inanimate too have their place in the scheme of things. The Buddhist knows this. He meditates on sacred truths and reaches heights of understanding. And I, as a non-Buddhist, know without question, too, that there is something beyond all this.

Following a trail among flame-coloured berberis and rhododendrons limp-leaved after the frost, we climb among pine groves to reach the Japanese-built Hotel Everest View, which nestles unobtrusively on a ridge and has the most stunning view of any hotel I've ever visited. At around 200 dollars a night it's way over our budget, but it's worth a visit to sit on the balcony with a cheese omelette, a pot of tea and a view to drool over that includes Everest, Lhotse and Ama Dablam. Sited at about 4000 metres, the hotel was built in 1971 by a consortium of Japanese businessmen who either overlooked or ignored the altitude and its affect on those who were not acclimatised. Wealthy businessmen and women with tight schedules were flown from Kathmandu to an airstrip at Syangboche, above Namche, then transferred here by *yak*. Many visitors were so sick they were unable to enjoy the view and had to be evacuated to safer altitudes; some did not make it, and died.

Before long the hotel gained a reputation for being a very expensive place to come to die, and for years it stood empty. But after refurbishment it has now reopened, with bottled oxygen and a special pressurised room to bring comfort to those with neither the time nor inclination to visit this landscape in the proper way – on foot. Slowly.

At a little after seven in the morning we leave Namche. It's bitterly cold, but I love this time of day in the mountains, for the light is pure, the sky full of promise and almost unlimited hours of exercise stretch ahead. Today we plan to leave the main Everest trail and head north into the Gokyo Valley. Years ago, long before Solu-Khumbu became peppered with trekkers' lodges, I was told about this magical place with its string of turquoise lakes trapped in an ablation trough beside Nepal's longest glacier. I'd been told of the big white massif of Cho Oyu on the Tibetan border; told about *yak* pastures sliced with streams that froze each night, the simple yersas and drystone walls, and views of peaks to dream about. Last night my dreams had been full. Today we're about to make them come true.

At first the trail is the same as that which we took yesterday, but its repetition is more than justified by the views, with which it would be impossible to grow jaded. This morning, though, we're an hour or more ahead of yesterday's departure and have the trail to ourselves. A small herd of musk deer flits across the path and disappears into the undergrowth. Moments later we turn the spur to be confronted once more by that panorama. My fingers are wooden as I adjust the lens

131

of my camera and, having taken several shots, tuck it inside my down jacket to save the batteries.

While we drift in frost and deep shadow Everest and Lhotse burn in sunshine, and it's not until we reach Kyangjuma that we step into that same light and pause to enjoy the rising temperature. Our trail then plunges into woodland, crosses a dried stream-bed and joins another path coming from Khumjung. Minutes later we mount an abrupt stone stairway built against an exposed band of rocks, then continue by angling across an open slope towards a ridge spur, beyond which lies Gokyo's valley.

At the high point of Mong Danda we stop for tea and biscuits. Beside an old *chorten*, the *bhatti* is a simple one; smoke from the cooking fire drifts throughout the room, but the eastward view is dominated by Ama Dablam, wrapped in a shawl of mist rising from the river, and Alan and I are content. Thyangboche Monastery can be seen below, backed by Kangtega, whose sharp iced peak threatens to puncture the sky – that alone is sufficient to make the effort of this trek worthwhile.

Outside coloured flags shake out their prayers, and when we leave my fingers trail lightly across the carved stones that rest against the *chorten*.

Losing all the height we'd gained, we now descend a steeply twisting trail to a handful of buildings at Phortse Tenga, the first in the Gokyo Valley. Twice we're forced from the path by heavily laden yaks with sharp horns. Black-haired and with scarlet tassles fitted to their ears, the hefty beasts lumber up the trail, their herder close behind giving whistled commands through his teeth, backed up by a well-aimed stone or two.

After having our permits examined at a national park check post, Cho Oyu appears, blocking the valley ahead with its gently angled cone and extensive ridges like huge outspread wings. We continue through patches of woodland, across numerous streams and a *yak* pasture in autumn rust, and finally arrive at the few lodges of Dole. Barely have we entered one before a dense cloud sweeps along the valley snatching every view. The temperature plummets. It's just turned

1 o'clock, but we've been on the go for six hours and, mindful of the need to acclimatise, and with no visual reasons for continuing, we're content to stay. For the remainder of the day we hug the stove and consume endless bowls of garlic-spiced soup while clouds brush the grass outside.

It's only a very short trek from Dole to Machhermo, but – determined to obey the rules of acclimatisation – we resist the temptation to continue as far as Gokyo. Once more we wake to a sky full of promise and set out with an easy step, regaining views of Cho Oyu sparkling in the early light while we crunch through overnight frost. On coming to Luza, with its drystone walls and two simple lodges, we stop for mugs of milky Sherpa tea and biscuits and pass the time with a friendly lodge-owner who's eager to talk. While Alan and I perch on low stools in the sunshine, the lodge-keeper squats on his hunkers beside us, drawing deeply on his cigarette and exhaling the smoke through a bombardment of words. It's not always clear what he says, but we build a relationship on smiles and words of no significance.

Beyond Luza a high bench of pasture is crowned by a *chorten* and prayer flags on sticks. Around us mountains jostle for attention, and I'm willing to give all they demand, for there is no haste, no need to be anywhere but here. Nearby a little hanging valley emerges from screes, an elegant rock peak bursting from its headwall. Machhermo lies at its entrance on the far side of a stream – three stone buildings and a grid of drystone walls and neat pastures in which several yaks are grazing.

From our first glance we're won over by Machhermo's location, and with every hour we spend here the enchantment grows. It's an idyllic place. Snug out of the wind, it captures sunlight, and we're seduced by its beauty. Although our lodge is extremely basic, it's reasonably clean and the *Sherpani* in charge has a shy, friendly nature I find most appealing. I love the way she hangs her head, but glances over high cheekbones with lights in her eyes. I'm captivated by her smile, the way she busies herself, feeding the fire with dried slabs of *yak* dung, or tosses her head to shake a strip of wayward hair, then patters about the room in split trainers that disappear from view beneath the long thick *chuba*.

Dragging a bench towards the fire she invites us to sit, then reaches for a smoke-blackened kettle. Through the window afternoon mist can be seen drifting along the valley, above which the tops of Kangtega and Thamserku peer over the ridge, where two tiny figures morph into trekkers silhouetted against a bank of cloud. For the second day in succession low cloud brings early twilight, and with the sun being hidden the air has lost its warmth. I'm glad of my thick down jacket in a room with a fire – even a *yak*-dung fire that makes my eyes smart and nose run.

As a meal of fried potatoes, spinach and grated *yak* cheese is being prepared, we're joined by Tendi, the *sirdar* from a French group camped in the walled enclosure nearby. Pouring *chang* from a kettle, he makes himself comfortable beside the *didi*, where we four become cocooned within a glow of firelight that dances shadows into every darkened corner. Tendi blows on his hands, shuts the door and returns to the fire. The *Sherpani* lights a hurricane lamp that purrs softly to cast a yellow, inconsistent glow, and scooping the food onto two metal plates she hands them to us. '*Dhanyabaad.*'

It may not be cordon bleu cuisine, but I'm thankful for that. In this lodge on a cold November evening the last thing we need is large plates and small portions. The plates are big enough, with portions to match, and when we've finished we're offered more.

'Hey, Tendi,' I say when the meal is over and we're shoulder to shoulder in the firelight. 'What can you tell us about the *yeti*?'

In the back of my mind I recall hearing something about this legendary creature associated with Machhermo. The story is misty, the details unclear, so this may be an opportunity to learn something. In truth I'd prefer to let the *didi* tell us, but she has few words of English, and the sum total of my Nepali would not be up to translating the story. Tendi's English, however, is reasonable, and this is what he tells us:

'This true, let me say, *Yeti*,' (he pronounces it 'eti') 'he come here Machhermo many year since. Nineteen seventy-pour was. In that time young woman, *Sherpani* girl, was with *yak* – pive *yak* she has here, eat grass.'

Didi interrupts to reinforce Tendi's words in her own Sherpa tongue, pointing in the general direction of the uphill side of her lodge, then lowering her eyes once more and staring into the fire, a light flush to her cheeks. Although she does not look directly at him, it's clear that she's attentive to Tendi's words.

He continues: 'She hear noise and look up see big brown fella with long hair come down from mountain. That 'eti he hit her, knock her down near river. Very scared she lay there thinking dead, but she can see 'eti catch *yak* and, tchhhk, he break neck of one *yak*.' He mimes the *yeti* twisting the *yak*'s great horns. 'Next, 'eti he catch second *yak* and, tchhhk, break that neck too. Then break neck number tree *yak*. But number pour and number pive *yak*, they run way.'

All the time our *didi* solemnly nods her head, rocking gently to and fro on the balls of her feet, hands clasped across her knees.

Tendi takes another gulp of *chang*, wipes his mouth with his sleeve. 'Ha!' he continues. '*Sherpani* she hide all night, and next day run to Khumjung tell p'leece. They write report and come see. Yeah! They find tree dead *yak* with neck broke. *Sherpani* girl has bad mark on face long time since from 'eti. Still live in Khumjung. She come no more Machhermo!'

In the dark early hours, when the cold forces me outside for a pee, I water the frosted grass while the beam of my head-torch chases this way and that whenever I hear a sound. Then, instead of savouring the beauty of the night sky, I hasten back to my sleeping bag. For warmth, you understand. It has nothing to do with thoughts of what might be out there…

I'm not sure that I sleep at all, but I'm warm and comfortable enough and spend the restful hours in a state of time-consuming awareness.

135

With no grain of concern I drift among the stars – for their presence is an integral part of the Himalayan experience, and tonight they enter the lodge through tiny squares of frost-feathered glass to lighten the darkness with a soft and silvery glow that journeys across the vastness of space. That vastness is beyond my grasp, but I'm content to bathe in its goodness. All my days I've accepted a lack of intellect, and long ago learnt to live with ignorance – perhaps that's the key to my talent for joy! I've no qualifications, no driving ambition, no burning desire for material wealth or success as measured in Western values. I care only for simple things, and recognise riches in the natural world about me. Awareness of each moment is both the clue and the reward in the search for happiness. You have to know you've touched heaven when it's in your grasp. To look back at a golden age in your life is an illusion – unless you know it's golden at the time. And to look forward through blinkers towards a longed-for fortune is to sacrifice the riches of now.

For me, night-time in Machhermo polishes gold.

This morning we take our leave of the *didi* and puff our way with steaming breath that settles on beards in dew-like droplets. Moving slowly, we work our way deeper up-valley on a trail that leads to views of Cho Oyu once more. Half an hour after setting out we pass a small *yersa* below the terminal moraine of the Ngozumpa Glacier. The glacier itself is unseen, held in check, as it were, by the bulldozed spoil of the mountains. Alan leads the way, climbing into the left-hand ablation trough. Cascades pour through breaches in the moraine wall; at least half the stream is channelled beneath bulbous but transparent coverlets of ice, where bubbles of air are stretched and moulded by the surging pressure. Ice cakes the moraine. It adds a deadly veneer to exposed rocks, and where there's sign of a path it has the appearance of a crazy bob-run outlined with snow-dusted cairns. Perilously we skate our way uphill, and at the top of the rise enter the ablation valley proper, a stony landscape graced by a small green tarn. Once more Cho Oyu is in our sights. Beyond that bulk of snow lie the great open spaces of Tibet.

The trough broadens and a cold wind gusts from behind, but having achieved most of the height needed for today we stomp along the trail and remain warm enough. A second tarn is reached, this one turquoise in colour and larger than the first. We find a dump of rocks and, using them as shelter from the wind, relax for a while and simply enjoy living.

Beyond this second tarn we pass through a defile that suddenly opens to a third jade-green jewel – the main Gokyo lake marked on our map as Dudh Pokhari. A clutter of lodges spills against the lower bank of moraine, while beyond the western shoreline mountains ease generous space. Up there lies the Renjo La, a 5000 metre pass leading to the valley of the Bhote Kosi, but down here sunlight dances on the water, where a pair of orange-backed ducks with white blaze on the head and green-black tail feathers ride wind-ruffled wavelets.

At nearly 4800 metres, Gokyo is not the warmest place in Nepal, and our lodge has no heating in the room where we huddle with glowing noses and ears protected from the morgue-like temperature. Once the sun has gone from the valley, our only hope of warmth lies in the consumption of hot food and drink and the comfort of thermal clothing beneath good-quality down. But our days are well spent, for we wander the moraines and ablation valley, and the mountains too, with an appetite for beauty that approaches greed. Gokyo feeds us well.

We rise early to ascend Gokyo Ri, a notable viewpoint at 5340 metres, which claims one of the finest of all mountain panoramas. A light skim of ice edges the lake when we set out, but we want to be early on that summit to enjoy the clarity of light that sharpens not only every vista, but all of our senses too. Early though we are, we're not the first to be on the move, for halfway up the slope we overtake a young Swiss trekker from Solothurn in his mid-20s and his companion, an ex-Gurkha soldier acting as his guide, who staggers up the slope breathing heavily. Concerned by his movements I stop to check he's okay, and am assured that he is. For once roles have been reversed, with the Swiss client keeping an eye on his guide. But it's a salutary lesson that being born in the Himalayan foothills is no guarantee that a man is fit for the mountains.

It takes a little under an hour and a half to gain the summit, where coloured prayer flags merely ripple in a light breeze – red for rocks, yellow for the earth, green for water, blue for sky, white for clouds.

For two or three minutes I sit with a heaving chest, the cold dry air rasping in my throat, but as this subsides it's possible to take stock of my surroundings. Gokyo Ri may not be much of a mountain, as mountains go, but as a vantage point it's incomparable. Being a little over 20 kilometres to the west of Everest, my eyes naturally turn to the highest of all mountains. From here a section of the Tibetan flank is clearly visible, as is the Southwest Face on the Nepalese side – first climbed in 1975 by a team led by Chris Bonington. To the right of Everest the ridge linking Nuptse and Lhotse is a stairway of ice, and far off Makalu continues the crest, although intruders try to shut it out. Standing proud of those 8000 metre giants, Cholatse and Taboche appear to be tilted as though giving way to a fearsome wind – but they lean the wrong way for that. Jet-stream winds come from the west, and those 6000 metre peaks are straining from the south. Below them the turgid flow of the Ngozumpa Glacier is contained between walls of khaki moraine, while the string of turquoise lakes, alongside which we wandered, lead the eye towards those sublime mountains overlooking Thyangboche. At this hour the sun climbs behind them, painting shadows and inspiring overnight mists of the far Imja Khola to dance and disappear like a Nepalese will-o'-the-wisp.

This crowd of peaks, lakes and glaciers is thrilling beyond words, but it is Gyachung Kang that seems to me the ultimate mountain. Cho Oyu, with which it is linked by an extensive ridge carrying the Tibetan border westward, adds to the tally of 8000 metre peaks within Gokyo Ri's panorama, but for architectural elegance Gyachung Kang outshines them all, and in my judgement claims the medal for sheer beauty.

Alan joins me among a nest of rocks, his face stretched in a grin that says more than words. In 30 years we've shared countless summits and high passes, most of which have demanded more of us than the ascent of this steep black hill. But none has ever rewarded with such an astonishing panorama. Suddenly Tendi arrives too. Members of his group having called a rest day, the Sherpa could not sit still and he's romped up the slope on his own. His voice chitters non-stop as he puts names to the mountains bristling wherever we turn, so I hand him my binoculars and, drawing peaks, glaciers and snowfields into close focus, he becomes ecstatic. 'Ohh – look see, look see!'

Gokyo's east bank trail passes directly below Cholatse and Taboche and is something of a roller-coaster. Just outside Na, at the start of the trail, there had been a series of streams to cross and scrub thickets alongside the river loud with the chatter of tiny birds, but as the trek progresses so we lose all of that, and it's only when we stop to steady our breath that it's possible to capture sounds other than that of my wheezing chest and the soft pad of boots on the frosted path.

A little under an hour from Na, we arrive at a scattering of stone huts and a mesh of drystone walls. The huts are unoccupied, but just below the trail a prayer flag sprouting from the shallow pitched roof of a small teahouse invites us down. The location is dramatic in its solitude, which seems the more profound for the fact that the sole occupant is a young *Sherpani* who looks no more than about 13 years old. Dressed in an ankle-length wrap-around skirt as thick as a blanket, a blue nylon windcheater and a bright red headscarf, her face is flat, with narrow eyes that rise at the corners as she smiles a nervous smile.

'*Namaste.*' We exchange greetings at the door.

'Mister, you like Coke? Or *chiyaa*?'

Lord, fancy bringing Coke up here! '*Chiyaa* – two please.'

'Sherpa tea?'

Her timidity fades, so we rest our rucksacks against the outer wall and go inside. There are two shelves with a row of metal cups without handles, a few packets of Ra-Ra noodles, and on the bare earthen floor a plastic bucket containing three bottles of Coca Cola. At one end of the room a wooden frame covered with coarse *yak*-hair blankets serves as her bed. A flimsy strip of pink cotton material hangs by the solitary window, and on the sill are the stubs of two candles. She has a low stool to sit upon and a tiny table with about half a dozen plates stacked upon it. The wall behind the hearth has a dense coating of soot that marks the passage of years. In the absence of a chimney a blue mist of smoke hangs just below the ceiling at eye level.

On second thoughts I'll have my tea outside and enjoy the view. Alan too.

And the outlook from this elevated perch is worth studying – the depths of the valley where the river is no more than a hint; the glacier's snout back the way we've come and the white mountains beyond that; the way ahead where Gokyo's valley spills into that of the Imja Khola; the delicately sculpted peaks far off, and those backing Machhermo to the west; a ridge of sharks' teeth, aiguilles to remind us of Chamonix or Val Bondasca, hacking at the overall blue.

Each day in the Khumbu we're thrown into an ecstasy of visual delights.

The little *Sherpani* girl brings our tea and hovers three paces back. 'Do you have biscuits?' I ask.

Her narrow eyes disappear as the word journeys towards recognition. 'Biss-kit? Oh biskoot! You like?'

She returns with four small packets of Indian-made biscuits in waxed paper and places them in a neat row on the ground before us. 'You like biskoot?' We take all four packets and, unwrapping one, I offer it to the girl. Before removing two of the crumbling orange-flavoured wafers she glances over her shoulder as if to gain approval from whoever might be there. But there's no one.

We order more tea and wish it were later in the day and we had an appetite for a meal. It would be good to give her more business, but it's too early for that, and we have several hours of walking ahead of us before we reach Phortse, where we plan to spend the night.

'Where are your parents?' I ask. 'Your mother? Father?'

Again she squeezes her eyes tightly shut while she deciphers my question. When they spring open she gestures down-valley with a flap of her hand. 'That place.' I look, but see nothing she could be referring to. No villages, no houses, no habitation. Just a long sweep of mountain-walled valley, the scale still hard to grasp even after these weeks of wandering.

Phortse appears when we top a small pass graced by a *chorten* and strings of prayer flags. The village lies nearly 500 metres below, and views into the valley are tremendous. A steep descent takes us past the deserted settlement of Konar, with a number of stone-walled fields and a water-driven prayer wheel in a stream. I pause to listen to the chuckling of the water, to the leathery, creaking sound as the prayer-filled drum is turned, and to the tinkling bell that counts off devotions by the thousand. '*Om mani padme hum...*' We brush alongside *mani* walls and ancient chortens, traipse through open woods of juniper, birch and rhododendron, and notice springs gurgling from the dry autumnal ground.

There are only two lodges in Phortse, and we're directed to one round the edge of recently ploughed fields. Women are clearing other fields, their banter drifting in the crisp air like tin on tin. The village is handsome in a lost-world, medieval way, a scattered collection of long, traditional Sherpa houses facing south above the confluence of the Dudh Kosi and Imja Khola rivers. The harvest is over, and haystacks stand in some of the fields. Buckwheat is stored in open-sided outhouses; yaks snort from wall-enclosed yards. There's a frieze of berberis on the down-valley side of the village, but our eyes are drawn to the southeast, where Thamserku and Kangtega once more toss clouds.

We're away at seven. The house where we spent the night had been active for an hour and more, ever since light stole across the fields. Outside a deep frost has coated everything. Drystone walls look as if they've been dusted with snow – and the fields too, while bare trees wear hoary ribbons. A tan-coated *yak* rises from its overnight sleeping position, and when it turns to face us I notice its exposed flank is also white with frost. Our breath comes in bursts of steam, and my nose glows like a belisha beacon. Over every house there hangs a blue mist of wood smoke. But the sky is cloudless, there is no breeze and, but for the fluttering of a handful of birds, the morning is practically without sound.

It's our own fault for not checking first with our lodge-keeper, but we find ourselves on the wrong path. Instead of heading up-valley to Pangboche, a contouring trail takes us round a bluff to give a spectacular view into the gorge-like valley of the Imja Khola, across which stands the Thyangboche Monastery. As yet we have no idea that our trail does not lead to Pangboche, and continue in blissful ignorance. Only later do we sense betrayal when it plunges down the precipitous slope, in places narrow and always heavily exposed. But what a trail! Steps have been made here and there, yet these are mostly covered in grit and marble-sized stones which force us to tread with exaggerated care. A slip could be fatal, or at best give an extremely cold bath in the thundering Imja Khola.

Eventually down at river level a man at a *yersa* describes a direct route to Pangboche. He tells me what I already know, that we should have taken a high path from Phortse. There's another trail alongside the river, but he insists we will never find it. 'Thyangboche upway,' he says. 'Thyangboche–Pangboche good way.'

So Thyangboche beckons and, faithful to its call, we follow, cross the Imja Khola by footbridge, and begin to climb. Although we'd planned to visit the monastery on our return from Kala Pattar, it's pleasant going through the conifer woods this morning, and I'm content, especially as halfway up the slope we pause to watch two musk deer nosing in the scant undergrowth.

Thyangboche Monastery stands on a ridge above a clearing edged with pine woods, berberis and rhododendrons. 'It would be difficult to imagine, much more find, a finer site for worship or contemplation,' wrote

Tilman on his visit here more than 40 years ago. And it's true. Across an open meadow, busy this morning with trekkers, Sherpas and yaks, Alan and I are aware that we gaze on one of the world's most sublime vistas. The summit of Everest sneaks above the great Lhotse–Nuptse ridge, Ama Dablam stands to our right, Taboche across the valley to the left. Kangtega's ice flutings rise overhead, Kwangde seems to float behind us, Khumbila graces the view across the way. In the midst of such grandeur the sacred monastery stands as a symbol of peace. Monks gather here to study, meditate and pray.

In the meadow an American in multi-coloured trousers and orange down jacket skims a frisbee while laughter shrills from a cluster of yellow dome tents.

Climbing the steps we cross a courtyard and, after removing boots, enter the main building. Monks in claret-coloured robes have just finished their devotions and emerge to the brilliance of the morning, while we are drawn into a sanctuary of calm stillness where the eyes of a twice-lifesize Buddha follow our movements.

Smelling of fresh paint, this is the third monastery to grace the ridge-top site. Built in the early 1920s, the first was destroyed by earthquake in 1934, so a second monastery took its place. Like its predecessor it was lit by rows of butter lamps, but in 1988 a group of Peace Corps volunteers donated a small hydro scheme to provide electricity. Perhaps the gods were uneasy with technology, for less than a year later a wiring fault caused a fire and the second Thyangboche Monastery was burnt to the ground. Today its replacement is almost complete, and we treat this latest incarnation with the same reverence we would Chartres or Canterbury cathedrals, and gain enrichment from it.

We stop for an early lunch in Pangboche. Before trekking brought new opportunities, this was the highest permanently settled village in the Khumbu, but now both Dingboche and Pheriche, further along the trail to Everest, are occupied year-round. In upper Pangboche there's an ancient *gompa*, a square building with red walls and a pagoda-style roof; the lower village has a few simple lodges on the edge of cultivated fields enclosed by drystone walls. The houses themselves are typical of the area. Built of stone, some have a rough plaster of dung and mud caked over them. Most are two storeys high and roofed with long wood shingles or flat stone slabs. The ground floor is used as a *yak* stall, or for storage, while the living quarters are situated upstairs and reached by way of a wooden ladder.

Beyond Pangboche we cross a stream turning a prayer wheel, and at Shomare meet the twin German sisters and their boyfriends whom we'd last seen on the trail between Junbesi and Sollung. They've been as far as Lobuche, which they describe as a very cold and unhealthy place; trail-weary, they are glad to be heading back to lower altitudes where they can be warm again.

The trail forks, and for a moment we stop to confer. The direct route to Pheriche, Lobuche and Everest Base Camp breaks to the left, but we take the alternative path ahead, for it's our intention to spend a few days in Dingboche. Five minutes later we cross the Khumbu Khola and head up the west bank of the Imja Khola to enter a truly wild-looking valley curving beneath the huge South Face of Lhotse, the world's fourth highest mountain, at whose feet lies the dun-coloured village of Dingboche.

The *chaarpi* at our lodge has no roof. As it's neither raining nor snowing, that omission is of no concern. In fact, in the middle of the night it's a bonus, for you can't crack your head on a sky full of stars. By day, if you stand on tiptoe you can gaze on Lhotse over the wall, and for a few precious moments at dusk a blood-red stain slips down its face so rapidly that there's no danger of getting cramp in your calves.

The lodge itself is basic but clean and, like the one we stayed in at Machhermo, is run by a *Sherpani* whose very presence warms us. She has a young son who initially hides behind his mother's striped apron, but his confidence grows during the evening. Apart from Alan

The steep hill above Samdo makes a perfect acclimatisation hike, gaining views of Larkya Peak and the Larkya La (Chapter 3)

High above Tatopani on the Manaslu Circuit, the trail crosses this bridge over a deep tributary (Chapter 3)

Having crossed the Larkya La on the Manaslu Circuit, porters stop for a well-earned rest and food (Chapter 3)

At Lho (Lhogaon) Manaslu is revealed in all its twin-summited splendour (Chapter 3)

Khumbu trekking without the crowds – on the trail from Na to Phortse (Chapter 4)

Despite the close proximity of unseen Everest, it is Pumori that entices from the Khumbu headwall (Chapter 4)

The yak pasture of Machhermo, now an important overnight stop on the trek from Namche Bazaar to Gokyo (Chapter 4)

Mong Danda, the high point on a spur that gives access to the Gokyo Valley (Chapter 4)

Overlooking the Ngozumpa glacier, Gokyo Ri is one of the great vantage points of the Khumbu region – from its summit no less than four of the 8000m peaks can be seen (Chapter 4)

The classic view from Kala Pattar – Everest, outshone by the iced gem of Nuptse (Chapter 4)

Village elder in Syabru
(Chapter 5)

Bhatti owners at Thangsep,
on the way to Langtang village
(Chapter 5)

Beyond Kyangjin the valley opens to a stony plain before curving into an avenue of lofty peaks (Chapter 5)

Kirken Sherpa, who has masterminded so many of my treks among the mountains of Nepal

Amit Rai – porter-guide on the Langtang trek (Chapter 5) and cook on our journey across Dolpo (Chapter 6)

On our way to the Tarap gorges, the riverside trail is hemmed in by crowding mountains (Chapter 6)

and me, the only other guests are a couple from Boston with soft voices and a gentle nature. They have with them a picture book of Nepal, and after our evening meal, when darkness falls outside, a hurricane lamp is placed on the table, casting a glow on the *Sherpani* and her son, and a neighbouring *Sherpani* who has dropped by for company. Seven of us crowd round the lamp, yet my eyes are not on the photographs in the book, but on the faces of the locals with whom we share the light. Once again I absorb each moment.

Having climbed the terminal moraine of the Khumbu Glacier, we come to a row of cairns serving as memorials to Sherpas who have died on neighbouring summits. It's an impressive site with a breathtaking panorama that invites contemplation. Ahead lies the upper Khumbu Valley, a boulder-blotched landscape with Pumori acting as a buttress to the headwall that masks the vastness of Tibet. As the Himalayan chough flies, 13 kilometres from where we pant along the trail stands the highest mountain in the world, but hidden behind mountains of lesser stature it gives no hint of its presence as we stumble on to Lobuche.

Members of the 1953 Everest expedition described Lobuche as 'a delectable spot'. In the Himalayan spring they discovered cushions of moss campion, mauve primulas and magenta-coloured azaleas in bloom at almost 5000 metres. There was a clear stream flowing and redstarts hopping on boulders. Rosefinches, a wren, snow pigeons and stone martens were visitors. 'Everything called to idleness,' wrote one of the team, but four decades later, in the bracing chill of November, we arrive to find a handful of lodges, several low stone walls built around the tents of climbers and trekkers, and an unwelcome mess of discarded tins, plastic bags, food wrappers and strips of pink toilet paper. Instead of a mountaineer's site for rest and recuperation, it's a cold and uninviting wasteland.

We check the lodges without enthusiasm. One has been taken over by members of a Japanese expedition planning to tackle the Southwest Face of Everest in the coming weeks. The atmosphere is charged, and when the lodge-owner hands us mugs of lemon tea, resentful glances are directed our way. We are, of course, mere trekkers, and unwelcome. So we drink our tea slowly in defiance, then find another lodge where the ambitions of those huddled by the stove are more in keeping with ours. A large plate of steaming potatoes spiced with red chilli sauce adds warmth to the room, but later, as I watch the upper reaches of Nuptse burn gold with the setting sun, the raw chill of the mountains snaps from the shadows and I know that tonight not even the crowded lodge dormitory will be free from that cold.

The trail climbs out of the ablation valley and attacks a frontal of old moraine. Just ahead of us two Sherpanis are portering equipment for the Japanese, the monstrous loads hiding all but their lower legs, which taper into khaki plimsolls. We've spent the last hour leapfrogging each other, and whenever we share a brief resting place among ice-glazed rocks I'm wooed by their dark eyes and cheeky laughter. No doubt their chatter consists of rude comments, but that's okay by me. I only wish I had enough of their language to offer a similar response.

Now it's our turn to lead, and Alan kicks off along the trail which soon tops the moraine, then slopes down to cross the Khangri Glacier just above its confluence with the larger Khumbu ice-stream, alongside which we've been puffing our way since Lobuche. In the middle of the glacier a partly frozen torrent has to be negotiated, so we offer assistance to the Sherpanis before being forced to one side as a procession of yaks comes scuttling down the opposite moraine bank. The herder stops to flirt with the girls, and we see them no more until we're resting at Gorak Shep.

Out of the wind the white glacial sand of Gorak Shep reflects the sunlight. Tibetan snowcocks make curious patterns as they chase one another across the sand, their maniacal cackling breaking the peace of this little hollow below Pumori, a mountain named by Mallory when he first looked down into the Khumbu Valley in 1921. We look up at the summit, almost 2000 metres above our heads, and with the comforting knowledge that we have no need to accept its challenge discuss possible routes via its South Ridge. Then we turn to other peaks, and after that look at forbidden ways into Tibet. This mountaineer's game is a useful delaying tactic, merely putting off the need to shake ourselves into further action, for we've not come this far to leave without having a close view of Everest. Although this upper valley and the soaring peaks that contain it provide a memorable feast, we know that a minor summit about 500 metres above us will satisfy our ambitions for today. This minor summit on the slopes of Pumori is the black hill of Kala Pattar, whose 5623 metre crown is noted for its classic view across the Khumbu Glacier to the South Col and summit of Chomolongma, Mother Goddess of the World.

Gasping for breath, as though on the final assault of Everest itself, we stop frequently to give our hearts a chance to recover. Mine is thumping in my ears, but this day is a gift to savour, and each upward step unwraps a parcel of mysteries. Since yesterday Nuptse has been in our sights, but now it's revealed in all its glory. If there is a crystal mountain, this surely is it. Bounding into the deep blue heavens from the eastern side of the Khumbu, hanging glaciers lead the eye to an immaculately sharp point. Wilfrid Noyce, the poet–mountaineer who took part in the 1953 Everest expedition, said that in a galaxy of impressive peaks, it was Nuptse that had impressed him as the most noble. Who would disagree with that?

My trekking pole taps on the rocks, breath rasping, boots making a dull thud with each step, the slope broken into a succession of slabs and boulders as we scramble to a secondary summit. I've been glancing down, hardly daring to look up. Down below, the Khumbu Glacier carries away bits of Everest, Lhotse and Nuptse, carrying them back to the ocean of their birth. The wheel of life, as understood by the Buddhist, is being mirrored by the mountains among whose summits their gods reside.

Then I raise my eyes to the east, and there at last the earth's crown is revealed. Everest, a black pyramid wearing a snow plume. It looks enormous, as of course it is, although the nearer Nuptse gives the impression of being taller – and more elegant. I embrace the moment, but know there's a higher summit to gain from here, and should we choose not to reach it on account of the extra effort involved, we'll always wonder what we missed. So we continue up the ridge, scrambling on rocks until at last we gain the cairn that marks the true summit of Kala Pattar amid a flutter of prayer flags.

The South Col of Everest can now be seen, as well as the South Ridge, by which it was first climbed; there's the West Ridge too, a section of the Northwest Face in Tibet, the bulk of the prominent Southwest Face and, far below, the spillage of the notorious Khumbu icefall, with the site of the base camp on the glacier below that. With a height difference of something like 3600 metres between base and summit, all the middle section is lost from view behind converging ridges. We're studying one of the world's great views, and it's hard to take our eyes from it. I dig my binoculars from the rucksack, and for the next half hour Alan and I pass them from one to the other, studying in detail the mountain on which so much has been gambled, lost and won.

Having climbed many a mountain together, Alan and I have no dreams of climbing the highest of them all, but are content to let others follow that dream. We, mere trekkers, are drawn to its shadow. Because it's there.

CHAPTER 5

Langtang and Helambu

NORTH OF KATHMANDU
(1994)

*I trek into the heart of the Himalaya and out via holy lakes
on the way to Helambu.*

S erendipity is the greatest gift for travellers. After trekking to
Everest in the post-monsoon season of 1993, much of the following summer was spent working in Austria, wandering from one
mountain district to the next with camera and tape recorder in hand.
In July I was crossing the Ötztal Alps with my wife when we arrived
at the Braunschweiger Hut below the Wildspitze. As we pushed open
the boot-room door, the first person we saw was a Sherpa, broom in
hand, sweeping glacier grit into a neat pile. He looked up and gave a
welcome smile.

'*Namaste*,' I said. 'Where are you from?'

'Kathmandu.'

'No, I mean – where's your village?'

'It's in Solu district,' he replied.

'Where in Solu district?'

'Some place called Junbesi.'

'Junbesi! Do you know Ang Chokpa?'

The Sherpa's eyes popped. 'How do you know Ang Chokpa?'

'I stayed in his lodge last October,' I explained. And with that, Kirken Sherpa and I began a friendship that has lasted 20 years, during which we've shared a number of memorable journeys among the high Himalaya and I've come to recognise him as the ultimate Mr Fixit. Find yourself in a tight spot in a remote location, and there's no one you'd rather be with; no one better than he to find a solution to a problem; no one more able to get you out of a hole, to turn disaster into triumph – as I know to my benefit. But that's for another story…

As I say, serendipity is the greatest gift for travellers. Meeting Kirken was one more serendipitous moment to celebrate.

When his work in the hut's kitchen was finished that evening, he joined us at a table by the window with a view of glaciers and mountains growing dim with the fading light. Over mugs of hot chocolate we discussed mountains, summits, glaciers and passes. Inevitably the conversation turned to Nepal, and as he knew so much about trekking through remote parts of his country, we spent an hour or so discussing routes and creating dreams, feeding off each other's enthusiasm. Although we'd only just met he was surprisingly candid, confessing that drink had ruined his life – he'd become an alcoholic, lost his wife and family, all his money and the trekking business he'd built from nothing. Now he was determined to start again, to rebuild his life and his business, and when the summer season was over in the Austrian Alps, he would return to Kathmandu to pick up the pieces.

My plan for the coming autumn was to trek with Alan Payne among the mountains north of Kathmandu, for after Annapurna and

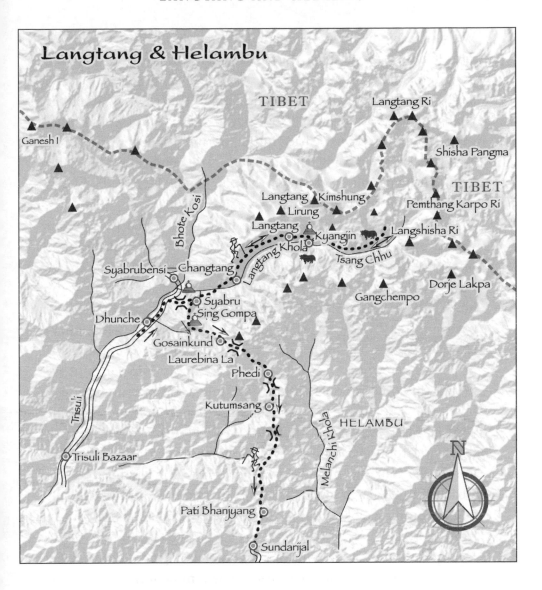

Everest, the Langtang and Helambu regions were the only ones with sufficient lodge accommodation to make independent trekking a viable proposition. Kirken listened to the rough outline of my route, gave advice and offered to help in any way he could, and before we left the hut the following morning, he handed me his card. 'I go home late September,' he said. 'Let me know if you want something.'

We miss each other in the crowds at Kathmandu's airport, but Kirken arrives in the evening at the Mustang Holiday Inn, where he'd booked a room for Alan and me. He looks fit and healthy, his eyes clear and alert, and he's eager to help. Draining a pot of tea he tells us about the young man he's arranged to be our porter-guide, discusses our other needs, and promises to be back in the morning. True to his word he arrives as we're having breakfast, hands us the application forms for our trekking permits, and when we've completed them he disappears with the forms and passport photos in his pocket.

Time in Kathmandu passes in a blur as Alan and I weave our way through the chaotic streets, locate the Biman Bangladesh airline office to reconfirm our home-bound flight several weeks ahead, buy food and gas for the days during which we plan to camp at the head of the Langtang Valley, and choose a couple of maps that should cover our trek. By now we're familiar with all the back streets, money-changers and most of the beggars of this most colourful and anarchic of cities where, every visit without fail, we bump into someone we know. This time is no exception, and only a block away from our hotel Alan spies Lionel and Françoise, the handsome French couple we'd met last year in the Khumbu. We're soon having lunch with them in a rooftop restaurant with a view through a fug of pollution to the Ganesh, Langtang and Jugal Himals in the north, while a background cacophony of car horns, the tinkling of rickshaw bells and the unmistakable whine of three-wheeled Tempo taxis drifts up from the street.

At 6 o'clock Kirken returns with our trekking permits and a shy young man, no more than five feet tall, whom he introduces as our porter-guide, Amit Rai. Kirken explains that Amit has worked for him in the past, and assures Alan and me that he will look after us. I'm not sure we need looking after, but make no comment. In a flurry of faxes before leaving home, I'd enquired about the possibility of hiring a man to carry some of the gear for our few nights' camping when the lodges run out; someone who might teach us a bit more about the country and its cultures, for in the brief amount of time I've spent out here with local Nepalis, I've learned to appreciate life from a different perspective and come to reassess my own values. The prospect of now having the company of a porter-guide for the duration of our trek is one that Alan and I both relish.

Amit's English is basic and monosyllabic, but is much better than my Nepali, and I'm confident we'll have no communication problems. He tells us he comes from a village out east on the way to Kangchenjunga, but moved to Kathmandu in search of work; he has a wife and baby son in a room near Boudhnath, and once had a restaurant, now 'dead' – by which I assume he means it's closed. He's brought a rucksack almost as big as himself, and starts to pack it with our tent, food and camping stove, then looks around to see what else he has to carry. Not a lot, is the answer. We're in this together and have equal loads, and since most of the time we'll be sleeping and eating in lodges, we won't need much gear. No doubt he thinks he's on to a good thing; if so, that's okay with me.

On the dot of 7.30 in the morning Kirken and Amit arrive in a Toyota Corolla, freshly polished for our inspection, although it'll no doubt be covered in dust long before we've cleared the outskirts of Kathmandu. Kirken introduces the driver, shakes us by the hand and, with a promise to meet us when our trek is over, wanders off towards Thamel.

We're out of town sooner than expected, weaving a slalom course along a pot-holed road through a landscape of low terraced hills, among which ochre-coloured houses appear through the morning mist. Once that mist has evaporated and the sun beats down, the windows come open and a warm breeze rushes in. On this late October morning we pass thin, straight-backed men on bicycles; others squatting beside the road staring vacantly ahead. Bare-footed women sweep the dust from their doorways, children splash water over grey buffalo, while snow mountains float above the foothills before being vanquished by balloons of cumulus.

We stop for lunch in Trisuli Bazaar, where the asphalt ends, then continue north along a dirt road (windows closed as dust covers the windscreen), with the Trisuli Khola flowing below to our left. Yesterday Kirken had warned us that at the tail-end of the monsoon last month, the road was cut by a massive landslide about four kilometres short of Dhunche, and a little over six hours after we drove out of Kathmandu we see the blockage ahead. It looks as though half a mountain has collapsed, but a bulldozer is tipping debris down the slope into the river, while labourers with bare feet and ragged trousers shovel soil and rocks into dokos.

I guess it's time to walk.

The four kilometres to Dhunche turn out to be at least 10, but since we came to Nepal for the trekking it's a relief to get some exercise at last, so the three of us pad along the dirt road in the Trisuli Gorge as thunder growls among unseen mountains and rain begins to fall.

No less than five check points interrupt our 10 kilometre hike. There are two army, one police and two national park posts, where our trekking permits and passport details are recorded in thick, well-thumbed ledgers, and whenever frustration threatens to boil over at the futility of repetition, I remind myself that it was we British who introduced bureaucracy to the Indian sub-continent in the first place, but Nepal has managed to refine such nonsense to perfection.

Although it's almost dark when we arrive in Dhunche, it only takes a few minutes to choose a lodge from several that line the dirt road above the original village. We soon have a room with three beds for the night and hasten downstairs to order a meal and a litre each of lemon tea, while the last light drains from summits of the Ganesh Himal across the valley, and a cluster of snow mountains to the north hovers beyond twilight. 'Tibet mountains,' says Amit. 'Not far, but no possible to go there.' In the morning Langtang peaks are added to the panorama, and with shadows melting on summit crests I'm eager to be out and moving.

We tread in the footsteps of the great mountain explorer Bill Tilman, for in the summer of 1949 he led a small expedition into the Langtang, Ganesh and Jugal Himals, and despite monsoon clouds and rain he was able to describe the Langtang Valley in glowing terms that excite my expectations today. Having read and re-read his account of that expedition in *Nepal Himalaya* I'm eager to get started. Leaving the lodge, we descend a stone staircase through the layers of old Dhunche, where rubbish is being emptied into the street and men clear their rattling morning chests with well-aimed gobs of spit. 'Ah, the sound-track of Nepal,' says Alan. 'I'm surprised you don't record it.'

Halfway through the village, women squat below a water spout and pummel their laundry on worn flagstones. Watching as we pass, they laugh in response to something Amit says to them, their voices fading only after we're out of sight on the road that winds down the hillside on its way to Syabrubensi, a township not far short of the Tibetan border. The road takes us as far as Thulo Bharkhu, a Tamang village whose stone-walled houses are protected by prayer flags that ripple in the flood of air coming down-valley, and there we begin the steady climb that should lead to Syabru.

The Trisuli Khola, the river that was born in Tibet as the Bhoti Khosi, is soon no more than a silver thread far below, its voice lost amid the shrill buzz of insects and the wheezing of my breath on an uphill trail. How good it is to be out once more with rucksack on back and boots scuffing the dust of a Himalayan hillside! Yesterday's rain shower was over by the time we'd reached Dhunche, and there's nothing to settle the dust this morning – the dust that belongs at this time of year. Tilman's party was ravaged by leeches and drenched by torrential downpours, yet in this post-monsoon season the vegetation is dry; there are no hidden horrors waiting to drop onto exposed skin or burrow through clothing to feed on our blood. We have no need to check for leeches when we rest beside the trail; the way to Syabru has been cleansed.

Our path takes us through oak, maple and chir pine forest; there are towering clumps of bamboo, and rhododendrons that will no doubt be magnificent in springtime. We pass one or two isolated *bhattis* and win a bird's-eye view onto tiny houses scattered below us among terraced fields – terraces that imitate the contour lines marked upon a map. According to my sheet, the houses represent the village of Mungra, and I'm bewitched by them.

Reaching a high point on a ridge, we pause for a moment to gather views of Ganesh peaks and summits that belong to Tibet. If what we see is merely a foretaste, as Amit seems to suggest, we're in for a treat when we enter Langtang proper. Standing on the threshold of another Himalayan wonderland, it means nothing that our man Amit and hundreds of others have trekked this way before us, for to Alan and me everything is new. Every hinted valley, every distant summit, every thatched house and landmark tree is registered in my mind as part of a landscape I shall carry with me in the years ahead.

Trekking, of course, brings all and everything into sharp focus. Living is given fresh meaning; life is instantaneous as trivia vanishes. All that matters out on the trail is the simple act of placing one foot in front of the other, breathing rhythmically, absorbing enough liquids to avoid dehydration, having sufficient food to fuel the body's engine, and finding somewhere to rest when night falls. That is all we need to concern ourselves with. Anything else is superfluous or superficial. My mind is free to capture the wonders of the world around me. And the world is full of wonders.

Crossing a stream, we rise again to a group of simple teahouses. 'This place Brabal,' says Amit. 'Let's eat,' says Alan in response, so we dump our rucksacks and enter one of the buildings to find a couple from Vienna having lunch with their guide. Alan and I order noodle soup for ourselves, *daal bhaat* for Amit and a 'big pot tea' for the three of us. The Austrians also left Kathmandu yesterday and, like us, are bound for Langtang. The teahouse *didi* cooks on an open fire and, as there is no chimney, by the time we've finished our soup the room has become too smoky for comfort, so Alan and I move outside where the air is not polluted, leaving Amit to finish his meal. Moments later a group of primary schoolchildren appear with their teacher, who explains that they're collecting donations for their school, after which they break into song, while six girls – no more than 10 years old – step forward and perform a graceful dance just for us.

On the outskirts of Syabru we're accosted by lodge-owners touting for business, but we resist their pleas and, with Amit's approval, enter Hotel Yeti, where the woman in charge beams a beautiful smile and offers a warm greeting. It's only 1.30, but we're going no further today.

Syabru is a line of two-storey houses built astride a prominent ridge, their shingle roofs overlapping one another. Wooden balconies are decorated with old food cans filled with plants, windows are beautifully carved with elaborate symbols; several houses have tall poles outside carrying long thin prayer flags. The front door of each building faces east, but when you walk through the house and open the back door, you'll find yourself peering down the western slope. On the western side of our lodge the *chaarpi* seems to be suspended over a wooded valley. This, surely, is the ultimate long drop.

Taking my journal I sit outside with the warm sun on my face. Millet is spread out to dry in front of the lodge; hens and their chicks scurry to and fro, marigolds cascade over a wall, while dozens of small terraced fields make a graceful arc below the village. Behind me the *didi* faces a small loom, her legs outstretched, back perfectly straight, while she weaves a colourful waist band, humming to herself. A local man a couple of houses up the way sits cross-legged in the sunshine splitting bamboo that he'll eventually plait into a *doko*. All is peaceful. This afternoon there are no strident voices, no crying children, no angry dogs straining at a chain, no unwanted shadows. Whatever it may be on other days, this afternoon everything about Syabru spells contentment.

That calm and sense of ease continues as afternoon fades towards twilight. The alpenglow gives its blessing to mountains walling the

Langtang Valley, and from the back door of our lodge I photograph Ganesh peaks catching the last of the sun as one ridge folds into another until the sky is no longer stained and darkness fills the valley. It's time to eat.

The Austrians we'd met at Brabal are also here. Tall, smooth-faced Ralph is a paediatrician in a Viennese hospital, and Isabelle works for an Austrian motoring organisation. They speak perfect English, while their guide, who calls himself Bonzo, is relieved to be able to converse with Amit. We're the only trekkers staying here, and the six of us plough our way through plates of *daal bhaat* sprinkled with bitter spinach. Alan and I drink bottles of Star beer, while Amit glugs water from a jug held above his open mouth, and when the meal is over I go outside once more and count the stars shining from a black velvet sky.

The early stages of any trek are days of adjustment as you come to terms with an unfamiliar landscape, its rhythms, traditions and the cultures of those who live in it. But, having made four treks in Nepal in the last five years, there's much that seems familiar already, despite the fact that this is my first time among mountains north of Kathmandu. These wrinkled foothills and the vegetation that clothes them offer few surprises, and I'm at ease wandering through. Here in Syabru village life seems little different from that of communities in the fertile hill country of Annapurna or Kangchenjunga, and I suspect that Buddhist values of the Khumbu region are in tune with those of Langtang and the remote villages in the shadow of Manaslu. Familiarity such as this does not breed contempt.

Today our route plunges below Syabru through bamboo thickets, then over the Ghopche Khola on a steel bridge above a water mill. Briefly framed by trees, the Ganesh Himal then disappears as the trail is squeezed by another dense screen of bamboo. We teeter across a huge landslide area, still unstable years after the 1987 monsoon undermined the hillside, and descend to hot springs on the south bank of the Langtang Khola, the river we'll now follow upstream as far as the glaciers of its birth.

The river thrashes its way among shiny black boulders in the gorge-like narrows of the lower valley. In a forest clearing we pass the inappropriately named Bamboo Lodge – a sturdy little building of stone construction, guarded by a troupe of grey langur monkeys staring at us from the trees – and half an hour later discover the suspension bridge we've been looking for. Simple lodges line both banks, but those on the sunny side of the river appear to be busy, so we enter one on the shady south side and order lunch.

Ralph, Isabelle and Bonzo have been with us since Syabru, and as an easy relationship has developed, conversation flows during the meal to delay our departure, but as soon as we cross the bridge in the early afternoon, the trail climbs steeply above rapids and out briefly into full sunlight. We're barely above 2000 metres, and the heat is trapped in the wooded gorge. The shade of prickly leaved oak and rhododendron filters the light and diffuses some of the heat, but even so I'm bathed in sweat and suddenly feel weary, so curse my greed for eating too much when there's still a way to go.

Having climbed 300 metres since crossing the river, we then slope downhill to a cluster of stone-built *bhattis* in a clearing known as Changtang and decide to call it a day. After checking in for the night at an unsophisticated lodge, I satisfy a raging thirst with a litre of weak black tea. Nearby several *yak* crossbreeds graze the clearing, while more lemur monkeys use the rhododendron trees as watch towers.

Our sleeping quarters are basic, just a single room separated into cubicles by partitions of woven bamboo, so every movement is heard by all. It's a restless night, and none of us sleeps well, and when morning comes we breakfast outside with a light dusting of frost on the ground. But it's a glorious start to the day, with a cloudless sky and shafts of sunlight breaking through the trees. It's another day to be out and moving. Birds tell us so, and the chatter of monkeys confirms it.

The trail plunges into forest once more to deny any mountain views, but orchids hang from lichen-wrapped trunks, the wayside banks are dense with moss, and ferns congregate among rocks and boulders. Mountains can wait. Ralph can't, and without a word he surges on and is soon out of sight. Isabelle looks perplexed and stays close to Alan and me.

Autumn has bronzed all leaves, and as we emerge to a broadening of the valley, with scarlet patches of berberis adding a sheen to the khaki grass, Langtang Lirung appears on the left-hand walling ridge, its chiselled ice sharply outlined against the blue. We also glimpse mountains crowding the head of the valley for, having left the gorge behind, we've now reached the U-shaped central section with all its mysteries about to be revealed. Unlike the majority of Himalayan valleys in Nepal, Langtang does not flow from north to south; instead it drains from east to west, parallel with the Tibetan border, whose frontier mountains gather at the valley's head near the 8000 metre giant Shisha Pangma. An alpine, glacier-carved world welcomes us as we arrive at the national park check post at Ghora Tabela.

We've already gained 500 metres this morning, and the valley continues to rise in a series of steps, enticing us on. Ralph is nowhere to be seen, but his details had been entered in the ledger at the check post, so we know he's ahead somewhere. Then, when we top a long rise to arrive at the two small *bhattis* of Thangsep, we find him relaxing in the sunshine outside the second of the buildings, so we join him for lunch.

The teahouse is run by a young Tamang couple whose toddler son has a cheeky face and a long slit in the seat of his trousers to simplify the act of going to the toilet. His mother has the distinctive features of a *Bhotiya*, with eyes that almost disappear when she smiles from the doorway, as her husband hands me a badly torn sheet of card that serves as a menu. The lettering is so faded and the spelling so erratic that it's difficult to read, and when we try to order, it appears that the only items available are *daal bhaat* or fried potatoes. Ralph recommends the fried potatoes, and while we wait to be served, the *bhatti*-owner offers me a fresh sheet of card on which I rewrite the menu for him in bold letters. He beams at his new price list, then shows it to his little boy, who bounces up and down, loses his balance and topples over squealing with delight. If that's all it takes to make him happy, he'll have a contented life.

At around 3500 metres, Langtang village is 1000 metres higher than where we stayed last night. It's a lot cooler too, especially when clouds drift across the sun, but it's a fascinating place – a real village, not a collection of trekkers' lodges; a community of shingle-roofed, stone-based timber houses, some of which have latticed windows with neatly carved surrounds similar to those we saw at Syabru. Some have scruffy wall-enclosed yards containing livestock – a *yak* crossbreed perhaps, or a few goats or sheep brought in from pasture. On the way into the village we passed the *gompa* and a forest of prayer flags; there were a couple of water-driven prayer wheels too, ignored (not surprisingly, considering her burden) by an old woman in black bent beneath a huge pile of firewood, and Amit tells us that a little further up-valley there are some of the longest *mani* walls in Nepal. Signs of the Buddhist faith are evident wherever we turn. During his visit in 1949 Tilman commented that the monastery here was in excellent preservation 'as befitted the sanctity of [the valley]'.

Sanctity; yes, the valley deserves our respect for it was once considered a '*beyul*', a hidden, sacred place to which Tibetan Buddhists would retreat in times of war or oppression in order to keep their faith alive, only leaving when it was safe to return to the homeland with their teachings intact. Like many remote places, Tilman said, the valley was originally seen as the home of the gods. Langtang village is its beating heart. Forty-five years ago he reckoned there were 30 families here, 'rich in cows, yaks and sheep', and the villagers reminded him of Tibetans, 'engagingly cheery, tough and dirty'. I find them quietly hospitable, and the *daal bhaat* served in our lodge is the best yet.

The lodge is just one of the larger houses, adapted to accommodate perhaps 10 guests, and despite the fact that dried *yak* dung fuels the stove that warms the communal room, we huddle round it as darkness falls, hands held as close to the heat as possible, but try to avoid drawing the acrid smoke too deeply into our lungs. I wonder, what would these mountain folk do without *yak* dung? It's used to plaster some of the walls, to fill the gaps between stones and to fertilise the soil. It's part of this room of a thousand shadows, where candles flicker and cast a yellow glow. Its smoke is ingrained in every rafter; its soot stains ancient timbers that meld into a black solidity in which there are no features. We've deserted the 20th century and live for a while in a medieval time-warp.

Out of the village we cross a damp pasture of pools and streams, then head up a slope of old moraine to a long line of *mani* walls, from where we gain a heart-stopping view of Gangchempo, a beautiful ice-crusted peak of 6387 metres that beckons from its dominant position on the south side of the valley, perhaps two days' walk from here. Like practically every other peak in the Langtang region, its name will mean nothing to any but the most dedicated of mountain fanatics – but who cares? From this distance it appears to have been sculpted with precision, and is so positioned as to be framed by foreground arêtes plunging from lesser summits. One glance is enough to understand why Tilman referred to it as Fluted Peak. If anything, it reminds me of the Weisshorn, but I quickly abandon the thought. Gangchempo is unique.

Our destination for today is Kyangjin, where the final group of lodges is to be found, and as it should only take about three hours or so to get there, we're happy to dawdle. But in any case, why would anyone want to hurry through such a valley? So we drift from one vantage point to another and attempt to identify peaks that gradually shuffle into range.

The river is now an icy torrent hastening among flat-topped rocks, with the path keeping to its north bank. The cropped sunburnt grass, and the tan and scarlet wayside shrubs, add colour to an otherwise monochrome landscape. Despite the trail, the odd building, *mani* walls and meadows contained by drystone walls, the valley has a wild, untamed character that rewards every step. Dr Ralph is ecstatic; his face beams with sheer delight.

After two hours we stop at a teahouse and sit with our backs to the wall, the sun on our faces, drinks in hand and a stunning view before us. 'It beats the view from my office,' murmurs Alan, and with that I plunder the well of memory and draw up a scene from 30 years ago, when I too worked in an office – not in Devon, where Alan is based, but in Essex. Three storeys up, the only view from my window was of a red-brick gents' toilet block just across the way; the only means of seeing the sky was to hang out of the window; strip lighting hissed throughout the summer as well as winter; the room smelled of dust and old manila-bound files of committee reports.

'I know what you mean,' I tell him, and shake the nightmare from my brain. Taking the plunge to try my hand at writing and lecturing was one of the better decisions I've made, but if Alan can juggle a conventional life in local government and escape to big mountains once a year, I wish him well. I'm not sure that double life would have worked for me. What I do know is that a lack of security and questionable income is a price I'm prepared to pay for times like this. It's something I'll never take for granted.

The lodges of Kyangjin are grouped together below a strip of moraine on the edge of a large mountain-rimmed plateau, once planed smooth by glacial action. Coloured prayer flags and chortens bestow a blessing on our arrival. The sun does the same thing, as does every mountain and glacier that forms part of the backdrop. Only five days from Kathmandu, we find ourselves in the heart of the Himalaya.

Again I think of Tilman's visit and his description of camping among anemones near the *gompa* which stands above the lodges; he mentioned a few stone huts and turnip fields, and the graceful lines of Langtang Lirung, which soars up to the north. He had first seen this fine peak from Kathmandu, from where he thought it looked climbable, but seeing it close to he was forced to admit that the south face now appeared impregnable. Like Tilman, we have no plans to climb the mountain, but having plenty of time this afternoon Alan and I decide to trek into the glacial amphitheatre behind the *gompa* for a better view. A narrow trail climbs above a stream to lure us ever upwards until we come onto a crest that looks directly out at a scene of icefalls, hanging glaciers and monstrous walls of rock and ice, and there we concede that Tilman was right to leave it alone.

Three years after Tilman was here, Kyangjin was visited by Toni Hagen while undertaking his geological survey of Nepal for the government. In 1955 Werner Schulthess, another Swiss adviser to the UN, established a cheese factory here, which is now run by the Nepalese government in a building behind some of the lodges, and this afternoon, while Alan and I were studying Langtang Lirung, Isabelle was at the factory buying a slab of *yak* cheese. It's a hard cheese, hard as Cheddar left for several months to dry; it takes a lot of chewing and has a distinctive flavour, and within minutes of biting into it I swear that ulcers are forming on my tongue.

Our stone-built lodge has a few twin-bedded rooms and a communal dining area whose stove is similar to the one we huddled round last night in Langtang. The window of the room Alan and I share looks directly out at Gangchempo, and the prospect of camping somewhere below that fluted peak tomorrow is one that I relish. Amit will come with us until we've found a site for the tent, then he'll trek back to Kyangjin and wait for our return. He tells us he knows a good place to camp, having trekked beyond these lodges a year ago, and with his words building anticipation, I fall asleep to dream of glaciers and frolicking yaks.

The temperature is eight below this morning when we breakfast on porridge thick enough to re-sole my boots. It has to be said that some of the meals in these lodges are pretty much hit or miss; there's little consistency from day to day, and tomorrow the porridge could be watery, as unpalatable as glue, or reminiscent of ready-mixed concrete. None of this matters much to Alan and me, for we'll not be here, and as soon as the sun explodes into the valley and melts the frost we're eager to be off.

Isabelle wants to come with us; at least some of the way, so she says. Neither Alan nor I voice objection, so, leaving some of our gear in Amit's room, the four of us turn our backs on the lodges and leaping ice-glazed streams we strike across the broad *yak* pasture with a clear view south up to Naya Kanga, flanking the Ganja La, a pass that leads into Helambu. Gangchempo dominates all and everything from its prominent position to the southeast, and yet, when we look back the way we've come, Langtang Lirung appears to have grown another thousand metres. We drift like insignificant shadows in a land of giants.

At the eastern end of the plain the valley narrows to make a gentle curve to the left, creating a monstrous natural trench whose flanking walls carry Nepal's border with Tibet. Gangchempo withdraws, but other fine-looking mountains make their appearance. At our feet tiny grey-flowered edelweiss pepper the grass like a sprinkling of quartz crystals, and as we meander through the valley I notice gentians whose petals alternate light blue with a soft pinky-white, while low-growing juniper trees and clumps of berberis grow on the opposite bank of the Tsang (or Kang) Chhu. Below Kyangjin, that milky torrent is transformed as the Langtang Khola, but up here it has all the vibrancy of glacial new birth, and the Tibetan name '*Chhu*' seems to suit its mood better than 'Khola'.

As we approach a *kharka*, a number of long-haired yaks can be seen chasing one another across the grass snorting steam from their nostrils. Although they appear to be skittish and surprisingly playful for such weighty beasts, I can imagine the damage one recalcitrant beast could inflict on a passing trekker, so we make a diversion to avoid them and, with the sun spilling into the valley, the snow- and ice-caked Pemthang Karpo Ri draws us on. However, it's the nearer peak, which our map names as Langshisha Ri, whose towering face of rock, topped by a crown of fragile-looking ice, is the most impressive, while hidden some way beyond these, on the far side of the Nepal–Tibet border, stands the 8000 metre giant Shisha Pangma. Whatever attraction these peaks may hold for climbers, today I'm more than content to be here in the valley, wandering through an avenue of palatial summits on a narrow trail that makes no physical demands.

The Chhu leads us on towards its birthplace, passing one or two stone-based shelters for *yak* herders, then nothing; nothing man-made; nothing but the perfection of nature in the raw. We're flanked on three sides by rock, snow and ice. Gangchempo stands to the south of us. Ahead stark moraine walls converge, squeezing the valley and restricting views to its head.

Amit's stride increases, and Isabelle tries to keep up with him. Alan and I stick to our own pace saying little; like me, he's looking for a pitch for the tent. Then three minds are in harmony as we come to a flat area of grass amid a scattering of rocks and recognise this as a prime site. 'You like to camp here?' asks Amit, knowing the answer even before he speaks. Isabelle says, 'It's a lonely spot – isn't it?' But she's not staying.

We pitch the tent with a view down-valley, collect water from the Chhu, and make a brew. The sun's warmth is tempered by a chill breeze, but the four of us sprawl in the grass and share a lump of *yak* cheese, a few biscuits and a couple of chewy bars, washed down with black tea poured into our two plastic mugs. Then Amit stands, wipes his hands on his trousers and addresses Isabelle. 'We go Kyangjin, you and me. We wait there.'

Alan and I watch them go, then zip the tent closed and make our way in the opposite direction. We are soon scrambling over a great moraine tip to explore a chaos of rock and dried mud, rubble-strewn ice and the miracle of minuscule flowers daring not just to exist, but to thrive in such a hostile environment. It is a wild and uncompromising scene and it's good to have it to ourselves, but before we realise it, the light turns milky, clouds gather where minutes before all was blue and welcoming, and a sudden squall of sleet stings our faces like shotgun pellets. Sod's Law, maybe, but the unexpected change in the weather could not be more fitting up here.

Once back in the tent, snow begins to fall as evening draws in. We make soup from a packet bought in Kathmandu, then Alan hands over a couple of boil-in-the-bag freeze-dried meals that claim to be Beef Ragout. One is – or at least, it could be with a vivid imagination – but the other definitely is not. That one turns out to be a breakfast cereal, and is disgusting when I mix it with the so-called ragout. Although I force it down, I spend the night with regret as my stomach churns and balloons with foul air. The only saving grace is when I crawl outside to find that snow has stopped falling, and through a hole in the clouds half a dozen stars and a thin slice of moon appear.

Our time in the upper valley is well spent. There is no set plan, no schedule we need to adhere to; just a simple desire to see as much of this corner of the range as possible in the time available. So we fill our days skirting grassy moraines, scrambling over others, crossing streams and glacier tongues and admiring the views. In 1949 Tilman and some of his party explored these upper reaches, visiting three high passes with a theodolite with which to survey the valley. Sadly we do not have the same amount of time to spend here as Tilman did, but every hour is special. We find a few cairns and wind-torn prayer flags among scenes of utter desolation, made eerie by a cold mist that sweeps up-valley. By contrast there's a tiny rock-rimmed meadow that in better light evokes in me a spiritual calm. It snows on and off, and heavy overnight frosts form, then melt, inside the tent to drip on sleeping bags, and before we make our return to Kyangjin, we spread them out to dry in the weak sunlight, then amble slowly down-valley to where Amit is waiting.

I'm up shortly after six o'clock, begin the day with movable porridge and scrambled egg, and soon after set off alone for the summit of

Kyangjin Ri, immediately above the lodges. It's a steeply twisting path, and with the early sun in my eyes I find myself taking a different route from the one I'd planned. This one leads into a long grassy gully in which the sun has yet to enter. Frost makes everything brittle, and my boots crunch with each upward step, but when the gully broadens near the top, it opens to a slope carpeted with alpine plants, mostly devoid of flower now that November is here.

Just over an hour and a half from the lodge I break out onto a narrow ridge at a saddle giving magnificent views in every direction. To my left the ridge climbs to a crown of rocks sprouting prayer flags, so I romp up to it and find myself with a grandstand view of Langtang Lirung and its neighbour Kimshung, their glaciers peeling into a deep basin. I can see way into Tibet, across to the Ganja La and to mountains below which Alan and I have been camping. Wherever I turn there's a ragged horizon that makes my heart sing. My altimeter tells me I'm at 4775 metres. I have the world to myself, and it feels good. No sounds drift up from Kyangjin, whose lodges are out of sight; just the whisper of distance and the mountain's breath. With my back to the rocks, the sun on my face and prayer flags shaking their benediction with every passing breeze, I gather the moment and savour it. At this moment, on the summit of an easy mountain, I'm aware of being alive.

As if on cue, a yellow-billed chough circles overhead, then lands a short distance from me. If he's looking for breakfast, he's out of luck.

'Sorry, fella. I've got no grub. Try one of the lodges down below.'

He cocks his head, as though he didn't hear, and takes a couple of hops towards me, but I reach out an open hand to show there are no tit-bits.

'I told you, I've got no food with me. Try below.'

Disgusted by my lack of generosity, the bird launches himself over the side of the mountain to shame me with his agility. I follow him down, but by a much longer and safer route than the bird's headlong dive, and when I reach our lodge I find that Alan and Amit have packed their rucksacks and are ready to depart.

Two days later we receive a warm welcome from the *didi* at Hotel
Yeti in Syabru, who greets us like old friends. We have the same room
we stayed in before, and cups of sweet milky tea and a tin plate of biscuits are waiting for us when we've dumped our rucksacks and return
downstairs. Once again Ralph, Isabelle and Bonzo are here, and, sitting
outside with our drinks, we're joined by a Danish couple staying in a
neighbouring lodge, who tell us that a few days ago a German trekker
had fallen to his death after losing his way on an alternative trail near
the landslide. The Danes had joined the search party looking for the
body and they are angry, for they tell us that for three days they and
other trekkers had searched for the body, while Nepalese army person-
nel based at Ghora Tabela had done nothing.

'Nothing,' they repeat. 'They were no help at all. They did not want
to know.'

The news casts a sombre mood. That trekker had been someone's
son, someone's friend. Perhaps someone's husband or father. No doubt
he came here, like us, looking for adventure and the rewards these
mountains offer. Trekking should be life enhancing; it is not supposed
to end in death.

By the time evening arrives, Syabru's calm has worked its magic and
lifted our spirits. The thicker air and comparative warmth, the half-
moon and our decision to spend two nights here all add to the return of
positive thought. Syabru has lost none of its charm during our absence,
nor has the *didi*, with her gentlest of smiles.

Morning arrives in stealth mode, sliding over the mountains
and slowly filling the hollows with light. I watch as shadows melt to
reveal colours, textures and all the multi-dimensional features that
make this land such an intoxicating place. A cock crows, but he's late
today, for a chorus of small birds have been at it for ages; they were
tuning up long before dawn's first colouring, and now they're in full
voice. But I'm reminded that this is not springtime in England; it's
November in Nepal – late autumn-almost-winter – yet these sounds

have all the vitality of a different season. I guess the birds of Syabru care nothing for the calendar; a new day is something to rejoice over, so they sing beneath projecting shingles on the roof and chatter in fields of stubble. And as the village wakens around me other sounds intrude too, none of them suggesting urgency or discord to break Syabru's spell.

Breakfast over, I sit in the shade of a tree whose branches are used as launching pads for the birds of daybreak. A primus stove purrs in a lodge kitchen; a couple of porters pack their loads nearby and secure them with thick string; Isabelle wrings out her washing over a flower border, while Ralph writes a letter to his father. Alan is immersed in DH Lawrence's *Women in Love*, which he must have read at least twice since leaving Kathmandu, and Amit and Bonzo gaze into the distance as a local woman wanders past, her face twisted as she chews the inside of her mouth, her feet slapping the ground in a pair of short blue wellington boots. There's nothing I need to do, nowhere I need to be, so I revel in the luxury of just living.

Is this real?

Sounds of threshing drift across the terraced fields as I stretch my legs and wander slowly past village houses interspersed with lodges and a handful of small shops to arrive at the *gompa*, where eight monks are bent over brick-sized rectangular texts chanting their mantras. As they do, an elderly woman with a goitre scoops a pile of small potatoes from a soot-blackened pot onto plates coloured with chilli paste and places one in front of each monk. Without any sign of acknowledgment the monks reach out, grab a potato to stuff into their mouths and continue their chanting. Shortly after, the floor is spattered with small pellets of half-chewed food.

Outside the *gompa* a group of seven men and four women sit or squat on the ground, making preparations for a Buddhist festival. Some are dressed in the simple robes of a monk or nun; the others are village elders with time to kill and nothing better to fill the hours than to sit, watch and grow old. One of the men kneads clay which, as it becomes malleable, he carefully moulds into a human shape, then sculpts the head and face with enviable skill. The sculptor says something which makes the others turn to me and laugh, and I realise his joke is that the clay face is modelled on mine. Stroking my beard then pointing to my glasses, I argue that some important features are missing.

A kettle of *chang* is passed round and a bucket of potatoes boiled in their skins. Someone nods to me as if to say: help yourself. I do and, peeling the skin with my thumb nail, I burn my fingers.

In the middle of the afternoon I drift away from the group at the *gompa* and stroll among harvest-bare fields. The air smells of warm soil and drying grain. A farmer's path entices along the top of a terrace retaining wall to a solitary house, where I stumble upon a scene that represents three generations in harmony. Two naked children play in the dust, while their mother combs the hair of an old wrinkled woman I take to be the grandmother. Both women sit facing the sun, and as she runs the comb through the old lady's hair, the younger woman searches for nits; when she finds one she nips it between thumb and forefinger, then flicks it to the ground.

Passing with a '*Namaste*' it strikes me that the simple scene I've just witnessed could have taken place at any time during the past 500 years. But not in my village at home.

Evening slides into the hills. Our *didi* at the Yeti stops work at her loom and prepares a meal of garlic soup and yet another *daal bhaat*, washed down with bottles of Star beer, after which Alan and I sit outside to find the moon has been cast adrift among long wisps of cloud. Amit joins us. Having been with us for a fortnight now, we have an easy understanding. As Kirken had promised, he's proved to be utterly dependable, and despite coming from completely different backgrounds and different cultures, I believe all three of us recognise there's much we can learn from each other. Amit may be in our employ for a few weeks, but we're equals on a journey. And, more importantly, we've become friends.

'You hear bell?' he asks.

We hold our breath and listen, and sure enough the tinkling sound of a bell comes wafting through the village. And with the bell, the low hum of a voice at prayer.

'I go see,' says Amit. Two minutes later he reappears, signalling for us to join him, and turning away directs us towards the *gompa*. But we don't get that far. Instead, he takes us into a private house and up a wooden staircase where a soft yellow light outlines a door. Amit pushes it open, and there we see into the *puja* room, where an elderly man is seated cross-legged behind a low table, on which a row of butter lamps dance in a draught. I recognise the smell of singed juniper. The old man mumbles a rhythmic chant, hypnotic and repetitious, and without pausing for a moment intimates that we're welcome to enter. Amit points to a shelf-like seat covered with a blanket, and the three of us sit down.

A framed picture of a Buddhist saint is propped against the back wall, with brightly coloured strips of tapestry hanging on either side; there's a *thanka* pinned to the wall opposite where we sit, and on the unpolished table lies a thick block of Buddhist text, from which the old man is reading aloud. In his left hand he holds a small silver bell; with his right hand he picks grains of corn from a tin plate and drops them one by one into a brass container, against which stands a postcard of the Dalai Lama. Undeterred by our presence, the old man sways gently to the rhythm of his prayers. He is at peace with his faith, and we with him.

Several hundred metres above Syabru we sit drinking lemon tea at a *bhatti* with a wind-driven prayer wheel fitted to the top of a tall pole; to the side of the building there's an orchard with a few wrinkled apples left hanging. It looks as though they've been attacked by birds. Ralph, Isabelle and Bonzo are with us yet again, although they tell us they'll go no further than Laurebinayak, which we should reach some time tomorrow. From there they'll return to Kathmandu by a different route, leaving Alan, Amit and me to visit the holy lakes of Gosainkund and cross the Laurebina La on the way to Helambu.

Hearing voices, I look up to see a couple of Sherpas coming down the trail. One offers '*Namaste*', while the other stops in front of us, thrusts his head forward, then throws his arms round me and beats me on the back. It's Tendi, whom Alan and I met last year on our trek to Everest; it was he who told us about the *yeti* in Machhermo, and with whom we'd spent an hour or so on the summit of Gokyo Ri. It's good to see him again, and the exuberance of his greeting suggests he's pleased to see us too, so we order more tea, exchange snippets of news and idle away an hour or so in the sunshine. When we part Tendi and his colleague head downhill to Syabru on their way to join a group to climb one of the Langtang peaks, while we continue up the trail towards Sing Gompa, where we'll spend the night.

Frost feathers patterned the window of our room at Sing Gompa, but this morning the sky is clear, and sunshine draws us up the ridge to Laurebinayak, from where Manaslu appears in the west beyond the Ganesh Himal and the frontier range north of the Sanjen Khola, while Langtang II and Langtang Lirung seem close enough to touch. But clouds are gathering, so Alan and I leave our Austrian friends with a promise to meet again in Kathmandu, and storm along the trail that takes us into an increasingly wild-looking landscape. Snow begins to fall in earnest, but we plough on, with the wind beating the rocks and stinging our faces, and are thankful at last to reach the group of stone huts and basic lodges above the north shore of the largest of the Gosainkund lakes.

Ours is not much of a lodge, and the rooms are only a degree or two warmer than the weather outside, but it does have a stove that offers a semblance of heat – if we could get close to it, that is, but this evening four Germans have beaten us to it. Alan and I glower from the side, hoping that a sudden down-draught will waft the smoke directly into their faces.

Darkness falls and the snow stops. Stepping outside to clean my teeth, I discover a silver pathway reaching across the black water of the lake from one side to the other; a shimmering line drawn by the moon. The water twinkles with frost as ice forms around the lake's edge. Low snow-patched mountains gather round; they're almost luminescent beneath a covering of stars. Night is bewitched, and the cold is forgiven.

Gosainkund lies at around 4380 metres, yet in the summer thousands of Hindu pilgrims gather here to bathe in its waters for ritual cleansing. I decide to retain my sins and keep warm, so burrow into my sleeping bag and barely move all night.

Up at 6.30, and strips of cirrus can be seen in a dome of blue. Half an hour later the clouds vanish, there's no wind, but the temperature is down to minus 12. We breakfast on porridge and weak black tea (Amit chooses noodle soup) and are away soon after, boots crunching on frosted snow as the trail rises at a generous gradient above the lake. From a tarn-speckled depression we continue across a land of high pasture, old moraines and scattered boulders to discover yet more lakes, one of which is frozen over, and a view west that excites with memories of Manaslu and Annapurna – could that be Machhapuchhare, the fish-tail, we see far off? The sun is on us, and stopping to list summits is a pleasure, but then we're on the Laurebina La before we realise it. An hour after setting out from our lodge we dump our rucksacks and wander up to the summit of a small hill adorned with prayer flags, a vantage point whose panorama is even more extensive than that from the pass. But out to the southeast, the way we're headed, spectacular cloud formations suggest we make a move.

With Amit scooting ahead, we descend more than 1100 metres before stopping for something to eat in a poor little teahouse at Phedi. In places the descent is steep and icy, and we pick our way with care. There are patches of snow as well as ice, but masses of gentians too, some white with frost. The sun has gone now and the chill bites deep, but it's surprisingly cosy in the *bhatti*, where we're squashed at a table with several forlorn-looking porters wearing unsuitable clothing. I'm relieved to learn that they're on their way down and not up.

I'm concerned about the weather and anticipate more snowfall. Or is my prediction governed by the knowledge that in the winter of 1991–2, James Scott, a young medical student from Australia, lost his way in a snowstorm not far from here? In trying to find his way back to Phedi, he made a near-fatal mistake by attempting to follow a river down into an unseen valley. The terrain proved too difficult and dangerous, so when he discovered an overhanging rock, he decided to shelter there until the weather improved. By the time it did he was too weak to do anything but wait and hope to be rescued. In all he spent 43 days sheltering beneath the rock before he was found, having survived all that time on a single bar of chocolate, but losing something like a third of his body weight. A few months later, a Thai Airlines Airbus crashed into the hillside nearby, killing all 113 people aboard.

Phedi has an unfortunate history.

Tearing ourselves away from warmth and shelter, and after crossing the Tadi Khola, we trek along the steep left-hand side of a gorge on a roller-coaster trail. It begins to snow once more. This time large flakes are shaken from clouds that are no longer above, but all around us. In no time they've covered the trail, and concentration is needed to keep on track as we cross a series of ridge spurs, so when we crest a high point and peer directly onto a couple of scruffy little *bhattis*, we decide to call it a day.

It's a tiny hermit's cell of a building with just a couple of rooms in which a young Nepali family is living. As we arrive the woman is breast-feeding just inside the doorway, snow wafting around her. Alan hums the refrain from 'Away in a Manger'. The carol fits, for the *bhatti* is barely more sophisticated than a cattle shed. But it's shelter. Snow has been falling now for about three hours, obscuring views, covering the ground outside and drifting through the open door – why do they insist on keeping the door open on such a day? A cock struts in, shakes the snow from its head, and having made its way into the sleeping quarters scratches at the bare-earth floor. Above the fire two glassless windows allow some of the smoke to escape and flurries of snow to enter.

We've stayed in some pretty rum places in the hills, but this beats the lot. Yet I'm content; at least it's better in here than outside – even with the damned door open – and it's only for one night. At least, I hope it is. Alan seems happy enough, hunched over the fire reading again by the light of his head-torch, while Amit's attention is on the tinny radio balanced on a shelf alongside two bottles of Star beer, a dusty Sprite, a packet of Ra-Ra noodles, and a pink toilet roll imported from China. Today Nepal is holding its second-ever democratic election, and Amit is hoping for news; but the reception is poor, and the radio crackles and fades. Perhaps the battery is dying.

This evening our *daal bhaat* is served luke warm, but cups of sweet milky tea help wash it down, and we creep off to bed at 7.30, our sleeping bags stretched over a bare wooden platform. For once I'm glad my wife is not with me.

Morning dawns clear but bitterly cold. Alan, Amit and I wear down jackets while eating breakfast, but the three-year-old son of the *bhatti*-owner wanders bare-armed and shoeless as though it's summer. We're away before 8 o'clock, heading downhill on an icy trail, and at the foot of a slope meet two young Frenchwomen having great difficulty staying upright. They curse the cold, the frozen snow and ice, and tell us they spent the night at Therapati and are planning to cross the Laurebina La today, which we warn them will be a lot colder than this. Amit advises them to study the clouds, and if the weather looks unsettled when they reach Phedi, not to leave until it improves.

When we stop for warming drinks at Therapati, Amit learns from the lodge-owner that it looks as though the Communists might be forming the next government. With no discernible expression, he suggests that could be a good thing. 'Communisties,' he says. 'They kick shit from guvmint.'

By the time we reach Kutumsang there's no more snow, the sun is warm and Helambu folds its hills towards the south. Down there beyond these abrupt post-harvest hills lies Kathmandu and another world. But Helambu is a different world too. Although we can see Himalayan peaks when we look back, this is not big-mountain country but an afterthought; an afterthought for us, but a prelude for anyone heading north.

Helambu's hills are golden brown and intricately terraced, its villages roofed with thatch or tin, its well-trod paths teetering along narrow ridge crests. After the chill of Gosainkund, Phedi and Ghopte, Helambu welcomes us with its warmth; for two days we wander through a fertile land bursting with plenty, gathering the sun.

We trek through ridge-top settlements lively with goats and scarlet-combed cockerels; there are chicks in upturned dokos, men working sewing machines at open-fronted shops, women slopping out in the street, children calling '*Namaste*' or hustling with cries of 'Hello-one-pen; gimme shim-shim.'

There's no such thing as level ground, except in and around the houses. Elsewhere all is either up or down, and most of the hills are brutally steep. Long flights of steps have been cut in some of the slopes, but using them disrupts my stride and jars the body. I get stabbing pains in my knees, and at the end of the day my calf muscles ache and disrupt my sleep.

Seated outside a *bhatti* in Chipling, overlooking a veritable staircase of terraced fields, we share a bench with an overweight American, his teeshirt black with sweat. He's in a bad way, and this is only the second day of an eight-day trek he's arranged through a Kathmandu agent. He has a Nepali guide with him who carries only the lightest of rucksacks, while the American is burdened by a backpack fit for a six-week expedition. He tells us he's never walked anywhere before, but as he was in Kathmandu he thought he'd sign up for a trek nearby, imagining he'd be walking through gentle river valleys. Did he get that wrong! Now he has blisters on both feet, and the prospect of more uphill trails sends him into a wailing depression. 'Shit,' he complains. 'I only git a coupla weeks' vacation, n'ahm done fer ahlready.'

177

Before tackling the long haul up to Chisapani for our last night in the hills, we stop for a cold drink at Pati Bhanjyang, a scruffy little settlement built on a saddle in the hills. A swarm of bees gathers over the thatch of a nearby house. Unconcerned, an old woman squats below them washing her hands in a stainless steel pot, then empties the water into the dust and litter of the village street. A goat trips past, followed by a dusty grey buffalo and a farmer who taps the buff's flanks with a stick. The old woman's voice follows him through the village; he answers without so much as a glance. He could be talking to himself.

Tomorrow this will be history. But now is all we have, so I suck it in and savour the moment.

CHAPTER 6

Dolpo

JOURNEY THROUGH THE HIDDEN LAND
(1995)

Following a long-held dream, I organise an expedition to cross the mystical land hidden behind the Himalaya.

While Nepal has made a transition from a country with a closed-door policy (pre-1949) to the tourist honeypot it has become today, it has only cautiously provided access to its more remote mountain regions. It was not until 1989, the year I first went to Kangchenjunga, that a few fortunate trekkers managed to obtain permits to enter remote Dolpo, northwest of Dhaulagiri and the Annapurnas. Before then it was practically unknown to all but a small number of foreigners, one of whom was David Snellgrove from the London School of Oriental and African

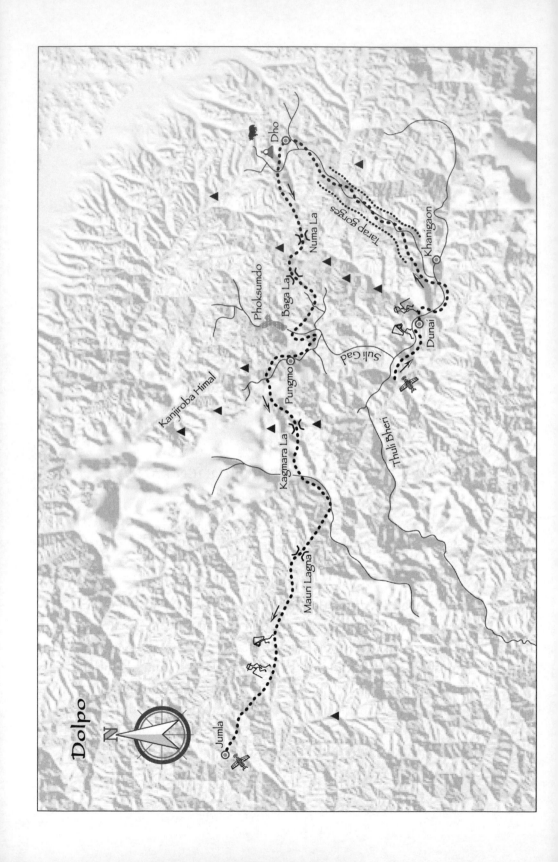

Dolpo

N

Jumla

Mauri Lagna

Kagmara La

Kanjiroba Himal

Pungmo

Phoksumdo

Baga La

Numa La

Dho

Suli Gad

Tarap Gorges

Thuli Bheri

Dunai

Khanigaon

Studies, who in 1956 made a seven-month journey through the Buddhist lands of west and central Nepal. When I came upon his account of that journey in a Kathmandu bookshop, I knew I'd have to go to Dolpo to experience some of the places he wrote about. That account, together with Peter Matthiessen's *The Snow Leopard*, effectively sealed my fate.

Dolpo – the name alone was enough to haunt my dreams.

Then, shortly before we left Kathmandu at the end of our Langtang trek, Isabelle handed me a gift. 'Thank you for looking after me,' she said. Bewildered by her comments, I unwrapped a copy of French photographer Eric Valli's *Dolpo: le pays caché*, whose images of other-worldly faces, extraordinary landscapes and *yak* trains crossing a barren land of lost horizons cast the final spell. I simply had to go to Dolpo. No question about it. My next destination among the mountains of Nepal was made clear, even if it meant organising my own expedition. It was time to have a word with Kirken…

The twin-engined aircraft Kirken has chartered to get us to the south side of the mountains has only eight seats, the rest having been removed to make way for large sacks of rice due to be transported to impoverished villages in some far distant valley. Where we're going is one of the highest permanently inhabited regions on Earth, a land where the annual harvest is insufficient to feed the whole population, so I guess this rice is destined, as we are, for the northern side of the Himalayan divide. Out there I anticipate a very different world, for the Himalaya forms a barrier not only between landscape and vegetation, but – with all its Tibetan influences – between cultures and racial identities. Dolpo will be a far cry from the humid lowlands of the Terai we've just left behind, where squadrons of mosquitoes gathered at dusk and the sticky heat made sleep all but impossible to achieve. Nepalgunj, where we spent the night just a few kilometres from the Indian border, was not my kind of town, and delay after delay there made us all edgy. But now at last we're dodging clouds as the flat lands below give way to hills that rise to bigger hills, and mountains dashed with snow appear through holes in those clouds.

Conversation is impossible with the loud droning and vibration of the aircraft's engines, but excited faces are pressed to the windows and fingers point to sudden views. Only Kirken looks ahead, his eyes fixed on the necks of the pilot and co-pilot, who search for the meadow on which we'll land. At least, I hope we will. But as everyone knows, flying in Nepal often involves navigating a way between mountains. And Nepalese clouds have a habit of disguising mountains that are hard to avoid.

Beneath us now I see a valley with dusty trails ribboned along the hillsides, a milky blue river below, a house or two, and the shadow of our plane rippling across the land. Then, suddenly, that land has gone and all I see is blue sky as the pilot banks, then momentarily straightens the aircraft before chasing down out of the blue towards a hillside that now fills the cockpit window in a moment of suicidal madness. This is white-knuckle flying for sure, and just as it seems we're about to bury ourselves in that hillside, the nose of the plane lifts and we hit the brown autumn grass and hurtle up the slope, bouncing and bumping like a crazy fairground ride as the pilot fights for control.

Once again I step onto Nepalese soil and feel the warm sun on my face. Nerves settle, and the relief of safe arrival washes over me as I notice a familiar figure walking across the grass. It's Amit, our friend from Langtang, who's to be our cook, approaching with a shy smile and garlands of marigolds to hang around our necks.

It's good to see him again. He grips my hand, then casts caution aside and gives me an unrestrained bear hug before greeting Alan, then Ralph and Isabelle in turn. He's comfortable with the four of us, but blushes when I introduce him to Martin, Steve and Wendy, who make up the rest of the group. Half a dozen porters appear, and with Kirken taking charge the plane is emptied of our kitbags, rice sacks and the bundles of fruit and vegetables we've brought from Kathmandu. Moments later the plane races down the slope trailing a long plume of dust, then rises towards the clouds. Peace settles and the sounds of Nepal return.

Amit takes us across the meadow to a house where a kettle of weak black tea and a few biscuits are waiting. A team of Sherpas stack boxes of food, porters test the weight of kitbags, kitchen-boys fill a *doko* with pots, metal bowls and a gleaming pressure cooker, while Kirken issues his orders. Like us, he's relieved to see that all the crew are here. He last saw them more than two weeks ago, when he put them on a bus in Kathmandu. 'Two days on a bus,' he'd explained, 'then they walk for 11, maybe 12 days with tents and all 'kipment for the trek.' Now he says with understatement, 'It's good they here, else we go hungry and sleep under stars.'

This is my first time on trek with Kirken, and I'm impressed by his organisational skills. Working out of a Kathmandu office on a noisy street, he runs a very efficient business in an understated manner. With just a handful of regular staff, he has the ability to call on as many freelance Sherpas and porters that might be required for a particular trek. With us now is one of his brothers, a carpenter from Solu district who's never been on trek before – but as he's short of work Kirken has brought him along to give him new experiences and a few weeks' wages.

Other members of the crew continue with their tasks, but give us the once-over when they think we're not looking. Some of our porters, I'm told, are subsistence farmers who grow just enough food to feed their families, but not enough to make a living, so they will earn much-needed wages by carrying huge loads over a series of high passes in an unfamiliar part of their country to enable a few 'wealthy' foreigners to enjoy a trekking holiday. I wonder if it makes sense to them – our spending so much money just to go for a walk. They walk because they have no option. We do so by choice.

In warm sunshine we follow a trail heading southeast among shallow terraces that slide towards the Thuli Bheri river. Dry stems of maize crackle as we pass, grasshoppers leap away from our boots, and brown moistureless hills of 4500 metres (that anywhere else would be classified as mountains) part briefly to give a teasing glimpse of distant heights spattered with snow – or could they be clouds? The mighty Himalaya, that ought to be seen as an arctic wall, is hidden, yet we're only a valley or two away from 6000, 7000 and 8000 metre giants. Strangely, I do not miss them. I know they can't be far away, but I can wait. We're on the move in an unknown country, and that's more than enough for now.

It's good to have Ralph and Isabelle with us again, and despite the fact that this will be a very different experience from last year's trek in Langtang I had no difficulty inviting them to join us on this journey. For one thing it's comforting to have a doctor with us, and Ralph's medical skills give me confidence that we'll be well looked after should anyone fall sick; as I understand it, there is no health care in Dolpo. There are no roads either, and no facilities for calling a helicopter in an emergency, which of course has added to the appeal. We must be self-sufficient in everything, and I find that strangely reassuring. Ralph's presence is like an insurance policy; I appreciate his company, but hope his skills will not be required.

Meeting the rest of us in Kathmandu, Ralph and Isabelle were soon at ease with Steve, Martin and Wendy, and I don't anticipate any personality clashes. On a commercial trek you take pot luck with a mix of complete strangers, but having been responsible from the start for this trip, I invited friends who I thought would get on together. Only Wendy was unknown to me until we met at Heathrow, but within minutes I was happy with her company. A divorcee with a home on the edge of Dartmoor, she's a member of the same mountaineering club as Alan, and he'd recommended her as someone who'd fit in. After 30 years of friendship I trust his advice.

As for the others, Steve Neville and I have known each other since childhood. We started climbing together, I was best man at his wedding and am godfather to his eldest son; since he came out of the army after a full 22-year career, he calls in whenever his work as an engineer brings him near my home. Until recently Martin Fry, a rights of way officer from Surrey, and I lived in the same village among the greensand hills of Kent, but although we've walked many a lowland footpath together, we've never shared a mountain trail. He and Steve are both first-timers in the Himalaya, and I know they'll make the most of every experience.

By contrast Alan is like an old-hand – but although this is his fourth Himalayan trek, it's his first as a member of a group with a crew of Sherpas and porters, and I wonder what he'll think of the large number of support staff making the journey with us. But he has other things on his mind this year and reckons he needs this time away from home even more than usual. His marriage is crumbling, and there are decisions to make that will affect his future; will this trek be a welcome distraction from that – or an escape he may come to regret? Only time will tell, but I'm hopeful that in a few days' time he and the rest of the group will become fully immersed in our journey, in the beauty of the trans-Himalaya and the other-worldly culture of the Dolpo-pa.

Lunging from its chain, an aggressive-looking dog barks furiously as we wander through a village of flat-roofed houses built in tiers, one above another, and linked by a series of log ladders with notches in place of rungs. Men, women and children stand in groups and watch as we pass. You'd think the circus had come to town.

Beyond the village the valley narrows, its walling hills broken with cliffs, the river carrying the cooler air and snowmelt of mountains we cannot see. Then we come to a small collection of houses protected by a crudely carved figure, placed at the bridge by which we enter, to keep evil spirits at bay. Shortly after, an army camp appears on the opposite bank of the river, overlooking a major tributary: 'The Suli Gad,' says Kirken. 'That way Phoksumdo and Shey.'

There's familiarity in those names. The Suli Gad – that's the river Matthiessen followed for a while on his journey to Shey Gompa and the Crystal Mountain in 1973. It comes from the Phoksumdo Lake, which we hope to visit later on our crossing of the hidden land, and although I'm in no hurry to get there, I'm excited by the recollection of Matthiessen's enthusiasm for the country to the north. 'I wonder,' he wrote, 'if anywhere on earth there is a river more beautiful than the upper Suli Gad in early autumn.'

A soldier clutching his rifle guards a bosun's chair fitted to a cable strung across the Thuli Bheri, but we have no need to cross the river here and continue on its right-hand side over a meadow fringed with pine trees, heading towards a solitary building surrounded by prayer flags on tall poles. Beyond it the valley opens its jaws to reveal autumn-brown slopes, a freshly laundered sky and snow-laced peaks far off. A few minutes later, we pass through a *kani* to enter Dunai, the administrative headquarters of the district; its paved street is lined with simple houses, shops, a school and a police post, but in the centre a statue of the king looks down on his people with what appears to me to be a sneer of disapproval. Between houses that back onto the river, a young boy squats naked upon a midstream rock, his teeth gleaming white in a healthy brown face. The merboy plunges into the water, splashes to the bank, then crawls out and scampers down the street shrieking with laughter as Kirken leads us to the edge of the village, where our tents are being pitched in a meadow beside an orchard of apple trees.

As is my custom, I'm awake at least an hour before the sun and outside before bed-tea arrives. A wreath of mist hangs over the river, but it's gone by the time breakfast is served. The mess tent has already been taken down and added to a porter's load, and shadows are being chased through the valley as Amit brings a large steaming pot to the table. Martin lifts the lid and scoops two or three ladles into gleaming bowls. 'Porridge anyone?' Several of us help ourselves and stir in liquid honey – only to discover it's not porridge after all, but scrambled egg.

We're slow to move today, for the routine of life on trek has to be learned by the rest of the group – bed-tea brought to the tent at 6 o'clock, followed by a shallow bowl of warm washing water; breakfast served shortly after 6.30, by which time kitbags should be packed and ready for the porters. While breakfast is eaten, the tents are collapsed and porters set off with their loads. Most days we're on the move shortly after 7.30; lunch is taken any time between 10.30 and 1 o'clock, depending on the availability of water; then we wander on through the afternoon until camp is pitched at around 4 o'clock. There's tea, coffee, hot chocolate and a few biscuits in the late afternoon, followed by dinner at six, and by eight most of us will be in our tents, dead to the world.

Ten hours in a sleeping bag! I think it was Tilman who once commented that the biggest health problem for the Himalayan traveller was bed sores. A bit of an exaggeration, of course, but nowhere else do I spend so much of my time in a horizontal position.

Unripe pomegranates, not much bigger than large plums, cluster on a grove of trees 10 minutes upstream of Dunai. Children stand beneath the trees and, without a word between them, watch as we pass, unresponsive to our 'Namastes'. Not so the miller brushing his teeth outside the low stone-walled water mill built astride a leat. Whipping the brush from his mouth, he gabbles a few words which Kirken interprets as a comment on my white beard: 'He says you must be very old!'

With the miller's permission I take his photograph, and although the rest of the group have moved on, we strike up a conversation that uses no common language, and when I enquire about his mill, he opens the door and, ducking his head, takes me inside. A coating of flour covers the walls and ceiling; it dusts the air I breathe, settles on my clothes, arms and face; I feel it on my hair and in my teeth – and all the time a rush of water along a wooden gutter spills onto the creaking wheel that turns the stone to transform grain into flour for a thousand chapattis. Everything I touch is covered with the creamy white dust, and I wonder at the condition of the miller's lungs, breathing this in, day after day, year in, year out. This is Old Testament technology, unchanged in thousands of years, and when I finally emerge to the bright, flour-free light, an Old Testament landscape lifts my spirits with its simple beauty. Once again I breathe fresh air transported by the river from snow mountains I cannot see.

For two unforgettable days we're enticed further into this land of deep valleys and crowding mountains. In sunshine and shadow the trail weaves a route among stands of blue pine and meadows of cannabis. On tenuous causeways built just above river level, it climbs over crags, descends to beaches of glacial sand and passes smoke-blackened caves, where for centuries porters and traders have sheltered for a night or two. We camp on shelves above the river, and crawl out of our tents through feathery grasses whose seeds snag on the hairs of bare arms and legs. Hundreds of metres above us a silent, cirrus-like flock of sheep drifts across a hillside; they appear to be no bigger than maggots.

We're not alone on the trail. One morning a long string of pack ponies comes towards us. Heavily laden and single-minded, neither they nor the pony-men with them care for us, so to avoid being knocked down the slope into the river we're forced to scramble up the hill or cling to rocks until they've passed, harness bells jangling, dust clouds rising from four dozen hooves. 'Traders from Pokhara,' says Kirken. 'They not local.'

In the early afternoon we come to a confluence with the Tarap Khola, whose gorges breach the main Himalayan wall, beyond which lies Dolpo proper. Although still very early on our journey, I sense this to be a major landmark and feel an added surge of excitement. Yet it's hard to believe that this river is born on the edge of the Tibetan plateau, for down here, flanked by slender birch trees, it has a European identity. As if to complete the picture, while I dream on the river's bank, a dipper bobs its tail on a midstream rock. Plunging into the water, moments later it emerges upstream, hops onto another rock and shakes the water from its feathers. In an instant I'm transported to the Spanish Pyrenees....

We pitch our tents in a grove of cedars across the river from Khanigaon, whose *gompa* was visited by Snellgrove almost 40 years ago. He described the way to it 'as though one were about to enter some hidden and idyllic valley, of which Tibetans love to tell, where men and animals live in harmony'. But this afternoon his words hang heavy as two of our Sherpas return from the village with a goat on a lead. After feeding it salt and speaking to it in hushed tones, a kukri blade flashes in the sunlight and the creature's head is separated from its body.

I'm shocked as much by my attitude to this slaying as I am by its swiftness, by the spraying of blood, the excitement it evokes among our crew of porters, and their eagerness to help with the skinning and butchery of the animal whose heart has barely stopped beating. Having spent all my life in the countryside I know all about the slaughter of poultry, pigs and cattle for human consumption, but to see it happen, here of all places, appals me. But oh, hypocrite that I am, this evening I tuck into goat stew that forms the main part of our meal, then ladle out a second helping.

It's a balmy evening among the cedars, yet the porters have built a fire – not for warmth, but for the comfort of its glow. Sparks lift into the night sky to mingle with stars, insects fill the black spaces beyond the trees with their unrelenting high-pitched sibilation, and the river thunders nearby. With eyes gleaming, laughter explodes from our crew as one after another retells the story of the goat's demise. It's the highlight of their journey so far, and they're drunk with its memory.

Our route takes us into the Tarap gorges, steadily gaining height as we climb from one level to the next. In places the trail is buttressed by drystone walls, with stairways of flat slabs that suddenly run out until we're stumbling among shrubbery and low-growing trees, leading me to suspect that the way ahead is work-in-progress. One section has been created by laying smooth stones on a timber frame wedged in a fault line of rock angling across a cliff high above the river. The trail, such as it is, gives airy exposed views before descending precariously to water level, where we cross from one bank to the other and back again on an assortment of bridges. There is no uniformity in their structure; each bridge is unique. But it is in such variety that our journey has added value. We trek without certainties; there's nothing we can forecast except the adventure of the unknown.

In the balmy warmth of late morning on our first day in the gorges I am lounging among the dried grass of October writing my journal while

Amit prepares lunch, when a silent flock of long-horned goats appears wearing panniers. With them are three traders from Dolpo carrying enormous sacks containing salt from Tibet. Dumping their loads, they set about removing the panniers so the animals can roam free and seek fresh grazing, before stacking the bags to create a shoulder-high wall. The men are dark-eyed and wild-looking, with long black hair that hangs in pigtails down their backs. They wear greasy jackets, calf-high boots and kukri knives in their belts, and with barely a word passing between them, they gather kindling, build a fire in the lee of the pannier wall, and in no time *tsampa* is bubbling in a smoke-blackened pot. Not to be outdone, Amit hands us plates of black pudding, coleslaw and chapattis. Martin takes one look at the black pudding and, knowing it was made from the blood of yesterday's sacrificed goat, he turns away. Feeling nauseous, he's been struggling all morning, and the sight of food is just too much.

On another day we camp on a small meadow beside a group of *yak* herders. They too have cargoes of Tibetan salt, but the sacks carrying these loads are a dozen times larger and weightier than the panniers fitted to the backs of the goats. But then their yaks are juggernauts by comparison. The herders tell Kirken they cannot use our trail as it's not sturdy enough for their animals, and instead must take a higher route across the mountains.

One morning we rise to find mist draped in the valley like an old lace curtain, the cliffs above our camp black and shining from overnight rain. A cold wind rushes along the river; surly and uninviting, it reminds me of wintry days in Snowdonia. But it was there and on such days that my passion for mountains and wild country was formed. Without them, perhaps, I would not be here today.

It rains for most of the morning. The temperature drops and sleet bounces off our waterproofs, but in the early afternoon conditions improve and sunlight explodes into the valley before the gorge makes a sharp bend and shadows fill the narrow spaces between walling cliffs. The sound of voices ahead echoes from wall to wall, and moments later we come across Dorje, one of our Sherpas, in conversation with Kirken's brother and two porters removing sheets of polythene from their dokos. 'Hey *Baje!*' cries one of the porters, and I flush with pleasure. The man whose name I do not know acknowledges me as his friend.

Where there's vegetation autumn is evident in every leaf, but with each hour of progress towards the hidden land, there's less of it. We're being squeezed by Himalayan mountains, and our eyes are attracted by different types of rock. I'm no geologist, but recognise sandstone, limestone and patches of conglomerate, and when we cross a minor pass within the confines of the gorge we find curious eroded lumps and domes of clay.

Once again our map is the product of a rich imagination, but I've grown used to fictional Himalayan routes drawn on poor quality paper, and rarely refer to it except at the end of the day, when Kirken and I will pore over it to speculate where we are and where we might be tomorrow. He came here with a naturalist several years ago to study the snow leopard, and remembers much of the route, although he's baffled by many of the names on the map and has little trust in its authenticity. This evening, though, he is adamant. 'Tomorrow', he tells us, 'we reach Dho Tarap.'

A final bridge takes us across the Tarap Khola out of shadows and into the warmth of a new day. Some of our porters are resting in the sunlight and, taking the hint, we remove a layer of clothing and sit for a few minutes with them. A circular, intricately carved *mani* with Buddhist motifs instead of Sanskrit letters leans against a crag. Prayer flags can be seen on the crest of a ridge high above us; everyone falls silent.

Excitement spurs me on and, emerging through the natural gateway at the head of the gorge, my eyes light upon the real Dolpo at last. Reality does not disappoint as I stand here a little moist-eyed and breathless, and gaze into a broad valley flanked by big brown hills lightly dusted with snow. A young boy wanders to and fro through the valley, stooping every now and then to lift something that he tosses over his shoulder into a small *doko*. What could he be gathering, I wonder?

191

At last I'm face to face with the boy, and peering into his *doko* I see it half-filled with dried slabs of *yak* dung. Of course! It's fuel for cooking and heating the homes. At around 4000 metres above sea level, this valley – like so many others this side of the Himalaya – is too high for trees to grow, so there is no firewood. There's neither gas nor electricity; no coal nor oil. The only fuel is that left by grazing animals. So each morning the children are sent out to scour the valley and lower hillsides to gather *yak* dung, while manure from sheep and goats will fertilise the soil for growing barley, buckwheat and potatoes. There can be no waste in this impoverished land.

The boy looks up at me, furrows his brow and tilts his head. How old is he? Perhaps nine or ten – who can say? His face has been blackened by seasons of raw winds and high-altitude sun, but when his homespun tunic opens at the chest, I note that his flesh is not much different in colour to my own. He seems just as bemused by my appearance, and in response to my 'Namaste' he offers a brief momentary smile before deserting me to inspect the rest of the group.

A long row of *mani* walls leads the way to Dho Tarap; chortens large and small, intricate and plain, waymark the valley, and above the village a white-painted *gompa* appears to glow like the stub of a candle. This morning the valley is full of life, for a shepherd leads his mixed flock of sheep and goats to pasture, yaks snuffle the dust of post-harvest fields, and the sound of threshing – so familiar now from half a dozen autumn visits to Nepal – drifts in the brittle air of high places. Large birds of prey form slow pirouettes above us; gliders, they are, with feathers.

Dho Tarap belongs to another age, another world, with its thick, grey stone-walled houses, tiny gaps for windows and flat roofs covered with straw. Over each one there hangs a strip of white cloth whose prayers have been bleached by the same high-altitude wind and sun that blackens the faces of those who live here. Narrow alleys squeeze between the buildings, and labouring within several walled enclosures women in striped homespun beat the harvested barley with long-handled flails.

Clouds of chaff hang in the air. Most of the women wear necklaces of turquoise and coral; the younger ones have coloured bangles round their wrists, while a few of the older women wear curious black bonnets studded with plates of brass or silver. Outside a threshing yard two men harness a pair of yaks to a wooden plough. Crows wait nearby for worms to be unearthed when the soil is turned, hopping from one foot to the other to underline their impatience.

With our tents pitched a little south of the village, we're quickly surrounded by snotty-faced children, one of whom – no more than four or five years old – has a deformed concave chest and a small humped back, but he has the brightest of smiles and quickest of eyes. Attracted by Wendy's voice he makes an innocent gesture of offering her a crust of *yak* dung. What other gift would a guest need here?

The children bombard us with questions, and Kirken is kept busy answering them all. But he warns us to leave nothing outside our tents. 'Sticky fingers,' he says. 'They take everything not tied down.'

Kirken, Alan, Wendy and I scuff our way up the hillside to visit the *gompa*, part of a complex of buildings with a tremendous outlook. The local *lama*, Amchi Namgyal Rimpoche, has only been here for a year, but today he's visiting another monastery within his jurisdiction, so we are shown inside by the caretaker. This ancient place is said to have been built around 1000 years ago, and as we step inside the centuries fall away. The dim light is only just sufficient to enable us to admire the decorations over the entrance, the three Buddhas and a larger-than-lifesize Guru Rimpoche that adorn an inner room, the row of butter lamps at the altar, and two black-and-white photographs of the Dalai Lama. But the *gompa* is more like a dusty museum than a place of worship; it needs the swaying of monks at prayer, the clash of cymbals and blasting of trumpets to give it meaning.

Outside, while standing on the rooftop, the beauty of the valley makes up for the *gompa*'s lifeless interior. Beyond Dho, to the southwest, the Tarap Khola is a silver thread stretching into the shadows of the gorge by which we arrived. But to the north, where our journey will soon take us, the valley is broad and flat, spattered with chortens and a prominent *kani*, and patterned with the bare outlines of harvested fields. It's a land with little colour at this time of year, but Snellgrove visited in a different season and found a profusion of flowers alongside the river. Legends speak of it as having once been filled with a vast lake, and it's easy to imagine a glacier pushing its way between the mountains, halting more or less where Dho stands today, then steadily withdrawing, leaving a great sheet of water blocked by a wall of terminal moraine. Eventually the dam would have given way, draining the valley of its lake and leaving behind a bed of semi-fertile soil, which is now used for crops of short-stalked barley and buckwheat that will not grow in neighbouring valleys at a similar altitude.

Kirken points out the direction our route will follow, and the three of us share excited anticipation for the days ahead. Although the landscape is totally different from any other Himalayan district I've visited so far, and there are no dramatic sky-piercing mountains to be seen, there's nothing second rate about this uncompromising land. Stark, dusty, a seemingly barren desert at this time of year, it would be folly to attempt to compare it with the Khumbu, Kangchenjunga, Langtang, Manaslu or the Annapurna regions; it would be as pointless as comparing a rose with an orchid. Each has its own beauty – and Dolpo does not disappoint.

This morning Ralph, our doctor, is sick. When I visit his tent I find him bleary-eyed in his sleeping bag while everyone else tucks into breakfast. Everyone, that is, except Isabelle, who shares Ralph's tent and his concern. He tells me he was up in the night, losing all his food from the past few days, and now nurses a bad headache. It sounds to me like early signs of altitude sickness – either that or food poisoning – and tell him that if the headache persists he'll have to lose altitude and go back down the gorge. He does not relish the thought. 'I'd prefer to call a helicopter,' he says without a hint of irony.

We delay our departure, and when I next visit his tent he assures me that he feels a bit better, the headache easing. I discuss the situation with Kirken, and together we decide to set off after lunch, in order to avoid gaining too much height too soon, and vow to keep a close eye on Ralph. We'll have a short and easy day.

We do. First we lunch on garlic soup, then fried eggs, potatoes, tinned meat and chapattis. And lots of tea. Ralph joins us but limits his intake to liquid – plenty of soup and as much tea as he can digest, for it's essential to remain hydrated.

On a beautiful early afternoon of azure skies and only the lightest of high clouds being shredded by a wind we cannot feel, we wander away from Dho. After days of trekking through deep valleys and narrow gorges, we now have plenty of space among mountains of almost 6000 metres disguised as little more than hills, across whose slopes a large number of yaks, sheep and goats drift as silently as cloud shadows. Although wearing neither glacier nor permanent snowfield, those hills have an undeniable allure. Beyond them, surely, lies a forbidden kingdom.

Less than an hour after setting out we come to the Crystal Mountain School, financed by a French charity. Now almost a year old, the head teacher explains that it's the only school to serve Inner Dolpo, and so far has 30 pupils. Because distances are so great, and the school is intended to serve such a large area, a dormitory block has been built next door to enable most of the children to board. The teacher speaks excellent English, and tells us that emphasis is put on teaching Tibetan and Nepali as well as English, but he's also determined to enhance the Dolpo culture. Throughout the Himalayan regions, cultures that have stood the test of time are in danger of disappearing, being overtaken by what is perceived to be a better way of life represented by visitors just like us.

'We need tourists like the rest of Nepal,' he says. 'And if they respect the environment and our way of life, they are welcome.' The alternative is left unspoken.

Making a donation for the school's upkeep we move on, our porters now well ahead of us striding towards a village Kirken says is called Tok-khyu. The map suggests there are other villages too, but Kirken is adamant: 'Many names, one place,' he insists. 'Tok-khyu.' Its houses are dwarfed by the landscape, and it's difficult to come to terms with the scale of this land of wide horizons.

The Tarap Khola is now little more than a shallow stream turning stones in its bed, and I sit for a moment on its bank to listen to the timeless music it plays. Water on stone, stone against polished stone, it has a rhythm all its own. Then that rhythm is joined by human voices, and looking up I see four Dolpo women walking towards me, spinning *yak* wool and singing a strange melody, their weather-black faces creased with humour. As they turn to cross the bridge, their singing gives way to a wild dance that takes their breath. On the opposite bank they break into laughter, then pull themselves together and waltz down to their village, singing once more.

Beyond Tok-khyu the way forks. Kirken indicates a pass leading to Saldang, but that is not for us; we have no permits for that route, so bear left and enter a sloping moorland of tussock grass, boggy patches and scores of small domes of what look like cushions of saxifrage. Some way above this we pitch our tents in view of the Numa La, which we aim to cross tomorrow. Our tents are 300 metres higher than at Dho, yet Ralph insists he feels a lot better, his headache gone. The rest of the group seem okay, and although my head tightens as we arrive, three mugs of tea soon put that right.

Shortly after 10 o'clock I'm woken by Ralph, who comes into my tent, trembling. 'What's wrong?'

'I thought I was suffocating,' he tells me, but his eyes say more than those few words.

'What happened?'

He describes waking, unable to breathe, choking and gasping for breath, and when Isabelle joins us she explains that she'd heard him breathing rapidly for what seemed ages, then suddenly he'd stopped. There was no sound, not a single breath. 'I thought he had died,' she says. 'It was very scary.'

Sounds like a classic case of Cheyne–Stokes to me, and I tell him so. It's not uncommon to have this abnormal breathing when sleeping at altitude, although it would be much more serious at sea level. Checking my high-altitude first-aid handbook, it confirms my diagnosis, and I suggest he takes Diamox. In truth, after his bad night at Dho I should have recommended Diamox anyway. But he's the doctor, and I'm hardly qualified to give medical advice to someone in his profession.

Isabelle is relieved and returns to her tent, but Ralph needs a lot of reassurance, and it's another hour before he goes back to his sleeping bag – by which time I'm wide awake and sleep no more. For a while I lie worrying about our Austrian friend, then realise there's nothing to be gained by worry, and instead think about the Crystal Mountain School, and what the head teacher had said about the need for tourists. We are tourists, but what benefits do we bring to the Dolpo-pa on our trek through the hidden land? Unlike most other regions I've trekked in, there's nothing for us to spend our money on here. No gifts, no souvenirs, no food – not even a teashop, where villagers could earn a few rupees selling tea and biscuits. We had to bring all our own supplies from Kathmandu; our own porters too. So we wander through Dolpo, gaining in experience, but leaving nothing that could benefit the local communities.

It's a sobering thought.

Shortly before dawn breaks over the mountains I hear Ralph's voice outside. This time he's telling Kirken he cannot go on, that he must return to Kathmandu and wants helicopter evacuation.

'Helicopter impossible,' says my Sherpa friend. 'I will arrange for a Sherpa to go with you. You can walk; you will be okay.'

'Belli too,' says Ralph. 'She wants to go back with me.'

I can see there's no use trying to argue, so after eating breakfast with the rest of us, Ralph and Isabelle say goodbye and set off with Dorje and two porters carrying a tent and enough food to get them safely back to Kathmandu. Watching them go, I'm forced to admit that altitude sickness is not their only concern. I'd suspected several days ago that they were struggling to come to terms with the strangeness of Dolpo, its landscape and culture – the very things that make it so special for me and the other members of the group – and that they longed for something more familiar. Last year, Langtang was acceptable because they could stay in lodges, were meeting other Europeans almost every day, and knew they were never more than a few days' walk from a bus journey back to Kathmandu. Dolpo does not provide that reassurance, which they find disturbing.

They turn and wave farewell, and the hidden land takes them from us. I'm sorry to see them go.

Much later than intended, we set off for the 5320 metre Numa La. It's not a difficult climb, for we follow tracks used by *yak* herders for much of the way, but we have something like 1000 metres of height to gain, and the altitude is affecting me and the group. The sound of rasping breath is with us throughout the ascent. Once again I envy the energy and lung capacity of the Sherpas, who maintain a conversation as they mount these slopes, when it's all I can do to suck in enough oxygen to take the next few steps.

The mountainside is bare and open to the wind. Crossing numerous folds and spurs, we come to snow. It lies at first in patches, where it has settled on slopes of black shale and grit, then as we approach the pass it spreads more evenly; but if we step outside the trough created by those who have gone before us, we flounder in thigh-deep drifts.

Suddenly Dhaulagiri appears in the southeast like a monstrous dome above a series of intervening ridges. I'd last seen that 8000 metre giant four years ago when trekking round Annapurna with Alan. Although it looks slightly different from this angle, it's unmistakable – the same Dhaulagiri we'd gazed on from Muktinath and a dozen different places along the Kali Gandaki's valley. Only moments ago we'd been scanning scenes that consisted of numerous desolate brown hills spreading north and east into Tibet; now we have the Himalaya of dreams – snow mountains that both challenge and inspire.

A bitter wind storms over the Numa La, carrying spindrift and shredding the prayer flags fitted to a cairn, yet we're all relieved to be here and, finding brief shelter from the wind, enjoy a fresh vision ahead, where the Kanjiroba massif continues the Himalayan line in the north-west. This is another world…

Slithering down a slope of wind-packed snow we meet a *yak* train lumbering up towards the pass carrying sawn timber, their herd-ers whistling through their teeth to spur the animals on. Ten minutes below them, at the foot of the snow slope, Kirken, his brother Tashi and Kumar beckon us over to a large rock, behind which they're sheltered, and hand us welcome chapattis with boiled eggs, slices of cheese and tinned fish, which help stoke our inner fires and replace lost energy.

The descent continues over rocky slopes and bare dusty bluffs before twisting into a tight V of a valley at the headwaters of the Chhadha Chu, which Kirken tells us drains into the Phoksumdo Lake. In its upper reaches the stream cuts its way through mini-gorges of rus-set-coloured rock and, as very little sunlight can penetrate, everything is glazed with ice, demanding extra care when we cross and recross from one bank to the other, for this is no place to slip and break a leg.

After what seems an eternity, we turn into a fine valley blocked at its head by the graceful Norbung Kang, plastered with ice and snow, where our tents are being erected in a meadow of scant grass. Checking my altimeter I discover that we're still 200 metres higher than our camp on the far side of the Numa La. It feels much higher, and my heart is racing. Despite the beauty of this meadowland, it's in a frost pocket, and we all know we're in for a cold night. I wonder where Ralph and Belli are, but reckon they'll be warmer than us.

Last night the temperature dropped close to minus 15, and this morning our porters huddle round a fire of *yak* dung, clutching mugs of tea that Amit passes to them. The sun tops a ridge to spill its goodness into the val-ley, banishing shadows and glancing off jewels of frost, and after bowls of cinnamon-flavoured rice pudding we set off up-valley, our breath steaming.

Having crossed the stream on semi-submerged rocks, we ascend a long spur on a clear *yak* trail that eventually takes us round a hollow, from which we gain our first view of the Baga La. We're on snow now; snow with an icy crust. In places the track made by yesterday's *yak* train is hard-packed polished ice. What with the altitude and the effort of staying upright, the approach to the pass is more exacting than it warrants. At about 5170 metres the Baga La is not much more than 600 metres above our camp, but this morning I find the going tough and look forward to reaching what appears to be a long saddle marked by a pile of stones and prayer flags.

As on the Numa La, an icy wind hammers across the pass, where we linger only long enough to capture the scene through the lens of our cameras. Steve has two, and his fingers are soon wooden with the cold. This is no place to sit and dream, so we make our way down the western side on slopes of scree and rocks bereft of snow until we're directed into a hollow, where an alfresco lunch is waiting. This time Mingma, Tashi and Kumar hover over a cooking pot of fried rice (no longer even warm at this altitude) with pilchards, which they ladle onto plates for us. I'm amazed, as are Martin, Steve, Alan and Wendy. Here we are, crouching in a rocky hollow at around 5000 metres, eating cold rice and fish off tin plates. Okay, it's not a gourmet meal, but it's filling – and far more than we have a right to expect. No doubt working under Kirken's direction, Amit has come up trumps once more.

As soon as we've finished, the three Sherpas take our plates and the empty pot and dash off down the mountainside. Half an hour later we meet Mingma returning towards us. This time he's carrying a large kettle in one hand and half a dozen mugs swinging from his fingers. Amit, star that he is, has stopped at the first stream and made a brew for us, so we stand overlooking the idyllic valley of the Maduwa Khola and slake our thirst on mug after mug of hot lemon-flavoured tea.

So different from anything we've seen so far in Dolpo, this valley could have been transported from the Alps. Flanked by immense rock slabs on one side and mountains wearing hanging glaciers on the other, meadows, streams and waterfalls focus our eyes towards pinewoods and a barrier of big snow mountains far off. There are no bare brown hills this side of the Baga La; this is part alpine, part Himalayan, and we're enchanted by everything we see. Having dropped below 4000 metres, vegetation seems unbelievably lush as we wander across meadows among juniper and dwarf cypress trees, avoiding the burrows of Himalayan marmots.

On such a meadow our porters dump their loads and within moments our tents are shaken from their bags. Kirken beams with pleasure. 'Good place for camp?' he asks, indicating the luxurious nature of the valley. A waterfall sprays down a crag nearby, and when the last rays of the sun catch it, individual diamonds linger in the air for a brief moment. 'It'll do for now,' I answer with a grin.

Phoksumdo Lake is only a morning's walk away. But what a walk it is! It takes us past a group of low stone buildings patched with dung, across more meadows and through stands of blue pine, always on the right flank of the valley with the river cutting far below to disappear in a narrow gorge. Our trail squeezes between clumps of berberis, cotoneaster with tiny red berries, and ground-hugging juniper; we look down on the houses of a small village set among low terraced fields, the harvest having been taken and stacked on rooftops. And as we turn a spur, we're pulled up short by the sight of the Kanjiroba range dominating a scene of innumerable mountains, ridges and hinted valleys fading into infinity.

Narrow and exposed in places, the trail eventually turns more to the north, where we catch sight of the Suli Gad waterfall, reputedly the finest in Nepal, and several minutes later see the turquoise Phoksumdo Lake ahead, flanked by steep brown crags with the huddled buildings of Ringmo nearby.

Ever since reading *The Snow Leopard* I've dreamed of this lake – and the narrow ledge of a trail above the western shore that Matthiessen took on his way to Shey Gompa via the Kang La. Both

Matthiessen and Snellgrove before him spoke highly of this great sheet of water stretching back some five kilometres into the mountains, and seeing it for myself at long last is a revelation. The water is so crystal clear and of such a luminous colour, it holds our attention; but only briefly, for a gusting wind scuds across the lake and stirs the dust around our tents into miniature whirlwinds. There should be a meadow here, but it's been overgrazed by goats that have churned the ground, destroying plantlife and reducing what apparently was once a beautiful greensward into a small desert of ankle-deep dust. Yet it's the only place we're allowed to camp. Within half an hour of our arrival, dust has thickened our hair and invaded our ears, eyes and nostrils. I can't remember the last time I felt so dirty, so escape with Karma, Tashi and Mingma to the Tshowa Gompa, which stands on a natural shelf above the southeast shore, where the dust is less pervasive.

Apparently the old Bon monastery is 800 years old – its location idyllic. With the lake below and the crags behind festooned with prayer flags, the *gompa* is guarded by a row of 11 chortens. In one of its buildings religious murals fade into darkness, but when we hear chanting and the beating of drums, Mingma leads the way to a neighbouring building. Climbing a notched-log ladder, we duck through a doorway to enter a room where four monks are going through their devotions.

The Suli Gad drains out of the Phoksumdo Lake, and we cross the river on a bridge below Ringmo to trudge downhill on a dusty eroded trail through poor meadows amid low-growing trees and scrub. Half a dozen pack ponies come towards us, disturbing the dust that settles on the ragged clothes of the group of pony-men who follow behind, and who pass with barely a glance our way. The trail rises again, as we walk through a grove of silver birch a backward view reveals the lake glistening in the sunlight, with the waterfall exploding far below. So loud is its roar that we can barely hear each other speak. Of Ringmo's houses there is no sign.

In order to reach a valley that should lead to our next pass crossing, our descent reverses part of the journey made by Matthiessen and George Schaller in their search for the elusive snow leopard. But shortly after passing their bridge, which takes the Dunai trail to the left bank, and having had our permits checked at the headquarters of the Shey-Phoksumdo National Park, we reach Sumduwa, turn our backs on the Suli Gad (and Matthiessen's route) and enter the valley of the Pungmo Khola.

In its lower reaches this is a narrow wedge of a valley, but as we approach Pungmo village the flanking walls ease back as if to bid us welcome. Entering through a *kani* we hear the sounds of chanting coming from the *gompa*, and within moments we're surrounded by villagers – adults as well as children. There is no begging, no tugging at our clothes. The villagers of Pungmo are polite and friendly, but naturally inquisitive. Kirken strikes up a conversation with one of the older women who totters off to gather a large basket of apples for us. They're among the crispest, juiciest apples I've ever tasted, but they won't last long as the porter given the job of adding them to his loaded *doko* suddenly becomes a generous soul and offers them to all and sundry.

Small birds dart among trees wearing autumn colours as we continue up-valley, the river chuntering off to our left, and about half an hour above Pungmo we come to Doju, whose few houses stand haphazard fashion among bare fields. Outside one of the buildings three teenage girls giggle behind scarves placed demurely over their mouths, then one bravely offers me an apricot. Fortunately, before popping it in my mouth I notice a maggot crawling from it, and as I toss the fruit away the girls burst into laughter.

Kids, eh!

We camp on an almost flat meadow, with the sweet smell of pine lingering in the late afternoon. The Pungmo Khola sings to us nearby, and as we draw water from it a sudden flash of iridescent blue announces the presence of a kingfisher. To our left rise the mountains of the Kagmara range; to our right, those of Kanjiroba. It's a perfect site, and as I listen to the contented voices of my friends as they relax in the sunshine, hear the laughter of our Sherpas, and watch the porters gather dead wood for a fire I'm irrepressibly happy. If this trek were to continue for another six weeks, I'd not complain.

Our next camp is pitched about 600 metres higher, at the foot of Kagmara I. My altimeter reads 4300 metres, but we're all well acclimatised now, and no one even mentions a headache. To get here we had to climb through the steep and rocky Julung Gorge, the trail working its way up the left-hand wall. At around 4000 metres there was a narrow belt of rhododendrons – not in bloom, of course, but it was good to see them, for they were our first on this trek. On the far side of the gorge half a dozen *bharal* tripped across a seemingly featureless rock face; we saw them later grazing a meadow as we made our way towards the head of the Julung Valley, the Kanjiroba massif behind us spreading its snowy mantle over a sea of jutting peaks. It was on that meadow, surrounded by unnamed mountains of 5500 metres, that Amit spoilt us with a lunch of fluffy omelettes, freshly made cinnamon rolls and a spicy hot apple sauce. How does he do it?

An hour and a half later, Kagmara I fills the view from my tent doorway. It's an astonishing sight, and I wonder what Ralph and Isabelle would make of it. I hope they're happy wherever they are, and safely on their way to Kathmandu.

Kathmandu? I shake the thought from my mind and embrace the present, for one of our porters complains of toothache. '*Rakshi*' Joe earned his name a couple of evenings ago when he went with Karma to collect some food left in a bag at one of the villages, but he got himself so drunk on home-made *rakshi* that long after dark he was brought back to camp tied to a rope like a recalcitrant dog to stop him falling in the river. Now groaning with pain and holding his head in his hands, in the absence of Ralph he turns to me for help. Rakshi Joe was never the cheeriest of our crew, but I guess this afternoon he has good reason for looking unhappy. Toothache is lousy anywhere; at altitude, with frost creeping into the valley, it must be sheer misery. Checking his mouth for any obvious cause for his distress, and being unable to find any cavities, I give him a couple of ibuprofen and hope they'll ease his pain.

Borrowing my binoculars, Kirken sends two of his Sherpas to scout the route to the Kagmara La, and they return just before dark to report a safe and easy route. 'Two hours, plenty,' they say, which I assume refers to the time it will take to reach the pass – a climb of around 800 metres. They know nothing of the descent on the far side; that is for tomorrow to determine.

Our day begins by crossing the Julung Khola. The stream is covered with ice, but as it's not thick enough to carry our weight we search for suitable rocks to use as stepping stones. Of course, these are all ice-glazed too, and it takes 20 minutes before we're all safely across. In heavy frost we then wend our way up a dome of rock and grass at the head of an old glacial trough, cross a brief level of pasture, then follow a clear trail bearing west that has been used for decades by *yak* caravans.

Despite the cold and the wind that buffets the flag-bedecked cairn on the 5115 metre summit of the Kagmara La, we spend at least half an hour on the pass, soaking up the huge panoramic view that includes most of the Kagmara range to the south, Kang Chunne to the north, the Kanjiroba massif to the north and east, and far off to the southeast the impressive Dhaulagiri once more. And could that be Annapurna…?

Dolpo, a land unlike any other I've visited, seems to be melding into a more recognisable Himalayan landscape now, and for the first time it strikes me that our journey could be drawing to a close. This barren, gritty saddle is still part of Dolpo, remains within the Shey-Phoksumdo National Park, and yet – and yet, it gives the impression of being on the borders of something different, for a great arc of snow mountains appears to enclose the hidden land. Are we about to make an escape? If so, it'll be an involuntary escape so far as I'm concerned.

It's almost with reluctance that I follow Kirken's lead and descend into the valley of the Garpung Khola.

Tonight our tents are pitched on a grassy bluff starred with tiny edelweiss. There are edelweiss everywhere, and in the darkness their silver-grey heads glisten with frost to match in numbers and brilliance the stars of the Milky Way overhead. And after dinner, on our way from the mess tent to our sleeping bags, we're stopped in our tracks as a yellow moon rises out of the valley far below us. It's the first time I've ever looked down on the moon, and find it hard to drag myself from the scene.

At first the way down the Garpung Khola's valley is rough underfoot and demands full attention. Several tributaries are crossed, some of which are still iced over where the sun has yet to make its mark, but after making our way to the right bank on a bridge of birch logs and flat stone slabs, the trail eases a little. The sun is full on us now, the vegetation abundant. The scent of herbs rises as we walk; then the unmistakable smell of cannabis takes over. We pass through pockets of hot air where lizards sun themselves on wayside rocks. Tiny mice scamper in and out of shadows. The air becomes saturated with fragrance and is thick, too, after our days at altitude; there's no need to check my altimeter to know we've lost a lot of height. Both forest and hillside wear autumn colouring.

One of Amit's alfresco lunches appears near the army check post at Toijem. The midday sun has a delicious warmth, and in moments Alan, Wendy, Martin and Steve are fast asleep, while Kirken tells me about his schooldays in Junbesi. He recalls Ed Hillary building the school (one of the first he gave to the Sherpa people through the Himalayan Trust), and how he'd provided a scholarship for him to attend high school in Kathmandu. 'Good man, Sir Hillary,' he assures me.

A few minutes after we set off again, the Jagdula Khola rushes in from the north to dominate the lesser flow of the river we've been following all morning. The confluence is a thunder of wild water exploding against huge boulders.

Twenty minutes after having our permits checked at the Toijem army post, we have them scrutinised once more at the final check post of the Shey-Phoksumdo National Park, and an hour or so later arrive at the bustling village of Huricot. It is bustling too, this afternoon, for the last fields of barley and buckwheat are being harvested. There's the sound of threshing; straw is being stacked on flat rooftops; women pound grain with pestle and mortar; another sits at a loom in the yard in front of her house; hens strut to and fro among a scurry of yellow chicks. There's more activity here than we've seen since leaving Dho, and as the altitude is a modest 2600 metres, the air is thicker, warmer and filled with a potpourri of exotic aromas.

As we set up camp near the *gompa*, two chickens have been bought for dinner, along with a generous supply of *chang* and *rakshi* for the crew. The villagers have stacks of firewood, and Kirken pays for a load so that the porters can have another fire this evening. There's an air of end-of-trek about these preparations, even though we still have several days to go before we're due in Jumla.

'Now the big cold passes are behind us,' Kirken tells me, 'we make the boys happy. This is celebration time.'

And celebrate they do, with a fire whose flames leap into the night sky as mugs and bowls of *chang* and *rakshi* do the rounds. The *lama* from the *gompa* joins us for an hour and sits beside Kirken, his round Mongolian face shining in the firelight. A long tubular drum appears, and to its beat someone starts to sing. Before long the night reverberates to the sound of voices growing ever more excited as the home brews take effect.

Two days later we cross our final pass. At around 3800 metres the Mauri Lagna is the lowest of our journey through the hidden land, but it's a worthy one, with distant mountains filling horizons both ahead and behind. Back the way we've come, the Dhaulagiri massif once more climbs into view as it tops a familiar sea of ridge and summit; familiar, of course, from our efforts of the past days and weeks. We've earned that view, while ahead there's country still unknown to us where unfamiliar mountains jostle for domination. We stand there together – porters and Sherpas; Kirken with a delicate stomach this morning; Steve, Martin and Wendy, and Alan with whom I've shared scores of passes since we first climbed together 30 years ago. Aware that our trek is drawing to a close, the crew are happy and look forward to going home; I suspect the same can be said of my friends – and of a big part of me too, although I'm torn between a love of family and the comfort of home, and the glorious freedom of wild places. None of it should be taken for granted.

Kirken and I watch the others as they descend below snow-dusted peaks that tower over the bare hills of the Jagdula Lekh and are then swallowed by a dense bank of rhododendrons. He and I are reluctant to move, so we sit side by side and let the moments pass. The last sounds of porters working their way through woodland far below fade into the stillness of the morning. A bird calls; another answers. Then silence.

Far ahead, beyond converging ridges that fold one against another, a great block of snow and ice hangs in the sky. Divorced from its roots by a skein of mist, it has no connection with the Earth, but hovers like a cloud bank untouched by any shifting wind. I'm mesmerised by it.

'What's that?' I ask Kirken.

He looks over his shoulder, checking to see if anyone is within earshot. There's no one. We are alone.

Leaning closer until our shoulders press, he taps the side of his nose, and in a stage whisper tells me.

'Saipal. I must go there!'

And with those five words another dream is born….

CHAPTER 7

Api to Jumla

NEPAL'S FARTHEST WEST
(1997)

I journey through untrekked regions of the Farthest West, becoming lost,
hungry and physically wrecked.

That snowy vision of Saipal remained with me long after our journey through Dolpo's hidden land had ended, so a plan was hatched to devise a way for Kirken and me to trek there as soon as possible. But the following year I was committed to spending practically the whole summer in the Alps, and the autumn organising and leading a trek around Manaslu once more – this time for my wife and two friends on their first visit to Nepal, with Kirken taking care of the logistics. By now he was very much 'My Man in Nepal', with whom I'd developed both trust and understanding, and – since neither of us could get Saipal out of our minds – after celebrating our successful circuit of Manaslu we arranged to meet in Kathmandu the following spring.

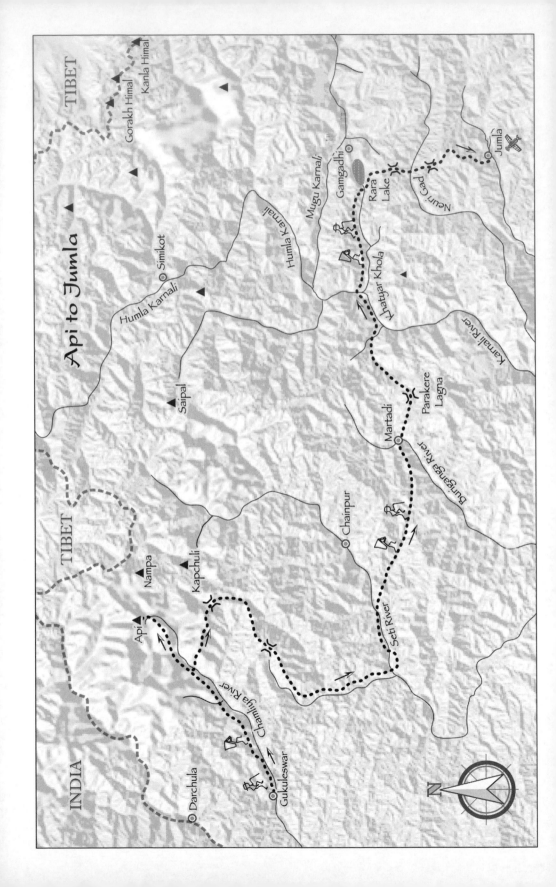

Api to Jumla

TIBET

Gorakh Himal

Kanla Himal

TIBET

Simikot

Humla Karnali

Humla Karnali

Saipal

Mugu Karnali

Gamgadhi

Rara Lake

Jumla

Neunj Gad

Khatyar Khola

Kamali River

INDIA

TIBET

Nampa

Api

Kapchuli

Chainpur

Martadi

Parakere Lagna

Bunganga River

Chamilya River

Seti River

Darchula

Gukuleswar

N

For three days and nights we make our way to Nepal's Farthest West on a succession of battered, garlanded, dust-engulfed, smoke-belching buses – horns blaring, music screeching; locals throwing up out of the windows; livestock and baggage; and at least 30 passengers at a time perched on the roof. It's a nightmare of a journey, with the vehicles becoming more crowded the further west we travel. On one of these buses, Kirken and Chombe are crammed into the driver's cab, which they share with no less than 15 other passengers, while I and the rest of his crew whom Kirken has brought along to act as porters are wedged inside the main seating area. No sooner are we squeezed aboard than an urgent tugging at my leg tells me I'm actually standing on an old man squatting on the floor. Shortly after, at a bend in the road, I'm aware that Mila has no physical connection with the vehicle at all, and is outside, hanging on to Dorje, who clings to the open door. Thrusting an arm through the opening I grab Mila's wrist, and we remain like that for the next 20 minutes.

It's the most dangerous 20 minutes I have ever spent in the Himalaya – and we're still only on a road in the foothills.

At a three-way junction we wait for several hours in a dusty village for the next bus to come along. This is hot, low-lying country, but a line of shapely snow peaks forms the northern horizon; with the Indian border not all that far away, we speculate that what we gaze on could be Trisul, Nanda Devi, Api and Nampa.

Api, a shapely 7000 metre mountain towering over the India–Nepal–Tibet border, is where we're headed, for Kirken has a plan which goes beyond our original intention simply to trek to Saipal. Instead of making a direct approach from the south via the Seti or Karnali river valleys, we aim to work our way to it from the west – as far west as we can go in Nepal – and then, after reaching Saipal, we'll continue heading east until we come to Jumla, where we'd ended our trek across Dolpo 16 months ago. 'That way we fill all gaps,' he said. And who could argue with the logic in that?

This is not a commercial venture. Kirken and I will cover all costs equally, and the five members of his team who volunteered to join us to

211

carry the loads have agreed to do so for porters' wages and the adventure of the unknown. We've no idea how long it will take. Nor are there any guarantees that we'll make it all the way, but we carry food for three weeks, and when that runs out we hope to buy more from any villages we come to. In truth, we travel with little more than a wish and a prayer.

Ten kilometres from the Indian border, Gukuleswar is in festive mood. The small road-head township is almost lost amid the wood smoke of numerous cooking fires. There are tents and awnings, and a bustling, good-natured gaggle of brilliant saris and dazzling teeth; a cacophonous swell of chatter and laughter, of bells and trumpets and belching buffalo; of shrill cries and the joyous greetings of friends and family members all gathered here to celebrate a major Hindu festival. A bedlam of sound is hurled against a background of rushing water, as the Chamliya River surges over a makeshift causeway destined not to last much longer. It reminds me of Namche Bazaar on market day, but with the level of excitement cranked up several notches.

After three days and as many sleepless nights on the road, this is no place to recover from our journey, so after slaking our thirst and having a bite to eat, Kirken and I find the police post to have details of my permit entered in the ledger. That will enable us to move out of town to somewhere more peaceful. But first, the policeman has to find the ledger; then the all-important rubber stamp to give my permit the seal of approval. He searches through two drawers of his desk, rummages among piles of paper and shrugs. He has no idea where it could be. Yet without that stamp on my permit there could be trouble if we're stopped by other officials, so Kirken insists on the policeman signing and dating it instead. He does so with a flourish, then holds the grey card up to the light for our approval. Free to go now, we emerge from the wooden shack to the carnival of noise and colour that is Gukuleswar on a hot spring afternoon.

It's not easy fighting our way through the crowds, especially for our overloaded porters, but the policeman does his best to guide us to the edge of town and wishes us well with a handshake. We'd hoped to hire a man or two to share some of the loads, but no one is interested in leaving the festive atmosphere of town in exchange for a few days of hard labour in high temperatures, so it's a case of gritting teeth and making the most of it. But half an hour later, as we pause in the shade of a tree on the east bank of the river, Kirken enters into conversation with a local man who tells him he's twice been as far north as Api Base Camp, and when we set off again he joins us on the trail, carrying the two primus stoves from Dorje's *doko*. I don't know what Kirken says to him, but before long he has persuaded the man to porter a full load for us as far as Api for 200 rupees per day.

Above Gukuleswar there are no snow mountains on show, but the valley holds plenty of interest – with terraces of wheat and barley, bananas growing beside scattered houses, walnut trees throwing circles of shade, the trail bordered by drystone walls or cactus hedges, tiny water mills built over side streams, and a Hindu shrine with blood-red images and strips of yellow cloth. I try to take it all in, living today in order to relive it all in some distant tomorrow.

We camp early on a level patch of grass a step or two above the Chamliya River, and within moments I'm waist deep in the water, ridding myself of the red dust that had accumulated over the days since we left Kathmandu – already that seems like half a lifetime ago. It's certainly another world away.

Dusk settles over the hills and slides into the valley. No one speaks as we devour a pot of cabbage soup between us, tuck into plates of spicy noodles with tuna and grated cheese, and drink mug after mug of sweet black tea. Our new porter tells us his name is Gunasham, that he and his family live in a village somewhere between here and Api, and since he's on his way home with only a small bag over his shoulder, it makes sense for him to earn a few days' wages. Already he's been accepted as one of the team by Mila, Pemba, Dorje, Chombe and the man whose name I cannot fathom, whom I call JP. JP is new to me; the others I've

213

already trekked with, either in Dolpo or around Manaslu, for they're regular members of Kirken's staff who have proved their worth and are good company.

In the spring of 1980 an expedition from the British Army Mountaineering Association trekked through the Chamliya River valley to make an attempt on the South Face of Api, and a photograph of their porters and climbers striding along a foothill track, with the Api-Nampa range stretched across the horizon, was reproduced nine years later in *High Asia*, an illustrated history of the Himalayan 7000 metre peaks. It's an evocative image that gave me hope of seeing that same exciting view for myself; but, sadly, it's not to be. We're too close. Despite the landscape being broad and open, all big mountain views are obstructed by converging ridge systems to the north, while Gunasham warns us that the valley will soon narrow to little more than a ravine and reduce our views even further. But that's fine for now – my imagination has been stirred, and I'm happy simply to be here.

It's good to be on the move once more, on a journey full of unknowns. Chewing sticks of sugar cane as we walk, we cross numerous tributaries and pass through villages where locals stand and stare, for white faces are rare in this far corner of Nepal; there are no other trekkers, and it's clear that my presence brings novelty to their day. Long processions of laden goats and sheep bully past, hundreds to a flock, and squeeze between drystone walls. Dribbling by the trail, buffalo with bulging eyes flare their nostrils and shake their heads to disrupt the flies that taunt them. The smell of livestock is ever present; it's carried by shepherd and goat herder from one side of the mountains to the other. No doubt we smell of livestock too.

It's hot, and we pour sweat as we follow the trail high above the Chamliya's gorge. We're all desperate for shade; the temperature has settled at 36 degrees, there's not even a breeze, we've run out of water and every step is a challenge. But suddenly we top a high point and there, several days ahead, a great wall of rock appears, plastered with snow and ice and crowned with a bank of cloud. 'Api', says Gunasham, and for a moment I forget the pounding of my heart and heaving lungs as I absorb the vision. Then the cloud bank sinks and Api disappears.

The trail slopes downhill to a lonely teahouse, where we crowd inside to avoid the sun. A thick stew of ginger and cinnamon tea bubbles under an evil-looking froth, but it tastes like nectar when mixed with milk and enough sugar to destroy all the enamel on my teeth. The boys help themselves to endless jugs of cold water filled from a spring, but like me Kirken chooses tea and slurps the hot sweet liquid while chatting with two women standing outside. Both wear nose jewellery, extravagant earrings, and bangles on their wrists; their heads are covered in richly coloured scarves, one scarlet, the other mauve; their saris are summer pink; one wears flip-flops, and the other well-worn trainers. Their voices are shrill as cicadas, and they laugh a lot. Gathering the moment, I fill the well of memory.

The gorge is incredibly deep. In Dolpo I thought the Tarap gorges were narrow, but the Chamliya's is something else. So narrow, in places it's little more than a slice ripped through the land, and on both banks of the silver thread of water snow-free mountains erupt in crag and unbelievably steep slopes of grass. When I see two women cutting hay I find it hard to imagine how they maintain a foothold. There is no level ground, and teetering along the west side of the gorge our trail becomes the ultimate helter-skelter route that punishes anyone carrying a heavy load. Our boys are burdened with huge loads – even with Gunasham taking a share – and my heart goes out to them. And yet the moment we stop for a rest, their eyes flash and laughter echoes across the valley. They have my admiration. It's a privilege to travel with them.

Four days of hard going bring us to a woodland glade near the head of the gorge at almost 3000 metres, and here we make camp, surrounded by rhododendrons. The trees are in full bloom, while beneath them rag-ged-edged primulas emerge from the leaf mould of countless autumns. This is my first Himalayan spring, and although the weather is much warmer but less settled than in the post-monsoon seasons, the plant life is vibrant in its variety. Finding numerous species I do not recognise only serves to underline my ignorance.

There's plenty of dead wood available, so this evening we light a fire and, with plates of food before us, bathe in its glow and discuss the route ahead. We cannot be far from Api, but our map does little to inspire confidence. Contour lines are drawn at 500 metre intervals, and I swear we've seen at least one mountain of around 6000 metres that does not appear on our sheet. Gunasham also disputes the names of some of the villages we've passed through, so we're left with a certain amount of guesswork based on observation. Rather than being intimi-dated by that, I find it strangely encouraging.

For some reason I do not understand, Gunasham remains in camp with Dorje, while Kirken, Mila, Chombe, Pemba, JP and I set out for Api Base Camp. Since he's the only one of us who's been there, and his guiding has been impeccable so far, it seems odd that the local man does not come with us. But here we are, shortly before 7 o'clock in the morning, stum-bling up-valley on frosty ground, with a gusting wind and clouds hang-ing low with the threat of snowfall. Before long we have to fight our way through a screen of towering bamboo, beyond which lies an open patch of delicate mauve flowers. A flimsy bridge takes us over a torrent, followed by a tough climb up a wooded spur that forms a cornerstone of the side valley we've just crossed, but as we emerge from the trees there are none of the views we'd hoped for as the first snow flurries drift around us. A few days ago we were shrivelled by the heat; now winter threatens a return.

We sense mountains we cannot see, stumble through drifts of old winter snow, and disturb pheasants spooked by our approach. Suddenly Kirken lifts my spirits by pointing out the pug marks of a snow leop-ard. Having studied this most elusive of Himalayan animals, he knows what to look for, and we follow its trail until the snow drifts run out. Somewhere in the gloom there may be eyes upon us.

At well over 3000 metres my legs feel heavy this morning. Snow flurries thicken and settle on the damp ground. We continue nevertheless and come to a viewpoint overlooking a small ravine, across which there's a great basin of pasture and woodland backed by a mountain wall whose lower slopes are all that's visible. Could this be Api? I study the map, take a compass bearing and convince myself that it is.

Descending into the ravine by a slope of unstable snow, we then climb out the other side, spilling minor avalanches of loose rock and soil as we do, before advancing across the pasture to a stand of holly oak draped with lime-green lichens. A smaller summer pasture lies beyond the trees, patched still with winter, and as we cross to another belt of woodland at the foot of the mountain, snow falls more heavily to blur our vision. A grey misty light closes in. Flanked by a mystical world of rock, snow and ice, and unsure of where we are, we build a fire on the edge of the woodland, make a brew and discuss our options.

Shall we go on in search of a mountain we may not see? Or return to our camp? The boys don't seem to care one way or another; they express no opinions and appear to have no expectations other than to walk with Kirken and me day after day with heavy loads.

I admire that attitude of not caring, although it's not one I share. A year ago Api did not feature at all in my plans, but once Kirken and I began to discuss our journey to and beyond Saipal, this bastion of Nepal's Farthest West took on an identity of its own. It became a symbolic starting point for our adventure, although in truth that adventure began many days ago, so this is almost a diversion. It's not as though we have any ambition to climb the damn thing, but having come this far it would be rewarding simply to see it close to.

Not much chance of that today, though.

But as Kirken and I discuss what to do next, the snowfall eases, a vague patch of blue appears through a tear in the clouds, and mountains whose shapes have been hidden until now begin to show themselves. To the southeast Kapchuli (I think it must be) bursts through the mist to reveal a multi-summited ridge, while above us the shape we'd almost convinced ourselves to be Api shows that it's not – for a much bigger, more impressive peak rises behind and to the right of it. Through a dance of the seven veils a wall of rock and ice is displayed, soaring up and up to a seemingly level summit ridge. There's only one mountain it could possibly be.

So *that* is Api!

This all-too-brief vision satisfies both Kirken and me. We finish our tea, kick snow onto the fire and retrace our route back to the woodland camp.

In conversation by the campfire last night, Gunasham had asked Kirken about Kathmandu. He'd never been there, and had no prospect of ever going there, but was inquisitive about that distant city. Kirken said he could come with us. 'Carry a load to Jumla,' he urged. 'And I will fly you to Kathmandu, show you around and then pay for your journey home.' Gunasham was excited by the offer and, without hesitation, agreed.

Bemused by his spontaneity, by his readiness to grasp a fresh opportunity with no apparent consideration for its effect upon others, I remembered how several days ago we'd passed a trail that led to his home. He didn't bother to take it, or even to send a message to his wife to explain that he'd be delayed by going to Api Base Camp with us. And now he's prepared to trek for several weeks to Jumla, fly to Kathmandu, and eventually return home by bus – he could be gone for months. Meanwhile, as far as his wife and family know, he's just gone to Gukuleswar for a few days…

We backtrack for a long morning, stopping for half an hour in one of the highest villages to collect the bags of food and gear we'd stashed there on the way up. It's a friendly but extremely dirty place in which we're surrounded by numerous unwashed adults and children with snotty faces, many of whom have chesty coughs and openly sneeze around us. TB is rife in some of these remote, smoky villages, and I'm anxious to be away from it.

Leaving the village we continue in sunshine to a high point where we gain a clear view of Api – why couldn't the weather have been like this yesterday? Passing through more tiny villages, Gunasham then guides us away from the main trail to descend a precipitous twisting path to the Chamliya River. The gorge is almost at its narrowest point here, and it's a long way to its bed; despite the severity of the slope, a few terraces have been created two-thirds of the way down. Apparently they belong to one of the villages we'd passed on the main trail, so to work these fields would involve some epic labour, the thought of which only increases my admiration for the farmers who eke out an existence in such an unforgiving land.

Some way below the terraces we come across an attractive, neatly dressed woman in her early 30s resting on a patch of grass. Her jet black hair shines, dark eyes sparkle and her smile reveals teeth that will never know a dentist's drill. When she stands I notice she's several months pregnant, and Kirken learns that, coincidentally, she's a midwife on her way home from helping with a difficult birth in some far-off village. With a brief nod, she indicates that her home is high above us on the opposite bank. Since that's the direction we're going, she joins us as we wander alongside the river, with the walls of the gorge soaring overhead, then cross a bridge and begin the steep ascent. The hillside makes no concessions; it's a brutal climb, yet the woman chatters all the way. She eventually steers us along a contouring path that deserts the main trail and leads to a neat whitewashed house with a tidy yard screened by a row of trees full of pink blossom. A few more houses can be seen on the slopes above, while we're shown to a bare terrace on which we can spend the night. The tents are hardly up when mist spills off the mountains, thunder crackles and it begins to rain.

Gunasham has left us. Complaining of a fever, he's gone back to his wife and family. Last night he slept in the midwife's house, where Kirken reckons he was reminded of home comforts; weighing them against the rigours of a journey through unfamiliar country, he decided that not even the promise of a visit to Kathmandu was worth the effort and discomfort of our trek. Although we shall miss him, there are no hard feelings, but his absence means that the boys are left with full loads to carry once more.

It's not only Gunasham we will miss. Last night Kirken arranged for a local man to guide us over mountains to the east, but he doesn't show up this morning. We make enquiries, but there's no sign of him. Neither can we persuade anyone from the nearby houses to porter for us for a few days, so there's no alternative but to trust our questionable map, shoulder the loads and work our own way. At least the sky has cleared and visibility is good as we stumble among a veritable maze of little paths climbing over, around and alongside small terraced fields, gaining height as we do.

In the middle of the morning we emerge onto a high plateau of farmland, where fields are being ploughed by cows and scrawny buffalo. Women and children follow the plough with wicker baskets of potatoes and dung, dropping one potato at a time into the furrow, covering it with a handful of manure, then kicking newly turned soil on top of that. Our arrival does nothing to disturb the work; we could be invisible, as far as they're concerned, as could the mountains at the head of the valley, where Api is revealed once more.

A little later we arrive in a village of smoke-grimed, stone-built houses. Once again there are trees in blossom with livestock snuffling in their shade. 'If we can get food here, shall we stop to eat?' asks Kirken. That sounds like a good idea, and as the last harvest was a good one we're soon squatting outside one of the houses with eight kilos of piping hot potatoes in their skins and no less than 18 boiled eggs. At first glance it looks like a feast, but there are seven of us, we're all hungry, and we make short work of the simple meal, leaving only egg shells and fragments of potato skin uneaten.

Villagers stand before us, our presence being their only form of entertainment. Unlike the farmers we'd seen earlier, both adults and children are unashamedly curious, commenting on my glasses, grey hair and beard. And although I may not speak their language, it's not difficult to gather the gist of what they're saying. Meanwhile grubby hands fumble with my rucksack and camera, but I have no reason to suspect that any of them are light-fingered, although I'm concerned at the amount of coughing and sneezing that is going on. This is another unhealthy place, and as with the small village where we stopped briefly yesterday, I'm eager to depart. I sense Kirken's unease too. But first we need to gather information about the way ahead, and while no one is prepared to guide us, there's no shortage of advice about the route we should take, and I have every confidence in Kirken's ability to translate that advice into something tangible.

Above the village we work our way through a band of holly oak almost bereft of branches, then turn a spur overlooking a deep, narrow and heavily wooded valley. On the far side we can make out what must be the pass that we need to cross in order to reach Chainpur, southwest of Saipal on the Seti River. The pass is unmarked upon our map, but the compass tells us we're heading in the right direction, so when a narrow path entices us on, we shuffle warily along it before plunging steeply down for about 200 metres to cross a stream by a simple log-and-stone bridge.

Climbing the other side involves hauling ourselves up a tangled slope using the roots of rhododendrons and clumps of bamboo. If there ever was a path, it has long since been swallowed by vegetation, but this is definitely the way we've been advised to go – not only by the villagers at the potato feast, but by an elderly woman we saw on the spur opposite, who had pointed to the pass and insisted there was a way to it. So up we go, sweating, cursing, stumbling, and at last emerging above the shrubbery to broken rock and tongues of old crusted snow littered with animal droppings.

Clouds descend and it begins to snow heavily. The boys are dressed for warmer conditions, but make no complaint. Besides, they sweat with the effort until we come at last onto what must be the pass at about 3500 metres. A cold wind is blowing, and there's practically no visibility, but by sheer fluke I discover a path on the far side. Instead of descending, it cuts left, loses a little height, then contours across what I imagine to be the headwall of a deep but unseen valley.

With dense cloud and snowfall, light begins to fade. Our world shrinks to just a few paces, but we press on for another 20 minutes or more, fearful that if we stop too soon, all trace of the path will be lost. Then Kirken shouts against the wind that it's becoming too danger-ous to continue, that we should find somewhere to camp. He's right of course; we need to get some shelter while we know where we are, so turn back with wind-driven snow stinging our faces, drop down into the lee of the pass and put up the tents, by which time it's dark.

It snows heavily for most of the night, but when dawn makes a late appearance I'm relieved to find that only a few light flurries drift in the easing wind. Crawling out of the tent I'm surprised at just how much has fallen since we first arrived, and it's only when the clouds eventually lift a little and visibility extends to 100 metres that we discover yester-day's tracks have disappeared and a small cornice lips over the ridge. Having neither ice axe nor rope for security, we're not tempted to force a route that way, but instead peer into the valley on the far side to see what lies below.

Through my binoculars I detect a small meadow below the snow-line, and what appears to be a path leading from it. Together we discuss our options before Kirken sends Mila and Pemba to scout a possible way down. When they return half an hour later, Mila wears both a wide grin and a furrowed brow, so I'm unsure which one to trust until Kirken interprets: 'He says it *looks* possible – if we are lucky, and very careful.'

That descent is one I'm thankful not to have to face again. That we reach the meadow 900 metres below the pass with only a few cuts and bruises between us is cause for celebration. It goes to show that even in the most difficult, exposed and dangerous of places, Dorje's cherubic face can lift the tension with laughter; it echoes against crags, follows us down unplanned snowslides, and rattles through ravines.

Exchanging winter for spring we follow the narrow trail beyond the meadow, descending steep hillsides among blossom-haloed trees and tiny gentians that remind me of the Alps and Pyrenees. Snow clouds having disappeared now, we're treated to the sweet fragrance of damp grass drying in the sunshine. Although we have little idea where we are, I'm well content as we arrive at last below a settlement of five houses perched on a terraced bluff overlooking the confluence of two streams. Calling a halt, we dump the loads, and in no time at all the primus gives the welcome purr of a meal on the go.

I guess they can smell our *daal bhaat*, for two men appear from the village. One wears homespun, the other an old faded jacket that has been torn and darned so awkwardly it makes his left arm look deformed. Both have extravagant moustaches; one has a straggly beard and smokes a pipe, its bowl turned downward, which he cups in both hands so that the smoke escapes between his fingers. I've no idea what he's smoking, but it has a strange tangy aroma that hangs over him. As they squat on their hunkers, Kirken offers mugs of tea and asks them the name of their village. Since it's not shown on our map the answer is irrelevant, as is the name of the river, which they offer without hesitation. But it would be helpful to know where the valley leads.

'Where does this river go?' asks Kirken. They turn to one another as if to say: why would anyone need to know that? A shrug of the shoulders is their only response. But then the man in the homespun tells us that if we travel downstream for one day we will come to another village. That appears to be the extent of their local knowledge.

The trouble is, the valley drains southwestward, while we need to head east or southeast, and what appears to be an unbroken *lekh* stands

223

in the way, forming a barrier to progress in that direction. Perhaps we'd been too premature in our decision this morning to abandon the ridge path we'd lost in the snow. Had we been more determined to push on, instead of taking what seemed the safest option, we may have been well on our way to the Seti River by now. But 'if onlys' can weigh heavily, and regrets are futile; we've made our decision and must now deal with the consequences. Our only certainty is that we're not going to attempt a return to the ridge. We'll head down-valley instead and see what happens.

It takes three days to reach the Seti River. On the first evening Kirken complains of a fever. I give him my down jacket and tell him to wear it in his sleeping bag to sweat the fever out of his system. But the following morning I have the fever too. My chest hurts with every breath and my head is full of mucus, and for three days the two of us cough our way towards the Seti River valley while our five loyal porters remain annoyingly fit and healthy.

A hunter whom we'd met at a group of houses guides us over the eastern *lekh* on the faintest of trails which leads to a wooded saddle with a glimpse of Api and Nampa between the trees. Kirken and I leak sweat and ache in every limb. A woodpecker drills a dead branch as we emerge from the woodland, while our hunter-guide steams ahead over a grass-covered bluff where a panoramic view extends west of Api to an exciting line of snow peaks of the Garhwal Himal in India. The hunter continues to a pass at a little over 3000 metres, and after the briefest of rests he takes off again, storming up the ridge for another 100 metres or more. Kirken and I struggle to keep up with him, but the boys have found their second wind and seem unaware of their loads.

Where do they find that energy?

Now we stagger downhill, with blue foothills melding into a fuzzy horizon, and collapse on an open meadow that ought to have a stream running through it, but hasn't. Pointing to a valley far below, with the instruction to follow it for two days, our guide tells us this is as far as he's going with us, so Kirken pays him off and we watch him return

As our plane takes off from the meadow airstrip that serves Dolpo, with it goes our last contact with the outside world (Chapter 6)

Dolpo women at work in a threshing yard at Dho Tarap (Chapter 6)

The ancient gompa at Dho is said to be a thousand years old (Chapter 6)

A yak caravan laden with sawn timber approaches the Numa La as we make our descent (Chapter 6)

Bleached by all weathers, prayer flags mark the 5170m Baga La (Chapter 6)

Porters meet villagers in Pungmo (Chapter 6)

A local mother and her daughters rest beside the trail in the Chamliya Valley (Chapter 7)

A young boy from Dho Tarap out collecting yak dung – a priceless fuel in villages above the treeline

Sangye, the horse that carried me over half a dozen Mugu passes; Chongdi, man of few words, keeps a watchful eye (Chapter 8)

Munie, our ever-helpful porter with the winning smile who was with us throughout our Mugu journey (Chapter 8)

Mila sounds his crossing of the 2940m Parakere Lagna (Chapter 7)

Rising near Lake Manasarovar in Tibet, and passing round Saipal, the Karnali is the most important river of Nepal's Farthest West (Chapter 7)

Pack ponies cross the Neuri Gad in the golden light of morning (Chapter 8)

A satellite dish suggests that ancient and modern come together on a Mugu dwelling (Chapter 8)

The upper reaches of the Mugu Karnali's valley – a rugged, uncompromising land for trekking (Chapter 8)

Rara Lake, a serene stretch of water at the heart of a national park (Chapter 8)

The row of ancient chortens that guides the way to Mangri (Chapter 8)

uphill without so much as a backward glance. In no time at all he's little more than a speck of shadow on a distant hillside.

It's midday, there is no shade and our throats are parched. Hundreds of metres below, snaking through the valley we're aiming for, a green twist of river taunts our thirst. I have half a litre of cold tea left in my flask, but it doesn't go far when I hand it round; a couple of glugs each and it's gone. Shaking the empty flask I'm suddenly angry with Kirken and his boys. Why can't they think ahead, anticipate long hours without water and fill their bottles before we set out? What's the point of carrying empty bottles in a land none of us has trekked through, when we have no idea when or where we'll next find a spring or accessible stream? They're like stupid, irresponsible children, unable to think beyond this moment. Do they really need me to do their thinking for them?

Then, as quickly as it came, my anger subsides. I look at the size of their loads; I remember the laughter that accompanies each hour on the trail, and the way they pamper me in camp, accept my frailties, my ignorance and, yes, my innocence, and know that without them I'd never have got this far. They are the true heroes of the Himalaya.

But if only they'd carry drinking water of their own...

The valley we've seen from the sun-baked meadow is the key to our route to the Seti River – a lush green swathe, well watered and full of promise. What's more, it provides easy walking through a terraced land dotted with small settlements and sliced with tributaries. In one we pass a man fishing with a net; on the bank of another we come across a cremation site with two forgotten human skulls not yet picked clean. Our pace quickens as we pass.

One morning we come face to face with a smart-looking official carrying an umbrella, accompanied by two heavily laden porters and a colleague with a briefcase.

'Good morning, sir! I am the chief of police of this district. Let me greet you.' He takes my hand and holds it in his for a minute or more, his face beaming, beads of perspiration on his forehead. 'I am going to

Darchula,' he tells me. 'It is a very important town; on the border with India, you know.'

He's uninterested in who we are, where we've been or where we're going, but is delighted to have an opportunity to speak to me in English.

'You may take my photograph,' he says, and stands to attention when I focus the camera.

On another morning we come to a huddle of poor houses astride the trail, and when we pause for a moment, Kirken discovers that one of them has a satellite phone. 'Hey Kev, you could make a call to Min!'

For a moment I'm tempted. It would be so good to speak to my wife at home in Kent, to let her know that all is well, to hear her voice again…but, what if she's not there and I leave a message? How would she interpret that? Would she hear my laboured breathing and the rattling in my chest, and be concerned? Or what if she's at home, but there's a problem? There's nothing I could do to help and I would spend the next few weeks worrying.

'Bugger!' I say aloud, kicking the dust in despair, then decide it's better not to phone home at all. We had no expectation of speaking to one another until I'm back in Kathmandu, so that's the way it'll be. But for the next hour or so I'm riding an emotional seesaw.

By the time we reach the Seti River valley Kirken seems to have sweated the fever out of his system and only complains now of sore knees. I'm still wheezing and, if anything, my chest feels worse than it did a couple of days ago. I sweat and cough the hours away, so reckon it's time to break out the antibiotics.

At least we know where we are now, and in anticipation gaze north-east to where Saipal ought to be. Yet despite being 7000 metres high, it's concealed, like Api and Nampa on our walk-in from Gukuleswar, by an intrusive barrier of snow-free mountains, although Kirken and I remain optimistic that it will show itself in due course.

Tracing the Seti upstream through meadows rich with flowers we wander past an encampment of traders whose goods are stacked high in striped bags, their goats and sheep grazing the hillside nearby. As pack animals have become essential elements in the landscape of this journey of ours, a view down-valley would now seem almost incomplete without them. If not goats or sheep, it could be a string of bell-jangling pack ponies with bulging loads that forces us off the trail. But on the opposite bank of the Seti dark-skinned labourers carve a road through unforgiving rocks, which surely means that the days of the four-legged juggernauts are numbered – soon to be replaced by diesel-belching trucks. The thought weighs me down until we turn a bend, and there ahead snow peaks dazzle the sunshine. Could that be Saipal? It's been 16 months since Kirken and I last set eyes upon it. Though it was the inspiration for our journey, now that it's almost within reach neither he nor I recognise it. Nor, strangely, do we care!

Instead of continuing upstream, we break away from the Seti River to pick up our eastward trend, accompanied for a while by a trader from Humla carrying half a dozen fish hanging from a stick. Gabbling in a dialect containing no sounds remotely familiar to me, I'm impressed once more by Kirken's ability to communicate with strangers in so many different languages and dialects. And it's as well that he can, for the cross-country route we've chosen does not exactly correspond with its depiction on our map, so we rely on local information gathered along the way. I think of it as oral cartography.

Day by day we tramp across lekhs running with streams. Rhododendrons splash the hills with blooms that range from pure white to lemon yellow and the deepest of reds. We mount one pass after another and look down on terraces that fan across the hills, the rich greenery of young millet interrupted by the brilliant scarlet of women bent double at work in the fields. Buffalo complain in the heat of mid-day; there comes the far-off laughter of children; night-time is disturbed by the yapping of jackals. And despite the pain in my chest, the fever that will not leave me, and the constant hacking that almost makes me gag, I could wish for no more than this – this drifting through a poorly mapped land with six willing companions, only one of whom I can properly converse with. For ours is a journey full of unknowns, and that very real sense of mystery adds to its appeal.

One day we descend a steep, roughly made stairway of stone slabs. Ahead of us a farmer leads a pair of buffalo, one of which lifts its tail and leaves a steaming mess on the path. As I reach it a coughing fit makes me falter and miss a step; my right foot slips, I fall into the fresh dung and slide down another three slabs greased by the juicy buffalo shit that now stains my clothes and arm. Behind me I hear Pemba and the other boys howling with laughter, and when I look back at them, they can hardly stand, their giant loads swaying from side to side.

Late one afternoon mist covers the hills and rain begins to fall. We camp early on a grass shelf a safe distance above a stream, and while Dorje and Pemba prepare the meal a storm erupts overhead, and for the next hour we're treated to our own *son et lumière* show that sends arrows of lightning onto the ridge above us.

I wake early on another morning, long before light creeps into the sky, to hear what sounds like raindrops falling. But my tent is dry, and it's only when I peer out that I discover yet another vast flock of laden goats pushing along the nearby trail, their hooves tap-tap-tapping in the dust. There are hundreds of them, and as this is just one of many such flocks, the trails are being chiselled by hundreds of thousands of small cloven hooves. Low clouds of dust follow the animals, settling on trailside vegetation and the clothing of their herders, with whom we have a growing affinity. Although the reasons for our journey are different, we share the same trails, breathe the same dust, have our legs bruised by rock-hard panniers as the same anxious animals bully past, and sleep beneath the same stars as these wild-eyed traders. Once again I recognise the privilege of being here now to witness a way of life that owes its ancestry to some long-lost age, but which is destined not to last much longer.

The Buriganga River drains mountains of almost 6000 metres, which are enough to block any possible view of Saipal when we reach the township of Martadi, midway between the Seti and Karnali river valleys. Perched on a hill above the river, it's a dirty, litter-strewn place, its inhabitants surly and inhospitable, its buildings defaced with political slogans and symbols. Only the police station where I go to have my permit stamped gives any appearance of order. Painted white and standing behind a neat lawn, it's guarded by a uniformed policeman clutching a rifle. I'm impressed by the building. Until, that is, I go inside to find bundles of paper spilling over every surface. Flies cover the windows and dust coats every chair. But the officer in charge is pleasant enough, and when he eventually finishes entering my details in his ledger, he spits on his rubber stamp and presses it onto my permit, which now allows me to enter Bajura district en route to the Karnali.

The morning after we leave Martadi Dorje brings me a mug of tea at 5 o'clock, and we're on our way before light seeps into the hills. Each day that passes seems to be hotter than the last, so we determine to make the most of the cool early hours, and when we set out I tuck behind the shape of JP, whose pace is better suited to mine than that of some of the others who canter ahead, chatting as they go. As the morning matures and temperature rises, any views we might have had are lost in haze, but to make up for their absence I celebrate the banks of rhododendrons, individual trees full of cherry-like blossom beside valley fields, and a riot of fragrant pink daphne bushes on the edge of a woodland where monkeys look down upon us.

Midday finds us crossing the Parakere Lagna at a little under 3000 metres. On the pass itself an archway decorated with rhododendron flowers has a brass bell suspended from it, which none of our porters can resist ringing when they pass beneath it. There are no views, but a few minutes after we've moved on, a distant line of snow peaks emerges through the haze; although they're too far off to be included on our map, Kirken speculates that they could be part of the Kanjiroba massif in Dolpo. I have my doubts. But what do I know?

After weeks on the trail I've lost all sense of time, for since my anti-biotics ran out there is no routine to follow; the days are broken only by the need to eat, drink or to make camp. The drugs have made no difference to this damned chest infection – every day I'm weak and feverish, while every night is disturbed by a rattling in my lungs and a hacking cough that shreds my throat. I drink copious amounts of tea and sweat the liquid out again. But I'm determined not to let it ruin this trek, and as each day passes I'm fully aware of my good fortune in being here, sharing the trails with these unfailingly cheerful companions. What they expect to get out of this adventure is anyone's guess, but their hopes are probably not much different from mine.

The Karnali River represents a major milestone on our journey. The most important river of Nepal's Farthest West, it rises near Lake Manasarovar in Tibet, its watershed falling between Gurla Mandhata and the Saipal Himal. Like the Kali Gandaki that flows between Dhaulagiri and Annapurna, it was draining south long before the Himalaya was born. If we were to follow it upstream, it would take us round the east flank of Saipal to Simikot, the district capital of Humla, whose traders we've been meeting for days. But although that is a tempting option, we dismiss the possibility. We'll stick to our plan to walk to Jumla via Rara Lake. Doing so will at least provide us with a brief introduction to the Karnali, whose west bank we'll follow for a good part of the day.

Sometimes we're almost deafened by the thunder of this powerful blue-green river as it pours over rapids. At other times it glides as a gentle wash between gravel banks and hills peppered with the dusty-grey candelabra cacti – there are so many cactus plants that I'm reminded of Arizona. That's not the only similarity, for the heat is enervating. Trapped between the rocky walls of the valley we gain little respite when the trail climbs high above its bed. It's only when we come down to a sand-and-gravel bank and make direct contact with the water that we can appreciate the cooler air of high mountains being carried by the Karnali's current.

230

Once again we share the trail with Humla goat people and are soon caught up in their relentless caravans. There is the same familiar dust, the bleating, the whistles and yells from their herders; the same smell we carry with us. When we stop at a teahouse, one of the goat men joins us for cups of the ginger soup-like tea that seems to be the standard beverage in this part of Nepal. He has a kindly face, a wispy beard and moustache, and a two-coloured turban wrapped round his head. Seated next to me he fills and lights his pipe, a stubby black chimney-like model with a bulbous head, which he holds vertically against his face so that he can suck the smoke through a cloth placed across a hole in the stem to act as a filter. Every time he exhales, his face is screened by a blue drift of tobacco smoke.

When we leave he soon draws ahead of us to rejoin his animals, but it's not long before we catch them too and, wandering slowly behind the goats, come at last to a large pipal tree with a stone-built *chautaara* in a meadow, with a few thatched buildings nearby. Realising a group of people at one of the houses is from Mugu, Kirken is eager to quiz them about the route we must follow as far as Rara Lake, and is soon deep in conversation with two handsome, mahogany-skinned men and a short, dumpy woman who gives the impression that by sheer force of personality she's the one in charge. In common with many others we've seen on our journey, she wears nose jewellery, a chunky ring on her finger and several coloured bangles on her wrist.

As I say, she's in charge and issues orders to the men, one of whom hands us small clay bowls of *rakshi*. I decline, as do Mila and Dorje. Chombe and JP are unsure, but seeing Kirken and Pemba knock back theirs, they try a little for themselves. Chombe and Pemba refuse a second offering, but JP holds out his bowl for more and soon a strange bewitched smile spreads across his face. Kirken needs no persuasion, and as well as emptying his bowl two or three times, he buys enough of the spirit to fill his water bottle. Mila catches my eye, and together we suggest it's time to move on. Recalling Kirken's confession the first time we met in the Alps, that through drink he'd lost his family, business

231

and all his money, I grow nervous now that he's rediscovered a taste for *rakshi*.

The heat builds in intensity, and without shade we pour sweat. I'm still coughing, my chest rattling, my legs heavy as lead, so when we see the trail climbing high above the river, we stop for an early lunch on a gravel beach. At least we can splash water over ourselves to cool down. Not so Kirken. Within moments he's fast asleep, stretched out on a slither of grey silt while Dorje unpacks his *doko* and prepares a meal. I take Kirken's bottle, empty the *rakshi* into the river and refill it with water.

Chombe and I go ahead of the others, soon puffing our way up the steeply climbing trail until the Karnali shrinks below. The trail is flanked by more of the grey-green cactus with tiny yellow flame-like buds, the stems knitted with cobwebs clogged with dust stirred by the daily passage of numerous pack animals. Although we have few common words between us, we have easy means of communication, and when my breath allows, Chombe and I discuss in the simplest of terms our pleasure in this journey.

The valley kinks to the left, and for a few minutes we lose both sight and sound of the river. Then we turn a spur and it's back again, a thick blue ribbon twisting far below, its rush and roar carried unevenly on the breeze. Ahead a band of cliffs has been sliced by the Karnali like wire passing through a cheese, and beyond the cliffs a green oasis of cultivation can be seen; in it is a flat-roofed village that reminds me of Dho Tarap.

Across the face of those cliffs the trail has been chipped into the rock or built out over empty space. It's an exciting route with plenty of exposure that demands care with every step, but when we come to the end of a particularly delicate traverse, we leave the main trail and descend a precipitous route that leads to a suspension bridge spanning the Karnali. There we wait in the shade for the others, watching the swirl of the river below and the antics of children on a silver beach.

When Kirken and the boys arrive I point out the condition of the bridge, which looks distinctly dangerous, for many timbers are missing and the whole construction appears to be in need of replacement. It's by far the worst of our journey; probably the worst of any I've faced in the Himalaya; but there's no alternative. Usually we cross such bridges together without a thought. This is different. We go one at a time, fearful that the weight of two of us might be enough to destroy it completely, spilling both men and bridge into the river.

Once safely across we enter the valley of the Khatyar Khola which, if our map is to be believed, rises in Rara Lake, and although we still have several days of unknown country ahead of us before we reach Jumla, I sense that we're now on the homeward stretch.

Tonight I stand outside my tent and watch the full moon rise from some undiscovered land beyond the mountains. There's a calm purity about it that settles my mind. Physically I feel wrecked and in need of a long, long rest. But the moon has restorative powers, and as its bright white light floods the hills, far off I catch the now-familiar sound of jackals calling to one another and gain renewed confidence for tomorrow.

We start a new day with stars still shining. It's refreshingly cool as we make our way deeper into a valley so different from that of the Karnali. An hour before dawn no birds sing, and even the boys pad the trail without conversation until the stars go out one by one and a grey light steals across the sky. A cock crows from a village emerging from night. Suddenly children appear, carrying water containers to a stand-pipe. They stand and stare when we pass, return our 'Namastes', but offer no more than a questioning smile.

The trail has few demands as we swing along, lost in our own thoughts, and as the morning develops mountains in the west burn in the sunlight while we still savour the shadows. Now our path rises up the right-hand wall of a gorge, but descends when the valley opens to a wild and stony region in which we disturb half a dozen crows feasting on the carcass of a cow – a recent death by the looks of it, as the hide is still intact; just two bloodied gaping holes where the eyes had been.

233

Our food stocks have dwindled, and although we confidently expected to be able to buy fresh supplies along the way, now that we're in Mugu district there's little chance of that. The villages are poor and there's nothing to spare. But, stopping at a small thatched teahouse perched above the trail, we discover a string of about 15 small silver fish slowly singeing over the fire, while the owner's son holds a skewer containing several pieces of what looks like trout in the flames. When a few bantams scurry in and out of the building between our legs, Kirken asks if we can buy some eggs. We're offered five, and as he pays for them one of the hens lays another, as if to order. The eggs are wrapped in a cloth and placed carefully in Dorje's *doko*; then we settle down to a late breakfast of spicy smoked fish, a handful of dried noodles and endless cups of tea. We'll have the eggs in an omelette later.

Picking a piece of dried noodle from my teeth I recall a comment of Bill Tilman's: 'In Nepal one can live off the country in a sombre fashion, but it is no place in which to make a gastronomic tour.'

Early afternoon, and the sun beats down upon us. Every movement is an effort, for my lungs and limbs ache, my heart feels strained, and I yearn to lie in the shade and sleep. Every few minutes a coughing fit takes more of my energy; sweat drips from my brow onto the trail; and when I lean on my trekking pole and gasp for breath, the crackling sound from my chest is alarming. Then a large blue-and-black butterfly I've never seen before opens its wings as it draws nectar from a trailside flower, and for a moment I forget to feel sorry for myself. Instead I catch the fragrance of sun-warmed juniper, hear the lazy clatter of cowbells drifting across the valley, and remember where I am. I know why I'm here; why Kirken, the boys and I are making this journey. It's to gather experience – life's big gift. There's nothing else to be gained from it; no financial gain, that's for sure. Just the day-by-day wonders to be found when crossing a series of landscapes of which we know next to nothing; the daily activity of wandering and wondering, gathering a harvest of experience. And if the cost of that experience is to be measured in moments of pain or discomfort, like now, so be it. I'd have it no other way, for times of ease and plenty are those we forget, while I know I'll remember today for ever.

Weak and feverish I lie outside my tent with a view across the lake to a range of snow-capped mountains. I could almost imagine this is Switzerland. It's not. This is Rara Lake, which Kirken tells me is the largest in Nepal – a serene body of water at the heart of a national park bearing its name. Conifer-covered hills surround it; those on the south side rise to snow-dusted heights of the Ghurchi Lekh, while way to the north my eyes savour a view worthy of all the effort of the past few weeks. There, a ragged white crest marks the border with Tibet. Since arriving here at noon my last remnants of energy have drained away, but I'm content just to lie on the short-cropped grass a few paces from the shore and accept with grace the mugs of sweet black tea and a few boiled potatoes that Dorje brings to me.

Kirken reckons another two days will see us down to Jumla and the end of our journey. I'm not sure whether I take that as a comfort or a challenge. Sure, it'll be good to have a proper rest, to eat as often and as much as I like, to stand beneath a hot shower and lie in a clean bed. It will be wonderful to be home again with my wife, family and friends... but not for one micro-second have I wanted this trek to end. And as for a challenge – well, the thought of two more days and two more passes to cross is more than I want to think about for now, let alone an impatient wait for a flight to Nepalgunj followed by a night bus to Kathmandu.

Now if I had a magic carpet, that would be something else...

It's a frosty night on the lake shore, and at four o'clock all and everything is floodlit by the moon. It's almost as bright as day, but tonight the scene is even more tranquil than yesterday, and I'm reluctant to turn my back on it. Will I ever see it again? If not, I must live the moment now, in all its intensity.

Skirting the lake's southern shore, we descend steeply to a grubby village whose occupants stare down at us from their rooftops, and before long we're heading south to the penultimate pass of our journey. It's as tough as I'd feared. Eking out the last of our provisions has left no diesel in my engine, and every upward step is purgatory, to which the only solution is to put mind into neutral and stop thinking.

Kirken was right. It does take two days to reach Jumla; two days in which I'm lost in a thick fog brought on by a numbness of mind. But as the light is fading on the final day, with the township now in sight, I come upon a bright-eyed, silver-tongued doctor from New Zealand who, with her husband, is working at Jumla's leprosy clinic. She's eager to talk, to speak English for a change, but I'm so weary I just want to get to a hotel and sleep. Kirken and the boys are being swallowed by the darkness, and I don't want to lose sight of them, but as I take my leave, I remember today is Good Friday.

'Happy Easter for Sunday,' I say.

'Easter? On Sunday? Oh my, I'd forgotten! Say – you wouldn't have any Easter eggs, would you?'

Easter eggs? I wish…

CHAPTER 8

Mugu

FOUR LEGS ARE BETTER THAN TWO
(2012)

On horseback into unknown Mugu, Nepal's poorest district.

Sangye shakes his head and makes a gentle snort, the tiny bells fitted to his halter resounding with a now-familiar jangle. The unmistakable smell of mules drifts on a breeze, and as we emerge from pinewoods we spy them ahead, our pack-animals now unladen and grazing a large open grassland fringed with reeds that reach out to the sparkling blue waters of Rara Lake. My eyes moisten a little. When I last walked across this meadow I wondered if I'd ever see it again. It's taken 15 years. But I'm back.

The trek across Nepal's Farthest West all those years ago, when I first saw Rara Lake, proved to be a watershed. With consequences for my

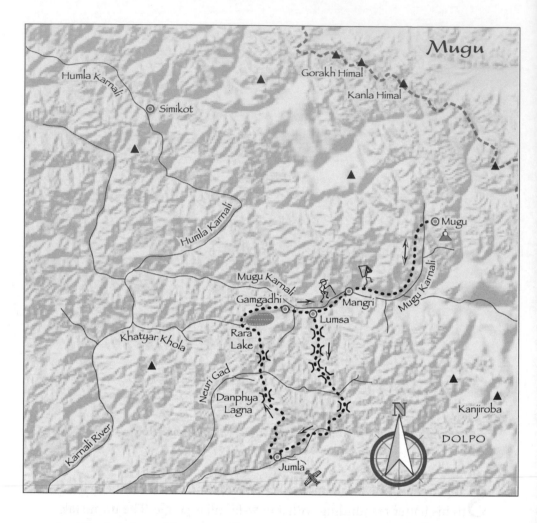

health that I could not predict at the time, it turned out to be quite literally a life-changing experience. Yet six months after I'd flown out of Jumla with a chest infection that left me totally exhausted, I was back in the Himalaya with Kirken, this time leading a trek to Kangchenjunga's North and South Base Camps for my wife, Min, and a group of friends. I thought I'd regained fitness, but crossing three passes between Ghunsa and the Yalung Valley had me puffing like a 90-year-old. A temporary blip, I told myself, it'll be alright next time.

It wasn't.

Despite this I had continued to trek in Nepal and Sikkim, led groups in Bhutan and Ladakh, and trekked in the Peruvian Andes. On top of this, each summer had been spent in the Alps and other European ranges. Every trip had been special; every day among the mountains a gift. But recurring chest infections haunted me, with each recovery taking longer than the last, and each high pass becoming more of a challenge.

In 2009 I was back in Nepal with Kirken to trek the Manaslu Circuit yet again. When I told him I had doubts that I'd be able to get over the Larkya La this time, but would be content to return alone from the highest village, he would have none of it and promised to find a horse for me to ride. True to his word, for two days I was carried to within 150 vertical metres of the pass, where the snow was too deep for my mount to continue. Sending the horse back to Samdo with its owner, I struggled on the final uphill gasping for breath like a fish out of water. But I made it, and there tried to come to terms with the fact that this would be my last Himalayan pass, my final trek in Nepal...

Kirken had other ideas and refused to acknowledge the problem, so when the Nepalese government announced that access restrictions to Mugu were to be lifted, he sent me an email at the end of 2011. 'Mugu to be open,' it said. 'Porters are hard to find there, but mules carry loads. Where mules can go, so can a horse. I'll get you one. When shall we go?'

Ah, Kirken the tempter! He knows me too well, knows how to dangle a dream. Hidden behind the hidden land of Dolpo, Mugu is a gap to fill – remote and mysterious. I know practically nothing about it, despite stumbling among its western reaches on my way from Api all those years ago, except that it's supposed to be Nepal's poorest district and Rara Lake lies within its boundaries. Beyond those two facts I'm ignorant. But it's the unknown that attracts, and if a horse can get me up the hills, I'm game.

As well as Kirken and a small crew of his from Kathmandu, which includes Pemba as cook, we have with us Ranga, an astute entrepreneur

239

from Jumla who's the owner not only of Sangye, my horse, but of our nine mules, plus a few local men to carry equipment and food that might not otherwise survive being strapped to the flanks of pack animals. There are six of us from the UK – my wife, Min, and me; John and Janette from near Glasgow, who spend most weekends scrambling in the Highlands; and Clive and Fran from Lancaster, both of whom are members of a mountain rescue team on the edge of the Lake District. Having enjoyed each other's company on previous treks, no persuasion was needed to sign up for this journey into one of the most remote corners of Nepal's Himalayan regions. 'Mugu? Never heard of it, but count us in.'

We arrive on the 3691 metre pass of the Danphya Lagna on a bright November morning. This time I have breath to spare, thanks to Sangye, but recall the last time I was here, heading in the opposite direction on the way to Jumla. I was totally spent then, a physical wreck, ignorant of the impact that trek was to have on my future activities…

'You remember this place?' asks Pemba with a grin that stretches from ear to ear.

Remember it? There is no sharp-edged clarity in a 15-year memory clouded with the dull grey mist of exhaustion; no detail – just a blurred sense of relief that there would be no more uphills to face.

Today is different. Today I can enjoy views that include Dolpo's Kanjiroba massif in one direction and distant snow mountains that shield Tibet in another. These views are exciting, for Kanjiroba inspires memories of Dolpo days, while those mountains on the Tibetan border build dreams. That those dreams may never be realised is neither here nor there. They're very much a part of my everyday living; they balance the seduction of memory and add spice to the promise of each new dawn.

Prayer flags shake out their mantras from a second high point a short distance from the Danphya Lagna, where a kettle of hot juice is waiting. As we relax in the short-cropped grass, a string of pack ponies appears from the woods that flank the northern side. Without slowing their stride, the men with them exchange a few words with Ranga and continue their journey, while Sangye watches them go. I know little about horses, but the expression on his face seems to be one of disdain. Perhaps he considers himself superior to 'mere' pack animals. If that's the case, he's probably contemptuous of me, too, for being a novice rider.

Since it's all downhill this afternoon I choose to walk. It's a long descent to the valley of the Neuri Gad – a thousand metres of sweet-smelling pine, juniper and rhododendron forest with roots intruding across the hard-baked trail – and half an hour below the pass a projecting spur overlooking the gorge-like valley gives warning that from here on down it's going to be steep. It is; steep enough to punish legs not yet mountain fit. So by the time we reach the valley, where a simple log bridge takes us across the river to its north bank, we've had enough. Our knees are like rubber, so a cheer goes up when we spy our tents being erected on a strip of grass just two minutes' walk away, our mules already unloaded. One of them rolls on its back, kicking four legs in the air with relief.

In the night I creep out of the tent and stand transfixed by moonlight flooding through the gorge. Individual stars rest on down-valley summits, and even the river seems to be hushed, silenced by frost that whitens the ground and stiffens the tents. I'm not dressed for the cold, but the scene is too good to miss, and it doesn't matter on how many dozens of Himalayan nights I've celebrated beauty like this, each one is unique, so I gather it all in before it's gone.

It's still cold when morning filters into the valley, for our camp is in shadow, while downstream the early sun beams into the blue-grey smoke of cooking fires that hovers over the village that our map names as Nauri Ghat. When I was last here all those years ago the village was known as Bumra or Bumri, and the river as the Tyor Khola.

Netra, who's been with us on several other treks, disturbs my memories with the call to breakfast, and with appetites charged by the cold we tuck into bowls of steaming porridge, followed by toast and omelettes, before filling our bottles for the day with tea. As we do, I hear the sound of pack animals on the move, and look out to see half a dozen laden ponies heading for the bridge. Anticipating a photo opportunity I grab my camera, dash outside and position myself beside the river. Upstream, mist swirls in the gorge after spilling over dark crags, while a golden wash of light drenches low-growing shrubs with the Midas touch of autumn. The six ponies trip across the bridge, below which the Neuri Gad tosses tiny jewels of spray as it hurries over the rocks in its bed. There are no mountains in view, no glaciers or snowfields, but this has to be one of the most romantic scenes I've witnessed in the Himalaya. Its beauty is poured into the well of memory, and I know I'll drink from it many times in the years ahead.

Today our trek takes us out of the Neuri Gad's valley, but not before we've met several mule trains carrying heavy-looking loads, and a woman with an infant in a sling on her back driving half a dozen buffalo along a narrow stretch between drystone walls. There are no caravans of goats such as we encountered in Dolpo and on the long trek from Api, and we're too low for yaks, but I wonder if we'll see any when we enter Mugu proper.

Astride Sangye it takes a while to break free of the morning's chill, for without the benefit of exercise to warm up I begin the day in gloves and down jacket, while Min and the others are soon shedding layers of fleece. Where the sun has not yet intruded, ice has formed across the trail, but out in the sunshine autumn colours are vibrant. Across the valley a wooded slope is blotched with scarlet. Tiny edelweiss spread their star-shaped heads on a wayside bank. A green woodpecker swoops into the open from a stand of blue pine, then turns away into a minor tributary with the same familiar hedge-hopping flight adopted by its European cousin. There's something of interest at every turn, for these Middle Hills are full of life, which I find as rewarding as the highest of the high mountains.

I need nothing more than this.

The morning continues to reward with a kaleidoscope of scenes and sounds as Sangye and I mount a rocky slope, near the top of which we arrive at a solitary teahouse built beneath an overhanging crag. Dismounting onto a nearby wall I wait for the others before ordering ginger tea. It arrives as a herd of black-and-white goats is driven down the hillside and into a pen below the teahouse, where their combined smell takes me back to the Chamliya River valley on our way to Api. If these goats are pack animals, their loads are nowhere to be seen.

Several cups of tea later, the group sets off with Kumar showing the way before I have a chance to mount my horse, so we follow up the slope to a high balcony path that gives extensive views back and across the Neuri Gad before turning a spur and descending into the mouth of the side valley through which our route will take us this afternoon. But before reaching the village at the valley's entrance, we pass a small huddle of houses where locals stand on a rooftop threshing and sifting grain, while a modern satellite dish creates a stark, 21st-century contrast to an otherwise medieval scene. Technology has arrived, leapfrogging several hundred years of little or no change.

Two days later we arrive at Rara Lake. Two days among lush alpine scenery – meadows and pinewoods – and views north to a line of the seductive, little-known snow mountains of the Changla, Gorakh and Kanla Himals. As for Rara, the lake is as restful to the eye as I remember; perhaps even more so. There's a bite to the air, but the water is calm as it reflects the sunlight – there's barely a ripple to disturb the surface. The path along its bank is lined with scarlet-leaved berberis and grey-green juniper trees, while a few reeds rim the shoreline. There are evergreen forests on all sides, as well as that ridge of snow mountains we'd seen earlier carrying the northern horizon. Our tents face the water, pitched as they are on the official national park site not far from an army camp, of which I remember nothing at all – although Kirken and Pemba insist it was here on our previous visit.

Without question, Rara is one of the true gems of Nepal, and no one objects to our plan to spend two nights here.

It's good to share trips like this with friends who'll accept without complaint any difficulty or discomfort; well-travelled friends who know the only guarantee for a journey into a remote land is the certainty that things will not go according to plan. It's when things go wrong, when you're cold, exhausted or unwell, that strength of character is called for. With John and Janette, Clive and Fran, there'll be none of the tensions that sometimes arise among groups drawn from strangers. Despite coming from disparate backgrounds, we all share a love of wild country and the challenge of working a way through it (even if their challenge on this route is likely to be somewhat different from mine and Sangye's). Our friendship was confirmed long ago on previous treks in the Alps and Himalaya, but living at different ends of the UK means that we rarely meet except on trips like this, so when we do come together we have fresh experiences and new stories to exchange – most of which are embroidered with humour, for laughter is the glue that binds friendship with adventure.

Distant mountains turn purple, and darkness settles over the lake as we gather in the mess tent for plates of goat-meat momos, cauliflower and a tomato-based sauce. While we eat, Kirken explains that when the Rara National Park was created in 1975, all the inhabitants of two villages on the northern shore were moved against their will to the low-lying Terai. Not surprisingly, being transported from 3000 metres to an alien, steamy, mosquito-rich jungle at a little over 100 metres above sea level led to fever, disease and many deaths. I wonder at the logic of such a barbaric, forced evacuation. If it was to return the lakeside to a natural state devoid of habitation, why build an army camp here, manned by soldiers from distant parts of the country? It makes no sense. No sense at all.

While Kirken is speaking, from the forest behind our camp comes the howling of jackals. By the sound of it there's a sizeable pack of these wild dog-like predators on the move, and they're coming closer – perhaps drawn by the smell of our goat meat. Clive and I shine our head-torches out of the tent doorway and a dozen pairs of green eyes stare back.

This morning care for Sangye has been passed by Ranga to his uncle, Chongdi, a quiet, smooth-faced man wearing a neat grey jacket and a striped turban made from a large scarf who says little, but misses nothing, and I warm to him immediately as he helps me mount up. Once more there's frost on the ground, but sunshine and a cloudless sky of Himalayan blue makes the morning sparkle as we work our way along the northern shore. After an idyllic rest day by the lake and two nights of howling jackals, we're now bound for the deep valley of the Mugu Karnali, which carves a trench between northwest Dolpo and Tibet. Unlike so many areas I've trekked in, I have no preconceived ideas of what it will be like, which only increases anticipation for the coming days and weeks.

Beyond the lake a trail takes us into woodland, at the far end of which an open glade grants a first view of the Mugu Karnali stretching far ahead. It's a view to savour, so we find sunlit grass and spend half an hour taking it all in. It's an exciting prospect, for although the great bowl of hillside opening below is full of terraced fields and scattered houses, the valley spreading from it narrows into a shadowed mystery that reveals no secrets.

When we're ready to move on Chongdi offers me Sangye's reins, but I decide to walk now, as it looks as though we'll be heading downhill for the rest of the morning. So Chongdi goes ahead and is soon out of sight as we step into the sun's full glare and begin the 1100 metre descent on a dust-laden trail eroded by the hooves of innumerable pack animals. It's an appallingly rough trail, despite the fact that it serves as the main street for several small groups of houses we pass through. Apparently having no concern for its condition, the villagers have simply left it to disintegrate, when it would only take a few days of focused labour to improve the way for everyone. If this is Nepal's poorest district, I sense that part of that poverty may be due to a lack of motivation, an absence of ambition.

And yet a single glance across the vast sweep of terraced fields is sufficient to counter that argument, for although a handful of men, women and tiny bare-bummed infants stare vacantly as we pass, buffalo plough the strips of post-harvest land in readiness for the next planting, while neat piles of animal dung freckle the hillside waiting to be dug into the soil. If husbandry is the heartbeat of Nepal, what we see now would suggest it's in good health. But of course, the *real* Mugu may prove otherwise.

As dust settles on our legs with every step, the distant yelping cry of a farmer comes drifting on a breeze, as does the laughter of children and the drone of a twin-engine plane coming in to land at an airstrip we cannot see. With that alien sound I'm reminded that food aid provided by the UN's World Food Programme is regularly airlifted to this deprived district. I admit I'm confused. Wherever we look there are signs of productivity – there's little sign of food poverty here.

Strung out in a line down the hillside, members of our crew step on their own shadows as the sun rises higher, but when we come onto a short stretch of dirt road it's possible to walk four abreast. Janette chats nineteen to the dozen, as though keeping in tune with her short but energetic steps; Fran's bright eyes are alert and gleaming; tall, long-legged Clive lopes along in conversation with John as Min points out three huge lammergeyer sailing the thermals above us, so close that we can see all their light underwing markings and hear the breeze ruffling their feathers.

Two-thirds of the way down the slope, Gamgadhi is a long bazaar village cascading its way along a narrow spine, barely more than a single street wide, the two- or three-storeyed houses with their blue-painted balconies facing one another across an alley crammed with goods – many of which have been made in China. Stacked beside a shop not much larger than a Welsh dresser, a precarious pile of television sets gathers dust; from another shop comes the tinny wail of ill-tuned radios. Large drum-tight sacks of rice form a barricade outside one building, while crates of beer with Chinese characters on their labels stand beside another. A mule train squeezes through the street, and a stray buffalo goes nowhere in a hurry. A tailor at his pedal-driven sewing machine looks down on us from a wooden balcony.

Such is everyday life in Gamgadhi.

At the foot of the slope a sturdy timber bridge takes us across the Mundu Khola, on whose west bank Pemba and Netra have set up their kitchen and are preparing lunch. With time to spare, we find a patch of shade beneath a willow and doze in the balmy warmth of midday. This afternoon we'll enter the valley of the Mugu Karnali, into which the Mundu Khola spills its goodness 100 metres from here. With that in prospect, I have a feeling that the character of our trek is about to change.

Deep and narrow, and with numerous twists and turns, the valley seduces us upstream – a valley gouged from mountains whose summits we may never clap eyes upon. To the north the map teases with its depiction of countless tiny lakes lodged among dandas around 5000 metres high; to the south, wooded hills climb to lofty bare ridges, while we pick our way in the oxygen-thick air of little more than 2000 metres above sea level. Despite our comparatively low altitude, for much of the day the air is cool, as our trail takes us deep in shadow along the south bank of the river, while the opposite side glows in direct sunlight. There's little cultivation to be seen, and the villages we pass through are dusty and fly-blown; very few could be described as tidy, most smack of neglect, and their children and adults alike are unkempt, staring at us with blank expressions. Their demeanour speaks of privation and a lack of hope.

Despite this, practically every building displays a small rectangular solar panel on its roof, provided by the Nepalese government to give each home a limited supply of electricity to enable rooms to be lit. But when I look inside some of the houses I wonder how many of these have ever worked for more than a week or two? In some rooms there are no light bulbs, or broken fittings hang from the ceiling; in others the wiring is faulty. For all their promise and good intent, the solar panels appear to be little more than a symbol of what might be – if only.

The largest village is Lumsa, where it seems the whole population gathers round as Kirken deposits some of our food and kerosene at the home of a friend of Ranga's – to be collected on our way back to Jumla. Although poorly dressed, the villagers are friendly but not intrusive, and it's a relief to be free of the begging hands and cries of 'Shim shim' or 'Gimme one pen' that are so ubiquitous among some of Nepal's more popular and prosperous trekking regions. We have the distinct feeling that very few trekkers have been here before us.

Our trail is rarely level; it's either climbing or descending, often on steep and rocky stairways, with Sangye lurching on the uneven upward steps and slithering where the path slopes downhill. No Newmarket thoroughbred could cope with this, but Sangye is a Himalayan work horse; this is his environment, and although I'm appalled at some of the challenges we face together, he rarely shies away from them. On every upward lunge I lean forward instinctively, coaxing him on; when we come to a steep downward slope I lean back – especially when confronted with overhanging rocks or branches of low-growing trees. Sangye is undeterred, but it's an obstacle course for me as a novice rider, and while I now appreciate just how much balance is required to stay in the saddle, my admiration for his footwork grows with each passing hour. And the fact that my heart and lungs are not straining is a huge relief. Four legs are certainly better than two in this valley.

Several times each day we meet mule trains coming towards us, and my legs are bruised from the battering they take from the wide loads, for the trails are seldom large enough to accommodate two-way traffic with room to spare. But when we see a string of laden yaks and *yak* crossbreeds heading our way, I steer Sangye into the shelter of a tree and dismount in order to avoid the sharp horns of the shaggy beasts when they pass. There must be at least 50 of them lumbering along the trail between drystone walls, each one steaming and dribbling in the thick air of the lower valley – these hefty creatures don't perform well below 3000 metres, which I guess is why they look so miserable. Sangye is uneasy, shifting against the tree, shaking his mane and snuffling. Following behind the yaks their herder is a black-haired Tibetan in homespun, listening to Western pop music on his iPod.

At Dhungedhara, a tiny huddle of houses above a strip of buckwheat, chillies and large orange pumpkins, I dismount, and together Chongdi and I encourage Sangye across a suspension bridge that takes us onto the north bank of the river. Here the afternoon sun is blissfully warm, so we sit on a grass bank for a few minutes, Chongdi and I, while Sangye grazes. Min and our friends are nowhere to be seen. Kirken and his crew are some way ahead of us. It's just Chongdi, Sangye and me, the blue rush of the Mugu Karnali, and an untamed valley full of unknowns twisting ahead. Once again, there's nowhere else I'd rather be.

Apart from a single night's camp on the opposite side of the river, we remain on the north bank for the next few days. There's very little habitation now, although the map shows a few villages spaced across the mountainside high above us. Of these there's little or no sign, so when we do spy a building it's worthy of comment. Beside the trail a house will inevitably be surrounded by a field or two in which poor crops struggle for survival. Where it's been turned the soil is dusty, friable and in need of feeding with manure, which raises the question: how do the folk who live here find sufficient nourishment to survive? There are no easy options, for although we're at no great altitude this is a harsh and unforgiving land – raw, rugged and uncompromising – but for those of us passing through it's also wildly attractive and every day has its rewards.

One day we meet several weather-beaten families making their way down-valley with mules laden with their belongings; they tell Kirken they're from Mugu village, which they've deserted until springtime. It's too cold to spend the winter at home, they say, and tell us we're crazy to be heading deeper into the mountains with snow predicted in a week or two. We also discover that some families have second homes in Kathmandu, financed by the sale of *yartsa gunbu*, a fungus-infected caterpillar found in a remote corner of the mountains and prized by the Chinese as an aphrodisiac and for what they claim to be its medicinal purposes. Demand from across the border has had a major impact on the local economy; hence the second homes of some of the villagers.

Once again I acknowledge the fact that Mugu is full of contradictions.

Early one afternoon the trail takes us up a long steep slope hundreds of metres above the river – a broken stairway of slabs and hoof-polished rocks, walled and overhung by damp crags. If I'd anticipated its brutal nature in advance I'd have dismounted at the bottom and struggled up the trail with the others, but once we've embarked on the ascent I can see no safe way to slide off my mount, so grip Sangye's flanks with my knees and hang on tight as he lurches from one rocky step to the next. Climbing the path just behind us Min is horrified to note that on one occasion the horse's four hooves are all balanced on a single small rock; should he slip or the rock give way, we'll both plunge to the river. Blissfully ignorant of this, I'm aware only that the exposure is formidable, and try not to allow my imagination too much free rein.

Near the head of the slope, as Sangye lunges for the next step, the saddle slips – fortunately to the left – leaving me hanging beneath the horse and crashing head, shoulder and arm against the walling crag on the way down. Had I fallen to the right, I'd have bounced twice before plunging into the river.

Bruised and unnerved, I decide to walk for the next hour.

Our camps are always placed close to the Mugu Karnali, and chosen with access to grazing for the mules in mind. From our tents we can see

the mules tearing at the rough grass or nibbling leaves on a neighbouring hillside, and as darkness falls they're brought back to camp to be
hobbled overnight. Sometimes we hear jackals. One morning we spy a
pair of *Himalayan tahr* perched upon a steep cliff high above the tents;
through binoculars we can see the wild goats' long hair ruffled by the
wind. On other days we catch sight of *bharal*, and once glimpse a very
large white-faced monkey staring down at us.

The valley makes a long leftward curve, providing a rare glimpse
of a snow-crowned peak far ahead; on the opposite bank a beam of
sunlight picks out a small *gompa* at the entrance to a valley Kirken tells
us leads to Dolpo. He came down through that valley many years ago
and now grows nostalgic as he discusses that journey with Sonam, the
local guide who joined us a couple of nights ago.

Kirken's memories feed my dreams; dreams of treks I know will
never be fulfilled. But knowing they'll never be more than a fantasy
does nothing to diminish their power to excite. Why harbour regrets for
today's limitations? I'll accept with grace those things I have no power
to control, and move on. These days my *mantra* has become: 'Maybe
not now, but in another life...'

In the lower valley there were few, if any, signs of the Buddhist faith, but
now we've entered the wild upper regions we come upon an ancient
looking *kani*, a few crumbling chortens and weather-bleached prayer
flags. With the frieze of saints and symbols of its archway fading with
age against the red clay, the *kani* reminds me of those I saw in Dolpo.
Exposed to every wind that blows, this one stands on a promontory way
above the river, which boils over a series of garage-sized boulders; the
roar of the torrent is filtered like a distant echo, while the *kani* betrays
an aura of peace.

Somehow nothing seems quite real; the past has a permanence
that's lacking in the present.

'D'you see what I see?'

Pointing upstream John directs our attention to five yellow kayaks being tossed through a channel of rapids in what appears to be a suicidal adventure. We're mesmerised by the sight. Three months ago I watched an inflatable raft being swept through the Zanskar Gorge in Ladakh, the river there being the colour of cold coffee. By comparison with the kayaks, that raft was part of a child's game. Riding these glacier-blue rapids must surely be the ultimate laxative. Not for the first time in my life, I'm glad to be a wimp.

Unlike the majority of treks in the Himalaya, our journey remains at a modest altitude. There are no glacier passes, our highest village will be just below 3500 metres, and the sight of snow mountains is a rarity. On either side of the valley we're walled by soaring crags whose summits can only be guessed at. Yet the trail is a demanding one, the landscape spectacular throughout, and each of us is fully absorbed in the experience of working a way through it. Every half hour the scenery changes, and with it the light. We sweat in sunshine, but are chilled the moment a cloud casts shadow. There are no consistencies, and I accept each moment for the gift it is.

Astride Sangye I'm often separated from Kirken, Min and the rest of the group. Sometimes I see them way ahead; on other occasions they're far behind me. There's a disconnection that's hard to come to terms with, despite the pleasure I gain from riding and from Chongdi's company. We may share the same trails and the same destination, but their day-by-day reality is very different from mine. It's as though we're on different journeys. If I were alone there'd be no problem, but my friends and I came to Mugu to share experience, yet my riding Sangye has put me at a distance from them. I appreciate Chongdi's silent friendship, but miss conversations with the others and have to make up for that lack when our day's trek is over.

Today Chongdi and I are joined by Sonam. Both men are quietly spoken and observant, and point out a herd of *bharal* picking a way across what appears to be a featureless rock face. Ten minutes later we turn a corner as two of the blue sheep drop onto our trail and, unconcerned by our presence, disappear into the bushes. Stopping to allow the group to catch up, we note a large dipper-like bird darting among rocks beside the river. With erect twitching tail and a splash of red on its rump, as it launches itself from one rock to another the tail expands to reveal a white stripe. By the expression on their faces, both Chongdi and Sonam are as pleased to see it as I am. Sonam catches my eye; he grins and nods his head as though we share a secret.

Further on, a metal bridge spans a tributary headed by a pyramid-shaped peak. A torrent thrashes through the gorge at its entrance, while slabs below the bridge have been decorated with large coloured manis. From nowhere a stray dog with a sleek black coat appears on the path ahead of Sangye and me, and 20 minutes later it guides us onto a beach of glacial sand, where two large bell tents stand beside a makeshift stone shelter overhung by prayer flags. From one of the tents a woman with Tibetan features and wearing a black *chuba* watches us pass. Neither Sonam nor Chongdi give her more than a casual glance, but the woman's eyes miss nothing.

Autumn colours the valley, but winter is in the air. Perhaps the prediction of snow given us by villagers heading down-valley will be borne out. Yet the sky remains clear for most of the day, and sunbeams create stepping stones as we pass through a woodland of semi-bare trees on a carpet of leaves.

Shortly after midday Chongdi grabs the reins: '*Baje*. We stop here,' he says, so I slip from Sangye's back in my usual ungainly fashion, straighten legs cramped from three hours in the saddle, and note that we've arrived in a small meadow close to a confluence of rivers. A *yak*-herder's stone hut stands nearby, while an arc of trees and shrubs gives shelter from the wind. Stained with lichen, two or three large boulders cast patches of shade. Had it been later in the day this would have made a perfect site for our tents, but no doubt Sonam will know of another place for an overnight camp. If so, it's hard to believe it will be better than this.

Kirken arrives out of breath. I can see at once that he's not happy, and he proves it by snapping irritably at Chongdi before turning to me. 'That place by the river,' he says. 'That place with trees and good water half hour after we pass the Tibetan camp – we should have stopped there for lunch. Everyone tired. Everyone hungry.'

Me too, but this is as good as anywhere to have a break.

'It's okay with you on horse. But walking is not so easy for us. You look see.'

He's right, for as the others arrive I note that even Janette is red-cheeked and has stopped talking! John removes his hat and wipes his brow with the back of a hand. Clive drops his rucksack with relief, but Fran's smile is as fresh as ever – I have yet to see her even remotely flustered. Min is nowhere to be seen.

'She's about 10 minutes behind us,' Clive reassures me. 'Don't worry, she's okay; just tired, that's all. Kumar is with her.'

Kirken sends Chongdi back with Sangye to find her, and returns 15 minutes later with Min looking weary in the saddle. 'I've got someone else's legs today,' she explains as we sprawl in the grass with the chapattis, boiled eggs and cheese that Pemba had prepared for our lunch.

'We all found that last stretch especially hard,' she continues, and with that admission I realise just what a difference Sangye has made to my physical experience of this trek. Throughout our journey the trail has made no concessions, and with its broken nature it's often been difficult to maintain a rhythm. Or rather, it's been difficult for the others to maintain a rhythm. Astride Sangye I've had it easy, for only when I've chosen to walk downhill, or on those extra-steep uphill sections when it's been necessary to dismount for the sake of my horse, have I had any personal contact with the trail. Truth is, had Kirken not arranged for me to ride, I'd never have got this far. It's a sobering thought, and one that makes me even more grateful for Sangye's four legs.

Our valley has made a sharp northward trend. To the east lies a route into Dolpo via a 5000 metre pass, and for a few fleeting moments I almost wish we were heading that way, yet this uppermost corner of Mugu is tantalising enough, and I'm more than content to be here. The last and highest village is within reach, and I speculate whether we'll find it deserted when we arrive – or will there still be a few hardy souls remaining there, prepared to sit out the winter in this tight wedge of land trapped between lofty but featureless mountains?

Tomorrow will tell.

It takes less than two hours to reach the village from our highest camp, passing above the treeline into a zone of raw beauty. A long row of chortens leads the way, from the last of which a crowd of 60 or more houses can be seen rising in tiers against the steep crags of the Tagi Danda, a waterfall cascading down the cliffs to one side and draining into the river that snakes its way in a series of braidings through a flat-bedded plain.

Mugu village is not deserted, but half the families that live here have gone for the winter, and more will leave shortly. Of those remaining, a few workmen are busy renovating the *gompa*, and I wonder if they'll finish before the snows arrive – or will they depart, too, in the next few days? With no light other than that which filters through the doorway, one elderly craftsman with thick glasses is creating a frieze of Buddhist symbols from a mix of grey clay and cement. Every breath escapes in a cloud of steam, yet he gives no impression of being aware of the cold or lack of light. With no form of heating, no direct sunlight, and no glimmering butter lamps, it's a bitter, unwelcoming place.

Outside the *gompa* Kirken recognises a monk in a claret-coloured robe whom he met 30 years ago when he came here as guide to a naturalist carrying out a snow leopard survey. It takes a few moments for the monk to realise who Kirken is, but then points out with a laugh that he has put on weight since those distant times.

'Come,' says the monk. 'Let's talk'.

The old man takes us along a pathway between dung-plastered buildings, then up a notched log ladder onto the roof of his house, which is protected by an open-sided porch, and while he and Kirken reminisce, we spend an hour or so on a dusty rug drinking Tibetan salt-butter tea and eating piping hot potatoes boiled in their skins. Out of the wind, and with the sun beaming directly on us, we gaze across rooftops stacked with firewood to mountains on the far side of the valley. Prayer flags drip their mantras onto yaks that snuffle in straw-littered yards. Directly below us Sangye is tethered to a post, and Chongdi and Sonam are laughing with a small group of villagers nearby. Children in ragged clothes chase one another through the alleyways; an old woman leans her back against a wall, warming her face in the sunshine. On a neigh-bouring roof another woman sits at a loom, while above her a large satellite dish is an intrusion from an alien world, confusing what is, in every other respect, a scene of great antiquity.

There's much about Mugu village that reminds me of Dolpo. Crammed close together on the east side of the valley, its two- or three-storey houses smell of smoke and animals. Wood smoke blackens the beams, seeps through cracks in the walls, or filters out through tiny glassless windows.

Big black crows and choughs perch on flagpoles; others swarm over the village in clouds of shining feathers, but it is the lammergeyers that hold my attention. There must be seven or eight of the great vultures aim-lessly floating in the thermals, heads down, wings outstretched, mocking human frailties. For several minutes they drift across the rooftops – ugly creatures they are, despite their grace in the air – then one after another they turn and sail towards what appears to be an island in the river, in the centre of which a tall gold-coloured Buddha is ringed by prayer flags. Making a *kora* around the Buddha, three devout women prostrate them-selves full-length on the ground in an act of penitence.

How many such koras will be required, I wonder, to add substance to their *karma*?

Apparently cross-border trade with Tibet continues in this remote backwater. Two days north of here, Chinese-made goods destined for Gamgadhi come over the Namja La. Thirty-odd years ago it was a two-way trade, with Mugulis taking Nepalese grains to Pong Dzu near the Tsangpo River's headwaters in Tibet, returning with salt, wool and bricks of Tibetan tea. But if the Mugulis now rely on international food aid, I cannot imagine grain heading north today, and suspect there's less salt and tea than Chinese-brewed alcohol and plastic footwear making its way south by *yak* train.

Having come as far north as our permits allow, we retrace our steps down-valley to Lumsa, trading the frost-pocket of upper Mugu for a more agreeable climate. Despite losing altitude the trail is not much easier heading downstream than it was going up, for it's a helter-skelter route whichever direction we travel. Sangye senses this, and on the first day after leaving our highest village he resents my company. I've no idea what I've done to put him in a bad mood, but from the start he makes it clear that I'm not welcome in his saddle by refusing to go where I attempt to steer him. He's clearly in charge and determined to prove it, forcing a way through bushes that tear at my clothes, bashing my legs against trailside crags, and even aiming for the lowest of overhanging rocks in an attempt to unseat me. Chongdi swears at him and yanks at his halter, but it makes no difference – Sangye has it in for me, that's for sure. Yet the following morning he's his old genial self once more.

Horses! I guess I'll never understand them.

After crossing the suspension bridge at Dhungedhara, Kirken directs us up an alternative trail to visit a large village he assures us is worth seeing. It's a steep and demanding route, with dozens of uneven stone steps that make it impossible for me to ride. So Chongdi takes Sangye, leaving me to struggle uphill gasping for breath with Min beside me, pausing frequently and inwardly cursing my shrinking lungs, while the rest of the group walk effortlessly ahead.

Mangri is a magical place in a magical setting. Standing on a broad sloping terrace way above the river, it's one of the largest villages we've seen since leaving Gamgadhi. There must be 70 or more houses huddled together and almost overhanging the alleys that twist between them. Constructed of timber and stone, nearly all the buildings have flat roofs covered with recently harvested straw. Many have small balconies; a number have wall-enclosed courtyards in which goats, hens or scrawny cows scratch at the grey, sun-baked earth. Tiny black bees hover around tubular wooden hives attached to some of the houses, and once again I notice the same rectangular solar panels we'd seen fitted to roofs in the lower valley.

It's a peaceful village. We hear no raised voices, and when children offer 'Namaste' they do so in hushed tones. A spell has been cast that none of us wants to break, so we wander slowly through under the gaze of inquisitive women and old men exhaling smoke from short-stemmed pipes. Three or four grubby-faced girls guide our way, and on the outskirts of the village stand aside to watch us go with eyes that peer over strips of once-blue cloth held over their mouths in a pretence of shyness.

Beyond and below Mangri the hillside expands with an arc of terraced fields tipping shadows from low retaining walls. All the crops have been taken, and a bare-earth path eases through the golden post-harvest stubble with a view overlooking the valley, which now makes a generous curve to the southwest. It draws us down; down into a forest of chir pine, rhododendron and a straggle of wild clematis; down at last to the riverside path deep in shade, where I mount Sangye once more and ride on to camp.

At Lumsa we leave the familiar trail to head south across a series of passes on our way back to Jumla. Ranga and one of our porters collect the kerosene and spare food that had been left here on our way up-valley, and add it to the porter's load. Munie is the oldest member of our crew, a simple man with a winning smile. Despite the weight of his load, he's usually one of the first to arrive in camp to help pitch the tents, collect water or assist with any other chores. In fact he's one of the most willing of all the porters I've had the privilege to trek with in Nepal, and the constant smile that lights his face – even when sweat pours from it when labouring uphill – reflects the warmth of his character.

Once again the trail above the village is too steep and broken to allow me to ride, but when the gradient finally eases, I use a section of wall to climb onto Sangye's back and sit there for a moment with a thumping heart. After more than two weeks of horse riding I'm comfortable in the saddle now, and enjoy the freedom it allows to study the countryside while on the move. Today my eyes range across a scene unguessed from our riverside route, where there'd been very few signs of agriculture, but up here a vast amphitheatre of terraced fields reveals a sun-trap of land put to good use. Not since the day we descended from Rara to the Mugu Karnali have we witnessed scenes like this, with buffalo dragging wooden ploughs through the soil, spurred on by farmers whose shrill commands form a counter-harmony to the songs of birds and ticking of insects. I swear it's something of which I'll never grow tired.

An hour or so above Lumsa we find Ranga and the mule driver lounging on a grassy bluff. It's a scenic spot with an immense panoramic view – all the more welcome as for many days we've been hemmed in by the valley's huge walls. Now we have space and unrestricted sunlight; spreading the map between us we attempt to identify some of the mountains on show. Sadly there's no detail north of the border with Tibet, and our sheet fails to include anything west of Rara Lake. Yet it's to the north and west that the most eye-catching summits hold our gaze.

'Look, Kev – Saipal!' says Kirken with a wistful smile.

He could be right. That great fortress of snow hovers above a maze of distant ridges – just as it did all those years ago when he and I had been captivated by it from the last of our Dolpo passes.

I wonder if he knows what I'm thinking…

After lunch above a stream, we continue to gain height. By now we've lost most of the terraced fields, for the slope is much steeper and houses are less frequent than before. Agriculture is a lost art up here, and the route more demanding, and when we come to a junction of trails Kirken confers with Sonam, who advises that Sangye and I should take the left fork, while he and the others take the alternative. Chongdi grabs Sangye's halter and guides us on a convoluted route that soon becomes less of a path and more a stream-bed. It squeezes through bushes and enters a narrow gully flanked by steep clay banks; it's so narrow that both my legs rub against the sides. Water drizzles through the gully digging thin channels in the clay, and although there's no sign that anyone has ever been here before, Chongdi never hesitates, never shows any doubt that this is the correct way, so I assume he knows where we're going.

At last we emerge at a small meadow where two young boys splash naked in a pond. Seeing us appear from what must seem like a hole in the ground, they drag themselves out of the water, grab their clothes and scamper away shrieking with laughter. Chongdi looks up at me and shakes his head with amusement, and a few minutes later we stumble upon a clear path that eventually leads to a village not shown on our map. There I dismount by a large pipal tree and wait while he quizzes a group of villagers as to whether Kirken and the others have passed through or have yet to arrive.

Reunited 10 minutes later, we continue and eventually camp for the night on a large rectangular meadow, from which we have an uninterrupted view of rank upon rank of mountains spreading north and west into Humla. With plenty of room for the mules to graze, and a clear stream a two-minute walk away, it's an almost perfect site.

Our journey has its own momentum. We'd been drawn to Mugu by the very fact that the district was unknown to us. That was its primary appeal. Apart from Rara Lake there are no recognisable milestones to mark the way, and even our highest village was merely a name on a map – the same name as the river we followed in both directions; the same name as the district itself. Practically every other journey I've made in the Himalaya has had a recognisable itinerary with definable goals. But not here. The journey itself is all – and I celebrate the liberty we gain from ignorance of the route. Kirken tells us there are no more villages for two or three days, but between here and Jumla we'll be crossing a series of 4000 metre passes. That's all we know. That's all we need to know. Day after day I have no idea where our trek will lead, nor where we'll camp tonight. Such decisions are left to serendipity.

And to Kirken.

High above the valley, and above all habitation, the mountainside is like a great tilted prairie, patched here and there with strips of forest reaching up to a 4000 metre ridge. Dwarfed as we are by the landscape, every horizon is beyond reach. Far, far away beyond the nameless hills my eyes scan distant unknown, unclimbed mountains, while around me more immediate hills rise to altitudes higher than most of the alpine giants I wander among each summer. They invite rather than challenge, and I, accepting their invitation, can imagine no finer country in which to walk or ride. With no restrictions Sangye takes advantage of his freedom to roam. I give him his head and share that sense of freedom too. I don't think I've ever been happier.

No longer confined to a single track, Kirken and our crew, Min and our friends, and the mules too choose their own routes to wander, and so far as I can tell there's little conversation to disturb the peace. Words are futile in places like this. The pass we're aiming for can be seen as a dip in the ridge a long way off, and there are no obstacles to avoid on the way to it. With perfect visibility, unrestricted views and our goal in sight for much of the day, the map is superfluous, discussion unnecessary. Without knowing it in advance, this is surely what we came here for.

After our coldest night so far we're anxious for the sun to pour its welcome light over the eastern ridge. Last night flames had swept across the slope below that ridge, and this morning smoke rises from the charred remains of trees and scrub that stood in their way. Kirken is scathing in his contempt for the hunters whom he suspects are responsible for starting the fire in order to drive wildlife into the open, where they'd be waiting with their rifles.

'They don't care if they destroy the whole mountain,' he rages. 'All forest burned just for a chance to shoot animals.'

It's not only wildlife that's under threat. With vegetation destroyed the whole mountainside will be vulnerable to erosion and landslide, and villages hundreds of metres below will be put in danger too. If Kirken is correct in his assumption that the fire was started on purpose, whoever was responsible has much to answer for.

Most mornings we've been on the move at around 7 o'clock. Not so this morning; it's a slow start, and the tents are down and loaded on the mules long before we set off, cocooned in down against the cold, heading towards what Sonam calls the Naulekh Pass, some 300 metres above our camp. By the time we reach it we've escaped the frost pocket, stripped off a layer of clothing, and now squint in the bright light that washes every east-facing hill, mountain and ridge. The warmth is as welcome as the view.

At 4127 metres the small grass saddle of the Naulekh Pass makes a tremendous vantage point from which to study the country to the north, east and west. The panorama is one of the most extensive any of us has ever gazed upon. So vast and all encompassing, it defies attempts to reduce or confine its content by mere words, but provokes instead an unfamiliar silence. My life among mountains has produced a thousand heart-stopping views; most contain recognisable summits. Not here, not today. While a sea of mountains reaches out to infinity, the only peaks we dare put names to are my old favourite Saipal, a huge and imposing block of snow and ice, and Gurla Mandhata, the 7000 metre neighbour of Mount Kailash in Tibet.

Absorbing the view, John recalls the comment made by a Lithuanian immigrant who joined him and some of his friends on the ascent of his first Scottish Munro a couple of months ago.

'He was so excited by what he saw,' says John, 'that on the summit he shook our hands and told us: "Every fibre of my being rejoices!"'

We laugh, but here on the Naulekh Pass I guess we could all echo those words.

On the south side we descend a little before contouring above a moorland-like basin that falls into the valley of the Sumpo Khola, the river which drains into the Mugu Karnali upstream of Lumsa. The way is mostly straightforward, and proves to be little more than a shallow link between cols, for at the far side of the basin an abrupt rocky gully leads to the Kala Munor, a second, slightly higher pass at 4250 metres, from where a faint trail can be seen winding along or just below other ridges that seem to go on for ever. It's an exciting prospect, the reality of which proves every bit as exciting to achieve, for I seem to be taking a ride in the sky to our third pass of the morning. Sonam says this is called the Buzi Lagna, and from it we can clearly see Rara Lake off to the northwest, contained by a dark green, almost black girdle of forest.

Three passes and we've not eaten since breakfast. 'Wait until we get to the next pass,' says Kirken, who was here only a few weeks ago when reconnoitring the route with Sonam. 'From there we can see Kanjiroba. It will be a good place to eat,' he promises. 'It's just around the corner.'

'Just around the corner' – you'd think he was describing a walk along the high street instead of a trek along the Kathana Danda in the Middle Hills of the Himalaya! All morning the air has had a bite to it, despite the bright sunlight, but now we're exposed to the arctic-like chill of a late November wind and hurry as best we can to cross our fourth pass of the day, where we crouch in the shelter of rocks to eat boiled eggs, cheese and chapattis, and wash them down with luke-warm juice.

Little more than a dip in an extensive ridge system, this final pass of the day appears not to have a name, but it's the finest of them all – with a stupendous view of the Kanjiroba massif to the east dominating a whole range of mountains that protect the hidden land of Dolpo. But that is simply one fragment of a panorama that has me spinning around 360 degrees, bamboozled by innumerable peaks and ridges cleft by mysterious valleys. Every horizon is fretted with summits; some are dashed with snow, but the majority are little more than anonymous pinnacles or domes nestling one against another. Nothing in our field of vision has been made by man. This is wilderness pure and simple.

What was it John's friend told him? 'Every fibre of my being rejoices!'

From a lofty ridge with limitless vistas, this evening we're brought down to earth in more ways than one when we camp in a deep hollow beside the Limi Khola. Hemmed in by steep wooded slopes, the site is claustrophobic, with a wreath of cold mist hanging over the river. That's not all. Since Kirken and Sonam pitched their tent here just a few short weeks ago, this tight wedge of a valley has been ravaged by gatherers of *yartsa gunbu*. Partly burned items of rubbish lie scattered between the blackened remains of numerous campfires, where we gather broken glass and rusting cans to bury safely away from our grazing mules. Two hours ago we made our way along what Clive claimed to be the finest ridge-walk he'd ever known. And now this. Instead of rhapsodising about the day, we're plunged into a sullen silence.

A new day, another pass. Cresting three minor ridges in quick succession, we then cross the wooded Mandhara Danda and emerge to the eye-squinting brilliance of a south-facing slope, then follow the mules as they disturb a million grasshoppers on their descent to a small patch of pasture at the confluence of two streams. Pemba and Netra arrived an hour ago, and the sound of a hissing primus lures us to them.

'What do you think?' asks Kirken. 'Should we make camp here and rest in the sunshine? Be nice and warm after the cold and damp of last night. And we have time enough.'

The others agree; there's nowhere else we need to be, and the pasture would make a decent site for our tents, that's for sure. But it's in another hollow, and I imagine it will lose the sun by mid-afternoon and won't be out of shade until long after we leave in the morning. We need somewhere with a more open aspect.

'How about up there?' suggests Min, nodding towards a ridge-spur a short walk away, and together with Kirken we scramble up the slope to inspect it.

There we discover a domed projection of grass and shrub with a pinewood fringe on one side, a rash of tiny autumn flowers along the crest, an infinity of brown rolling hills, and the distant blue ranges of Western Nepal filling every ragged horizon. The Himalaya – landscape of dreams and abode of the gods.

The site is perfect; it lacks nothing.

The light is so pure it's almost brittle. The fragrance of sun-warmed pine hangs in the air. I'm aware of the electric buzz of insects and the beating of my heart. In another two days we should be in Jumla. This journey, so different from any other, will be over. But I'm in no hurry for that to happen. That I may never be back is of no concern. Secure with memories of times past, untroubled by tomorrow, this moment is all that matters. Life is good.

'This will do,' I tell Kirken. 'This will do nicely.'

And it does.

GLOSSARY

Baje	grandfather
beyul	hidden valley, sacred to Tibetan Buddhists
bhanjyang	pass
bharal	so-called blue sheep of the Himalaya, in appearance resembling both sheep and goat
bhatti	simple teahouse, basic inn or rural dwelling
Bhotiya	Buddhist highlander of Nepal and Tibet
bokkhu	thick hooded garment worn as protection by honey-gatherers; it serves as both a cape and a blanket
chaarpi	toilet or latrine
chai/chiyaa	tea
chapatti	unleavened bread
chang	home-brewed beer
chautaara	porters' resting place, usually built of stones in the shade of a pipal or banyan tree
chuba	traditional black wrap-around robe worn by *Bhotiya* women
chhu	river

chorten	religious monument, similar to a small *stupa*, but it could be little more than an elaborate cairn
daal bhaat	the staple Nepalese meal – cooked rice (bhaat) with lentil soup (daal)
danda	extensive ridge in the Himalayan foothills
deurali	pass, or high point on a foothill ridge
dhanyabaad	thank you
didi	older sister; the word is also used to denote a female lodge-owner
doko	large conical basket of woven bamboo used by porters to carry loads
gompa	Buddhist monastery
himal	snow mountain
Himalayan tahr	long-haired wild goat with an exotic ruff surrounding head and shoulders
kani	entrance archway, often decorated inside with Buddhist symbols
karma	the effect of a person's actions on their fate in their next reincarnation
kharka	similar to a European 'alp' – a pasture and/or herder's shelter
khola	river
kora	circumambulation of a sacred place or object performed by devout Buddhists
kosi	river
la	mountain pass
lama	religious teacher or priest
lekh	long ridge system (see also '*danda*')
mani	from the Buddhist *mantra* '*Om mani padme hum*' ('Hail to the jewel in the lotus'); it is carved – and sometimes painted – on stones and boulders by the side of a trail

267

mantra	repetitive words or symbols of praise
Namaste	traditional greeting, given with hands pressed together in the attitude of prayer; it means 'I salute the god within you'
namlo	forehead tumpline or band by which a porter's load is carried
prayer flag	cloth on which prayers are printed; many prayer flags are coloured to represent the five elements – earth, fire, air, water and ether
puja	ceremony where prayers are offered
ramro	good
rakshi	distilled spirit
rimpoche	reincarnated *lama*
sadhu	holy man or ascetic
Sherpani	female of the Sherpa race; also used to denote a female porter on a trekking or mountaineering expedition
sirdar	head Sherpa who takes charge of the porters and staff of a trek crew
stupa	large Buddhist monument, usually with a square base and a dome topped with a spire; it often contains the remains of a revered *lama*
suntala	the Nepalese orange
tatopani	hot water
thanka	a religious painting, often created on silk, and found in Buddhist monasteries
tongba	a tubular container of fermented millet; also a traditional Sherpa home-made brew
tsampa	roasted barley or millet, mixed with salt-butter tea, milk or water to the consistency of porridge

yak   long-haired, wide-horned member of the Bos
             grunniens species; the female is a nak, and a *yak*
             crossbreed is known as a zopkyo (or zo)
yartsa gunbu fungus-infected caterpillar prized by the Chinese for
             its supposed medicinal value and as an aphrodisiac
yersa   collection of herdsmen's shelters or summer
             settlement
yeti   mythical creature of the Himalaya, often described
             as a hairy ape-like animal

FURTHER READING

Boustead, Robin: *The Great Himalayan Trail* (Himalayan Map House, Kathmandu, 2009) A pictorial guide to a series of routes that form a dream trek stretching from Kangchenjunga to Nepal's Farthest West. See also the author's guidebook *Nepal Trekking and the Great Himalaya Trail* (Trailblazer, 2011).

Duff, Jim and Gormley, Peter: *Pocket First Aid and Wilderness Medicine* (Cicerone, 2nd edn, 2014) An indispensable companion for anyone planning to trek among the mountains.

Freshfield, Douglas W: *Round Kangchenjunga* (Arnold, 1903) In 1899 Freshfield made a complete circumnavigation of the world's third-highest mountain.

Gilchrist, Thomas R: *The Trekkers' Handbook* (Cicerone, 1996) Long out of print, this entertaining handbook is full of good advice and is worth seeking out.

Harding, Mike: *Footloose in the Himalaya* (Michael Joseph, 1989) Thoughtful and humorous, Harding describes his treks in Ladakh, the Annapurna region and to Kala Pattar in view of Everest.

Hooker, Joseph Dalton: *Himalayan Journals* (Murray, 1895) A fascinating book recounting the great Victorian plant-hunter's journeys in Sikkim and northeast Nepal.

Matthiessen, Peter: *The Snow Leopard* (Chatto & Windus, 1979) One of the true classics of travel literature, it tells the story of an expedition into Dolpo in 1973 in search of the elusive creature of the title, with the animal biologist George B Schaller, whose own account (see below) also makes fascinating reading.

Murray, WH: *The Evidence of Things Not Seen* (Bâton Wicks, 2002) In this autobiography, the Scottish mountaineer describes his expedition to the Api-Nampa region of Nepal in 1953.

Pauler, Gerda: *Great Himalaya Trail* (Bâton Wicks, 2013) The story of an epic 123-day east to west trek across Nepal's Himalayan regions that the author undertook in 2012.

Pritchard-Jones, Siân and Gibbons, Bob: *Annapurna* (Cicerone, 2013) A guide to all the main treks in the Annapurna region by a highly experienced couple with almost encyclopaedic knowledge of Nepal.

Trekking Around Upper and Lower Dolpo (Himalayan Map House, Kathmandu, 2014) The title says it all.

Trekking Around Manaslu and The Tsum Valley (Himalayan Map House, Kathmandu, 2013)

Razzetti, Steve: *Trekking and Climbing in Nepal* (New Holland, 2000) The author of this collection of 20 classic routes is a talented photographer with many years' experience as a trek leader in the Himalayan regions.

Reynolds, Kev (ed): *Trekking in the Himalaya* (Cicerone, 2013) Twenty major routes across the Himalayan ranges described by an experienced group of mountain writers and travellers; it includes all the main Nepalese treks.

Reynolds, Kev *A Walk in the Clouds* (Cicerone, 2013) A collection of short stories recounting incidents from a lifetime of mountain activity, with several that take place on trek in the Himalaya.

Everest: A Trekker's Guide (Cicerone, 4th edn, 2011) One of a series of guides to individual treks in Nepal.

Kangchenjunga: A Trekker's Guide (Cicerone, 1999)

Langtang, Gosainkund and Helambu: A Trekker's Guide (Cicerone, 1996)

Manaslu: A Trekker's Guide (Cicerone, 2000)

Schaller, George B: *Stones of Silence* (Viking Press, 1980). An easy-to-read account of the naturalist's field work in Chitral and Hunza as well as Nepal, in which his journey to Dolpo with Matthiessen (see above) is described.

Snellgrove, David: *Himalayan Pilgrimage* (Shambhala Publications, 1981) A scholarly narrative of a seven-month journey across Dolpo studying the Buddhist monasteries.

Stevenson, Andrew: *Annapurna Circuit* (Constable, 1997) A highly readable first-hand account of the author's experiences along one of Nepal's most iconic trekking routes.

Swift, Hugh: *Trekking in Nepal, West Tibet and Bhutan* (Hodder & Stoughton, 1989) Hugh Swift probably knew the Himalaya from a trekker's point of view better than anyone. In this well-crafted handbook he describes not only well-trodden routes, but several that even today are virtually 'lost behind the ranges'. Pure dream-fodder.

Tilman, HW: *Nepal Himalaya* (Cambridge University Press, 1952; also included in the Tilman compilation The Seven Mountain-Travel Books, Cordee, 1983). This is Tilman's entertaining account of his visits to Nepal, in which he travelled to the Annapurna, Ganesh, Langtang and Jugal Himals, and became the first mountaineer to study Everest from Kala Pattar.

Unsworth, Walt: *Everest* (Oxford Illustrated Press, 1989; also several updated editions by different publishers) All you ever wanted to know about the world's highest mountain.

Valli, Eric: *Dolpo: Le pays caché* (Éditions du Chéne, Paris, 1986) A beautiful photographic book depicting the people and landscapes of Dolpo. Valli also made the award-winning cinema film 'Himalaya' (also known as 'Caravans'), which tells the story of a *yak* train carrying salt across the high passes.

INDEX

BRITISH ISLES CHALLENGES, COLLECTIONS AND ACTIVITIES

The Book of the Bivvy
The Book of the Bothy
The End to End Trail
The Mountains of
England and Wales:
1&2
The National Trails
The Relative Hills of
Britain
The Ridges of England,
Wales and Ireland
The UK Trailwalker's
Handbook
The UK's County Tops
Three Peaks, Ten Tors

UK CYCLING

20 Classic Sportive
Rides
South West England
South East England
Border Country Cycle
Routes
Cycling in the
Cotswolds
Cycling in the Hebrides
Cycling in the Peak
District
Cycling in the
Yorkshire Dales
Cycling the Pennine
Bridleway
Mountain Biking in the
Lake District
Mountain Biking in the
Yorkshire Dales
Mountain Biking on
the North Downs
Mountain Biking on
the South Downs
The C2C Cycle Route
The End to End Cycle
Route
The Lancashire
Cycleway

SCOTLAND

Backpacker's Britain
Central and Southern
Scottish Highlands
Northern Scotland
Ben Nevis and Glen
Coe
Great Mountain Days
in Scotland
Not the West Highland
Way
Scotland's Best Small
Mountains
Scotland's Far West
Scotland's Mountain
Ridges
Scrambles in Lochaber
The Ayrshire and
Arran Coastal Paths
The Border Country
The Cape Wrath Trail
The Great Glen Way
The Hebrides
The Isle of Mull
The Isle of Skye
The Pentland Hills
The Skye Trail
The Southern Upland
Way
The Speyside Way
The West Highland
Way
Walking Highland
Perthshire
Walking in Scotland's
Far North
Walking in the Angus
Glens
Walking in the
Cairngorms
Walking in the Ochils,
Campsie Fells and
Lomond Hills

Walking in the
Southern Uplands
Walking in Torridon

Walking Loch Lomond
and the Trossachs
Walking on Harris and
Lewis
Walking on Jura, Islay
and Colonsay
Walking on Rum and
the Small Isles
Walking on the Isle of
Arran
Walking on the Orkney
and Shetland Isles
Walking on Uist and
Barra
Walking the Corbetts
1 South of the Great
Glen
2 North of the Great
Glen
Walking the Galloway
Hills
Walking the Lowther
Hills
Walking the Munros
1 Southern, Central
and
Western Highlands
2 Northern Highlands
and the Cairngorms
Winter Climbs Ben
Nevis and Glen Coe
Winter Climbs in the
Cairngorms
World Mountain
Ranges: Scotland

NORTHERN ENGLAND TRAILS

A Northern Coast to
Coast Walk
Hadrian's Wall Path
The Dales Way
The Pennine Way

NORTH EAST ENGLAND, YORKSHIRE DALES AND PENNINES

Great Mountain Days
in the Pennines

Historic Walks in
North Yorkshire
South Pennine Walks
St Oswald's Way and
St Cuthbert's Way
The Cleveland Way
and the Yorkshire
Wolds Way
The North York Moors
The Reivers Way
The Teesdale Way
The Yorkshire Dales
North and East
South and West
Walking in County
Durham
Walking in
Northumberland
Walking in the North
Pennines
Walks in Dales Country
Walks in the Yorkshire
Dales
Walks on the North
York Moors – Books
1 & 2

NORTH WEST ENGLAND AND THE ISLE OF MAN

Historic Walks in
Cheshire
Isle of Man Coastal
Path
The Isle of Man
The Lune Valley and
Howgills
The Ribble Way
Walking in Cumbria's
Eden Valley
Walking in Lancashire
Walking in the Forest
of Bowland and
Pendle
Walking on the Isle of
Man
Walking on the West
Pennine Moors

For full information on
all our guides, books and
eBooks,
visit our website:
www.cicerone.co.uk.

Walking – Trekking – Mountaineering – Climbing – Cycling

Over 40 years, Cicerone have built up an outstanding collection of over 300 guides, inspiring all sorts of amazing adventures.

Every guide comes from extensive exploration and research by our expert authors, all with a passion for their subjects. They are frequently praised, endorsed and used by clubs, instructors and outdoor organisations.

All our titles can now be bought as **e-books**, **ePubs** and **Kindle** files and we also have an online magazine – **Cicerone Extra** – with features to help cyclists, climbers, walkers and trekkers choose their next adventure, at home or abroad.

Our website shows any **new information** we've had in since a book was published. Please do let us know if you find anything has changed, so that we can publish the latest details. On our **website** you'll also find great ideas and lots of detailed information about what's inside every guide and you can buy **individual routes** from many of them online.

It's easy to keep in touch with what's going on at Cicerone by getting our monthly **free e-newsletter**, which is full of offers, competitions, up-to-date information and topical articles. You can subscribe on our home page and also follow us on Facebook and **Twitter** or dip into our **blog**.

Cicerone – the very best guides for exploring the world.

CICERONE

2 Police Square Milnthorpe Cumbria LA7 7PY
Tel: 015395 62069 info@cicerone.co.uk
www.cicerone.co.uk and **www.cicerone-extra.com**